9/10/02

To: Mrs. Small CLU, ChFC

Thanks for your help!

[signature]

The Power of One

The Power of One

John Baird

The American College/*Bryn Mawr, Pennsylvania*

This publication is designed to provide accurate and authoritative information about the subject covered. While every precaution has been taken in the preparation of this material, the author and The American College assume no liability for damages resulting from the use of the information contained in this publication. The American College is not engaged in rendering legal, accounting, or other professional advice. If legal or expert advice is required, the services of an appropriate professional should be sought.

Library of Congress Catalog Card Number 97-70295
ISBN 0-943590-90-6

Printed in the United States of America

To Dr. Solomon S. Huebner

March 6, 1882–July 17, 1964

Contents

Preface

It has been over 35 years since Mildred Stone wrote her classic history of The American College that chronicled its growth from creation in 1927 to the arrival at our Bryn Mawr campus in 1961.

There was much to write about in the early years. The leaders of the College set the foundation in place and established the philosophy of education that prevails to this day. However, it was a much different era than currently exists in the life insurance industry. It was a more stable time, with a slow-to-change mentality, where promotion from within was the tradition and continuity of the past was the strategy for the future. These were also simpler times. The life insurance agent sold a few basic types of policies, and the career agency system was the dominant channel of sales that continued to grow and prosper.

The American College reflected the life insurance industry during those years. Its sole designation was the Chartered Life Underwriter with a five-course curriculum. The only other educational programs offered were management certificate courses that were designed for field managers. There was no full-time faculty specializing in the various disciplines of financial services and writing the textbooks for the courses. In the early 1960s everyone fit nicely into Huebner Hall with space for the American Society, the American Institute of CPCU, and its Society.

The decade of the 1970s was the beginning of a rapidly changing environment for life insurance. Perhaps 1978 was the pivotal year. It was the year that universal life insurance was introduced to the general public. It was the beginning of the "best of times and the worst of times" for The American College. Over the next 2 decades the College would experience its most rapid rate of growth but also the largest buildup of indebtedness in its history. The decisions to assemble a full-time faculty, construct a full-service library, and attain academic accreditation by introducing a masters degree program were made in the mid-1970s. In 1976, the College decided to change its name from The American College of Life Underwriters to simply The American College. At the time, this decision was highly controversial. In retrospect, however, it was a visionary decision of a vastly changing industry that would be greatly influenced by the public's primary concern shifting from the financial risks of dying too soon to the financial risks of living too long. A monumental decision in 1978

ix

was to build a modern, full-service conference center that included residency rooms.

Beginning in the 1980s, competition accelerated with a proliferation of new products. Annuities and mutual funds began to emerge as important financial products. The College's courses and curricula reflected these changes. In 1982 the College introduced its Chartered Financial Consultant designation and 13 years later added the Registered Health Underwriter and the Registered Employee Benefits Consultant designations. It also added a five-course track for those who want to take the Certified Financial Planner examination. By the late 1980s, the College had more than 40 courses in its various curricula, as well as a wide variety of continuing education courses.

The College no longer sees its constituency as a group of homogenous life insurance agents. Today its students represent a broad and diversified financial services industry. This is the new era of The American College.

In its 70th year, another history of the College has been written. It includes the past 35 years that have never before been set in print. Those years tell the story of new leaders, overseeing expanded growth, and complexity. The book is well written by John Baird, a local historian who met the challenge with enthusiasm, experience, and commitment. He has done us a great service because it is a story that deserves to be told.

We have much about which to be proud. The American College is worthy of our praise and esteem. This book gives us the opportunity to better appreciate the accomplishments of this unique educational institution.

Samuel H. Weese
President

Acknowledgments

Two and one-half years ago this book began with a conversation between the author and President Samuel H. Weese, who asked me to write the 70th anniversary history of The American College. Most nonfiction involves the contribution of other people who aid the author in his task, and this is the place to thank all who have helped me to produce this account.

The College acceded to my every request for information; made available its archives, files, and records; and provided access to alumni, faculty, staff members, and trustees. More important, the administration granted me complete freedom of thought and expression.

Special thanks go to Archivist Marjorie A. Fletcher who not only responded to my every factual request, but who also gave me useful material, the existence of which I was not even aware.

Vice Presidents Gary K. Stone, Charles S. DiLullo, William J. Lombardo, and Stephen D. Tarr were particularly helpful. Many faculty members contributed valuable data and perceptive opinions, as did administrative officers and staff personnel.

Mention must be made of Librarian Judith L. Hill, Professor Emeritus Clarence C. Walton, and Executive Assistant Victoria J. Doyle, who each rendered appreciated assistance. Both Mille M. Gregg and Helen H. Schmidt encouraged my efforts and furnished pertinent perspectives.

Present trustees added a crucial dimension to my research. Particularly helpful were Glenn A. Britt, William B. Wallace, Denis F. Mullane, John R. Driskill, and Paul F. Shevlin.

Among former board members who generously shared their opinions were John C. Bogle, Dan M. McGill, Joseph J. Melone, Jerry S. Rosenbloom, and Edmund L. Zalinski.

Edward G. Jordan, past president of The American College, also shared his experience and viewpoint.

Among a larger group of business and educational leaders who added their insights and shared their knowledge were William Bates, Jr., Linden K. Hustedt, CLU, ChFC, Stanley Liss, Ehrman B. Mitchell, Edwin S. Overman, and Ralph S. Saul.

Word Processing Supervisor Patricia A. Perillo and her assistant Virginia Marzano typed the manuscript, and their careful, enthusiastic work deserves the highest commendation.

Thanks go to Joseph L. Brennan, who designed the jacket and cover and was responsible for the layout of the photo pages throughout the book.

Thanks also go to Patricia G. Berenson for production assistance and to Lynn Hayes for editing the book.

John Baird

The Power of One

PART ONE

Philadelphia
1927–1961

SECTION ONE

Origins 1927–1934
Edward A. Woods
Ernest J. Clark

1

How It All Began

Do not squander Time; for that's
the stuff Life is made of.

Benjamin Franklin

A university professor and two life insurance agents had a dream that they brought to fulfillment in that period of American history known as the Roaring Twenties.

Solomon S. Huebner, Edward A. Woods, and Ernest J. Clark shared a vision that would benefit the business of protecting people against financial loss brought about by old age, illness, or human catastrophe. These three men and others within the life insurance industry realized the need to move salespeople from peddler to professional and to better inform and thereby better serve the public regarding this opportunity to manage the risks of life.

The second decade of the 20th century in the United States has been characterized as an "era of wonderful nonsense"[1] marked by flappers, bootleggers, and ballyhoo about sports stars and film figures. Al Jolson appeared in the first talking picture, *The Jazz Singer.* The popular song of 1927, "I'm Looking over a Four-Leaf Clover," reflected the optimism of those boisterous years.

Yet the 1920s was a time of genuine achievement, too. People in San Francisco and London could now converse by telephone for the first time. Henry Ford put America on wheels; Charles A. Lindbergh's solo flight from New York to Paris electrified the nation and advanced the aviation industry.

That same year a loaf of bread cost 9 cents and a gallon of gas sold for 12 cents. The Nash Motor Car Company offered a coupe for $865 f.o.b. factory, and the Dow Jones stock average stood at 175. Human life expectancy was 54.1 years.

Nineteen twenty-seven found business booming, the economy expanding, and the life insurance industry enjoying good times. After all, total insurance in force had increased from approximately $35 billion to more than $99 billion in just 10 years.[2] Beneath this patina of prosperity, however, serious problems existed in connection with selling the product.

These negative circumstances had existed for a long time. To be sure, the industry had recovered from the scandals that led to the Armstrong Investigation of 1904, but the major companies were slow to meet the long-range challenge caused by poorly trained agents who gave the business a bad reputation. As one writer put it, conscientious and forward-looking men in the field, "despairing of company leadership in training, turned to organized self-education."[3]

Most of these men were leaders of the National Association of Life Underwriters (NALU) originally organized in 1890. Ernest J. Clark, general agent for John Hancock, for example, served as the NALU's president in 1914. He gave Solomon S. Huebner, the ambitious and articulate Wharton School teacher at the University of Pennsylvania, a hearing among Baltimore life insurance underwriters in February of that year. Within months Clark had arranged for Huebner to bring his message of better agent and better public education to a wider audience at the NALU annual convention, which met in Cincinnati.

Edward A. Woods, the NALU's president in 1916 and a general agent for the Equitable Life Assurance Society of the United States, chaired an association committee that year to study scientific salesmanship. He helped form the Carnegie Bureau of Salesmanship Research "for the purpose of reducing the cost of selling through a cooperative study of the best methods of employing and training salesmen."[4] Seven years later Woods published his book, *Life Underwriting As a Career.*

During the next decade, NALU committees reported on higher standards, better sales practices, and college courses in life insurance. Solomon S. Huebner, who had first described his vision for an educational institution in 1914 at the NALU national convention, presented his human life value concept of life insurance at the Los Angeles meeting in 1924. Huebner's concept went beyond the traditional succor for family survivors to the creation of wealth through the capitalization of annual earning power.

Edward A. Woods's NALU leadership and industry prestige quickened the pace of discussion and negotiation as how best to achieve these ends. As a result, in January 1927 the NALU trustees voted to establish The American College of Life Underwriters. Ernest J. Clark handled the organizational formalities with the District of Columbia (where the NALU had been incorporated in 1921). He and a Washington lawyer, Edward S. Brashears, signed the official certificate in that city on March 22, and The American College was born.

The 12 incorporators met at the Palmer House in Chicago 3 days later as directors of this unique institution. They elected Edward A. Woods as president, Guy MacLaughlin as vice president, Ernest J. Clark as secretary, Franklin W. Ganse as treasurer, Solomon S. Huebner as dean, and Everett M. Ensign as registrar. Ensign also served as NALU executive secretary.

The group adopted bylaws prepared by Clark and Huebner, which stated these objectives:

- to cooperate with colleges and universities in training students for the career of professional life underwriter
- to cooperate with educational institutions in general life insurance education

- to conduct, if occasion demands, its own institution for the training of resident students for the profession of life underwriting
- to recognize properly qualified life underwriters with a professional degree[5]

There were further meetings in 1927, including a significant session of the Executive Committee held on May 3 at the Mayflower Hotel in Washington, DC. Clark, Huebner, and Woods stuck together, listened to contrary opinions, and finally secured approval for these important decisions: The name of the designation to be earned would be Chartered Life Underwriter (not "Certified," a term that reminded one member of high-grade milk); a high school diploma would be required for admission to the program; there would be no honorary degrees—right from the start the CLU designation had to be earned. Before adjournment, the committee also listed books to be read, defined the scope of examination material to be covered, and confirmed the details of taking the tests that would begin the following year.[6]

Encouraged by the success of these events, Dr. and Mrs. Huebner sailed for Japan in June where he would fulfill an exchange professorship commitment that had been planned for several years. His optimism about the CLU program, however, proved to be partially misplaced by an event that occurred when the NALU met in national convention at the Peabody Hotel in Memphis on October 13.[7]

On that occasion Edward Woods succumbed to pressure from some delegates who insisted on a supplementary program called the Accredited Life Underwriter plan for persons of "good character and sales performance" who did not wish to take the CLU examinations. For the payment of $50 such a member of a local life underwriters association could apply to The American College for recognition. With this concession to those who believed the CLU program too strenuous, the NALU approved both plans and the creation of the College.[8]

President Woods died of appendicitis and heart disease within weeks of that meeting. He was 62. A trade paper mourned him with these words:

> The news of his death was a bombshell to life insurance men, especially those who had seen him at the NALU convention in Memphis . . . where he was devoting most of his time to seeing that the new American College of Life Underwriters was safely launched under the auspices of the National Association.[9]

NALU sponsorship of the College never implied control. The association loaned the fledgling College a total of $2,000 at 6 percent interest the first year, but it later wrote off the amount as a gift to the College. Expenses by December 31, 1927, came to $1,889.16.

Originally, all directors of the College were NALU members, but within a few years the board increased its size from 12 to 21 persons, added home office executives and leaders from other insurance organizations, and dropped the requirement of membership in the NALU. The NALU, as historian Mildred F. Stone noted, "recognized from the beginning that an educational institution must be independent of any direction by a trade association."[10]

Early in 1928 Dr. Huebner returned to Philadelphia to experience the full impact of the NALU actions to authorize the controversial Accredited Life Underwriter plan along with the CLU program. Before his untimely death, Woods had warned Huebner by cablegrams of the NALU's interest in the certification idea, but actually seeing the concept in black-and-white proved to be more than the dynamic professor could endure. Huebner exploded to Ernest Clark and threatened to resign unless the NALU backed down and rescinded its action.[11]

Clark persuaded the indignant teacher to stay on the team. The College directors met within a month and elected the feisty Huebner to the board. Not long thereafter the directors agreed to separate the CLU and the Accredited Life Underwriter programs and discontinued the latter altogether.

In April 1928 the governing group elected Ernest Clark president of the College to succeed Edward A. Woods. John Marshall Holcombe, Jr., became secretary, and the officers moved ahead with dispatch to schedule the first series of CLU examinations, which were given in June. Dean Huebner and Professor Arthur M. Spalding (paid $100 per month as the first salaried College employee) worked out the details.

Forty-two persons applied to take the examinations. Three were rejected because they did not have high school diplomas; 34 actually took the tests, which were held at 14 universities from Boston to California. Dr. Huebner paid a young University of Pennsylvania professor named David McCahan $200 to help grade the papers. Twenty-one individuals were recommended by Dean Huebner to receive the CLU designation at the NALU convention in Detroit that September. President Clark presented the diplomas tied with blue and gold ribbons (the College colors) to the six graduates who attended the ceremony. Mutual of New York's Julian S. Myrick now headed the NALU and would later assume a prominent role in the life of The American College.

The College sponsored a second examination session in December. It is said that these examinations were more difficult than those taken by the first group. Fifteen candidates out of the 53 applicants who had been accepted were successful this time, which made a total of 36 CLUs the first year. Professor Spalding concluded that "underwriters often underestimate the knowledge and proficiency required" for success.[12] The College was setting high standards and maintaining them despite calls from some quarters for less demanding requirements.

In 1928, the year Amelia Earhart flew the Atlantic and Herbert Hoover defeated Alfred E. Smith for the presidency of the United States, it may therefore be said that The American College of Chartered Life Underwriters, by making education the foundation of professionalism for an entire industry, took what Julian Myrick described as "one of the biggest steps that has ever been taken for the development of life insurance."[13]

It is interesting to note that after the first conferments, the brand-new graduates organized an alumni association, which later became known as the Society of Chartered Life Underwriters with local chapters across the country.[14]

Events moved swiftly early the following year as the nation continued its economic expansion. The new College established an advisory council of 30 "ambassadors" from the industry to help Dean Huebner place The American College program in other educational institutions. The council also agreed to describe the CLU as a "designation" rather than a "degree," an action that enabled the College to retain NALU support and also be licensed by the District of Columbia Board of Education as required under a new law.

The American College not only survived the October stock market crash, but it also gained strength and influence throughout the Great Depression years that followed. The 1930 census recorded a population of 123 million persons. Despite widespread economic hardship and the geographically scattered College administration (President Ernest J. Clark in Baltimore, Vice President William M. Duff in Pittsburgh, Treasurer Franklin W. Ganse in Boston, Registrar Arthur M. Spalding in New York City, and Secretary David McCahan and Dean Solomon S. Huebner in Philadelphia),[15] matriculations reached 242 and CLU designations numbered 110.

Each passing year brought larger numbers, and by 1931 the increased volume required that something be done to provide more adequate College headquarters than the few file cabinets in Dr. Huebner's Logan Hall office at the University of Pennsylvania. Thus in the year when America's greatest inventor, Thomas A. Edison, died and America's tallest building, the Empire State building, opened its doors, The American College moved to larger accommodations in a nearby commercial structure. Nevertheless, spartan conditions still prevailed: To reach the attic domain of the dean and his assistant, who were on the sixth floor of the building, visitors had to climb a flight of stairs since the elevator reached no higher than the fifth floor.

Ernest J. Clark more than lived up to his reputation as a man of "ability, vision, and dedication"[16] during those early years of The American College, proving to be an effective president. Clark performed ceremonial duties at conferment. He made personal contributions to help pay for needed items for which there was no provision in the budget (for example, the $310 that he and a few other directors gave to produce and distribute 5,000 copies of an informational booklet about the College). More important, he supported Dr. Huebner at critical times, such as going with the dean to Washington, DC, to negotiate with educational authorities there regarding the license The American College needed as an institution registered in the nation's capital.

Clark also found opportunities to articulate the case for the College and to present its solid achievement record of the first several years. In 1931, for example, he told NALU convention delegates:

> The Chartered Life Underwriter course is probably the only course of study in the world that has been so perfectly standardized . . . We have

no record in the history of education of any other specialized course of study being established in this manner.[17]

The Depression deepened and many people's lives grew grimmer during 1932. The federal government established the Reconstruction Finance Corporation to stimulate business, but the move brought few apparent results. Angry World War I veterans marched on Washington on May 22 to demand immediate payment of a bonus for their service, which had been voted in 1924 to be paid in 1945.

Conditions worsened by 1933. Overseas, Adolf Hitler became chancellor of Germany. At home, Franklin D. Roosevelt closed the banks on March 6; the United States dropped the gold standard in June, but so much damage had already been done:

> One in four Americans who had previously been working was unemployed. Some 40 percent of the nation's commercial banks had failed, reducing their number from twenty-five to fourteen thousand, and two thousand investment banks and brokers had gone out of business.[18]

Throughout these distressing days and troublesome times The American College continued to score impressive gains. The CLU program grew each year, despite enforcement of the twin requirements of academic achievement and "selling, teaching, or management experience."[19]

In addition to its basic CLU curriculum, the College first offered management examinations in 1933 and decades later would expand this curriculum into an accredited degree program. Clark and Huebner were also gratified with the help from other colleges and universities in the struggle to improve life insurance education. Participating educational institutions in the examination process rose from 12 in 1929 to 63 only 4 years later.[20] Ninety-nine colleges and universities now offered their own general course in life insurance.

NOTES

 1. *World Book Encyclopedia,* 1966, vol. 19, p. 114.
 2. J. Owen Statson, *Marketing Life Insurance* (Homewood, IL: Richard D. Irwin), 1969, p. 817.
 3. Mildred F. Stone, *A Calling and Its College* (Homewood, IL: Richard D. Irwin), 1963, p. 29.
 4. Ibid., p. 40.
 5. Ibid., p. 69.
 6. Ibid., pp. 70–72.
 7. Mildred F. Stone, *The Teacher Who Changed an Industry* (Homewood, IL: Richard D. Irwin), 1960, p. 161.
 8. Stone, *A Calling,* p. 75.
 9. *The Eastern Underwriter,* December 9, 1927, p. 1.
10. Stone, *A Calling,* p. 133.
11. Ibid., p. 78.
12. Ibid., p. 90.

13. Stone, *The Teacher Who,* p. 169.

14. Ibid.

15. *Topical Outline of Subjects Covered by the CLU Examinations*, The American College, p. 3.

16. Stone, *A Calling*, p. 68.

17. Ibid., p. 103.

18. *The Economist*, vol. 335, no. 7910, p. 27.

19. Stone, *A Calling,* p. 138.

20. Ibid., p. 108.

SECTION TWO

A True Pioneer 1934–1954
Solomon S. Huebner

2

Taking the First Steps

Time and the World are ever in flight.

William Butler Yeats

On the international scene in 1934 United States troops left Haiti after a military occupation that had lasted 19 years. In Philadelphia Ernest J. Clark declined reelection as president of The American College after 7 years in that position. The directors elected him chairman of the board with responsibility for financing the school, made Solomon S. Huebner president, and appointed David McCahan dean.

Dr. Huebner had 30 years' experience in higher education, beginning with the introduction of his pioneer insurance course at the Wharton School in 1904. During the next decade, he established and built up the Insurance Department of the University of Pennsylvania and became its chairman. He spoke at NALU conventions and published his book, *Life Insurance: A Textbook.*

An early CLU graduate described Dr. Huebner as "the man who has, since the early beginning of the College and for many years before, done more than any other layman to promote the best interests of life insurance, and through years of tireless effort has spread the gospel of The American College up and down the land."[1]

David McCahan, with three academic degrees from the University of Pennsylvania, earned his CLU in 1929 and became assistant dean of The American College that same year. In the mid-1920s he joined the Wharton School faculty, served on the Registration Board of The American College, and began a public relations program for the new academic organization. For example, he sent notices of CLU conferments to the hometown newspapers of each proud graduate.[2] The enterprising new dean also published articles about The American College in the *New York Journal of Commerce.*

Huebner and McCahan worked well together. As mentor and protégé they attended to most of the operational details in the early years of the infant institution. Theirs was a labor of love, as each man received an honorarium of only $50 per month as dean and assistant dean, respectively. They even wrote a book together in 1933, titled *Life Insurance As Investment.* Another writer said of this remarkable team, "In a sense Dr. Huebner was the architect of The American College and Dr. McCahan the builder."[3]

The election of new officers offered a good time to recall the four basic principles upon which The American College had been founded in 1927 and that had been carefully observed since that courageous beginning: The College resolved to preserve its independence from control by life insurance companies or trade associations, to insist upon high academic standards, to have an educational program that was broader than technician training, and to function through established, respected educational institutions.[4]

The new president realized, however, that the initial momentum that had been effected by volunteers and two marginally paid officials would not suffice for the future. Dr. Huebner soon pressed the board for a larger staff and more money. The board rose to the occasion and appointed one of its own members, John Marshall Holcombe, Jr., of the Life Insurance Sales Research Bureau, to address this challenge. Holcombe's organization created a working committee to study the matter and take appropriate action. It named Henry E. North, vice president of the Metropolitan, as its chairman. North enlisted executives from Northwestern National Life, Massachusetts Mutual, the Equitable, Guardian Life, The Prudential, and Penn Mutual to serve as members of the group. He also brought in as a staff assistant another person from the Metropolitan, Earl R. Trangmar, who had fundraising and public relations experience that proved invaluable to the effort. Trangmar became progressively more involved with the College and later earned the distinction of being made a life trustee.[5]

Dr. Huebner's first years as president gave him both a change of pace and genuine satisfaction. In 1935, the year the Social Security Act became law and America's popular humorist Will Rogers died in an Alaskan plane crash, Solomon S. Huebner completed a 5-year, nationwide visitation program for Massachusetts Mutual. The grueling schedule took the intrepid professor to that company's agencies across the country to present his human life value concept and other fundamentals of life insurance education.[6]

Meanwhile, the College enjoyed greater press coverage. *Life Insurance Selling* dedicated an entire issue to this new institution and its CLU program, giving both an enthusiastic endorsement.[7] There were also other accolades. Paul F. Clark, CLU, a successful John Hancock Mutual Life general agent (and the nephew of The American College board chairman, Ernest J. Clark) who later became its president, completed an industrywide agency survey that revealed extensive enthusiasm for CLU capacity and prestige. According to Clark, the survey dispelled "the doubts and fears expressed from time to time by certain general agents as to the effect of the CLU movement upon immediate sales of their agents and the profits of the agency."[8]

By 1936 Henry E. North's committee determined that the College required at least $30,000 per year for present and future needs. The committee developed a gift solicitation plan known as the Cooperative Fund for Underwriter Training. Committee members would seek annual company contributions based upon a formula of size. The fundraisers presented their request to hundreds of home office executives, and within 90 days most of the leading companies had pledged a total of $30,000. The contribution entitled their representatives to half charge for the examination fees through the use of credit certificates. Metropolitan Life not only made a leadership commitment but paid for the campaign expenses as well.[9]

The mid-1930s brought a blend of good and bad news to Dr. Huebner. On the positive side, he completed a 2-year term as president of the American Association of University Teachers of Insurance. CLU matriculations had more than recovered from their slight dip in 1933–1934, moving to a new high of 594 persons. The number of actual graduates receiving the hard-earned designation had also increased. Huebner loved to lead the candidates in repeating the CLU pledge at the annual conferment exercises. The pledge (which he had written early in the College's existence) reflected the Golden Rule as it "set standards for professional service in life underwriting, but provided also motivation for achievement of the ideals."[10] The Professional Pledge reads as follows:

> In all my professional relationships, I pledge myself to the following rule of ethical conduct: I shall, in light of all conditions surrounding those I serve, which I shall make every conscientious effort to ascertain and understand, render that service which, in the same circumstances, I would apply to myself.

Yet sunshine brings shadows, and as Solomon Huebner enjoyed these and other happy experiences he also suffered from an infection caused by tick bites he had received on a vacation to the Mayan ruins in the jungles of the Yucatan. Beginning as hives and progressing to neuritis and kidney disease, the affliction worsened, could no longer be treated at home, and eventually required Dr. Huebner's hospitalization and a long convalescence in those days before antibiotics.[11]

Joe Louis won the heavyweight boxing title of the world in 1937; George S. Kaufman and Moss Hart shared a Pulitzer Prize for their play *You Can't Take It with You*. The American College reached the age of 10 years and marked the milestone with a number of decisions that caused a contemporary commentator to declare, "Ten years after the small beginnings we see The American College emerging into its second decade as a vital and ever-strengthening factor in American life insurance."[12]

Specific College actions that year included opening a full-service life insurance library, issuing a policy statement reserving the right to define the CLU program and prohibiting individual agents from doing so, and creating an Educational Advisory Department headed by John P. Williams, professor at Davidson College.[13]

The National Chapter of CLUs did its part, too. That loyal group sponsored a brief book about the College, and it held 39 different dinners across the country to commemorate The American College's 10th anniversary. Moreover, its alumni worked together to prepare quality agents to do a better job for themselves, their companies, and the general public.

As the College continued to grow in reputation and influence, even more recognition came to its respected president. For example, the Philadelphia Association of Life Underwriters created an annual President's Cup award and named Solomon S. Huebner as the first recipient.[14]

In 1938 the College's Board of Directors again asserted its leadership responsibility in a series of significant actions designed to further improve the respected young institution. The board members (increased in number from the original 12 in 1927 to 21 in 1930 and from then on including home office executives and other insurance leaders) were now to be known as *trustees* rather than directors. Another bylaw change provided for 21 *term* trustees to be elected in three classes of 3 years each; *life* trustees, not to exceed five in number; and *ex-officio* trustees, which at that time consisted of counsel for the College and the president of the National Chapter of what would later be called the American Society of Chartered Life Underwriters.

Ernest Clark, after 11 years in the successive roles of American College incorporator, president, and then board chairman, requested relief from this ultimate leadership responsibility. He resigned as chairman but would continue to serve as a trustee for another 20 years until his death at age 86. The board elected Clark, Huebner, and Treasurer Franklin W. Ganse as the first three life trustees, praising them for "outstanding, constructive, and devoted service to the College."[15]

The trustees, in a related act, elected another of their own, Julian S. Myrick, as chairman of the board. As we mentioned earlier, Myrick was a Mutual of New York agency manager who had been associated with The American College since 1928. As NALU president at that time he participated in the first CLU conferment ceremony. Soon thereafter he became a member of the College's first Advisory Council, and he joined the board in 1929. A few years later he chaired the Pension Committee and served with Paul Clark and John A. Stevenson to develop a retirement plan for the employees.

With this running start of enthusiasm for and service to the College, Julian Myrick started a span of board leadership that would extend for 22 years and far exceed the tenure of any other person elected to the office of chairman. Within a year the board made him a life trustee in recognition of his experience, ability, and panache.

These last years of the 1930s marked the end of the Great Depression. John Steinbeck's powerful novel *The Grapes of Wrath* dramatized the plight of migrant workers during that troubled time, but economic conditions were improving. Congress passed the first minimum wage law, and The American College experienced a dramatic upturn in student matriculations for the CLU program. In 1939 more than 1,100 men and women began their studies for the challenging designation, a number almost twice the total of any previous year. The life insurance industry as a whole could also rejoice. Only a few small companies had failed during the decade-long economic collapse, and the losses experienced by the policyholders came to less than one percent of the total assets of all life companies.

The United States hosted the World's Fair in New York that summer to celebrate the accomplishments of civilization and to herald the promise of the future. Before the festivities ended, however, Germany invaded Poland to begin World War II, and President Franklin D. Roosevelt proclaimed a national emergency on September 8, 1939. The country at large, the life insurance industry, and The American College would soon be tested as never before.

While the College had scored impressive gains in student enrollment, the actual number of CLU designations awarded had not kept pace. The colleges and universities that gave the courses lacked sufficient teachers with life insurance credentials. Something had to be done. The American Life Convention, the Institute of Life Insurance, and the Life Insurance Association of America agreed to work together to raise funds from cooperating companies "to advance the cause of insurance education."[16]

Concurrently, many people within the industry continued to be concerned about the poor health of Dr. Huebner. They sought a way to honor the determined pioneer before his contribution might end.[17] The $25,000 being raised from life companies for insurance teacher education was designated for a Huebner Educational Fund. What could be more appropriate therefore than to announce this program as part of a broader testimonial occasion being planned for the NALU convention in Philadelphia on September 26, 1939?

The American College designed its annual conferment dinner that year as a tribute to Solomon S. Huebner. Twelve sponsoring organizations and their representatives from the entire life insurance industry were listed in the souvenir program, including the following: Charles J. Zimmerman, president of the NALU; David McCahan, president of the American Association of University Teachers of Insurance; and Holgar J. Johnson, president of the Institute of Life Insurance.

Julian S. Myrick served as toastmaster. Dr. Huebner, who arrived in a wheel chair, gave the conferment address, and Charles Zimmerman presented gifts "from the field forces of America" to the guest of honor and his wife. Thomas J. Parkinson, president of Equitable Life Assurance Society of New York and chairman of the Cooperative Industry Committee that raised the money, announced the establishment of the teacher training fund as a tribute to Dr. Huebner.[18]

Representatives from the American Life Convention, the Institute of Life Insurance, and the Life Insurance Association of America formed the S.S. Huebner Foundation for Insurance Education on December 18, and three men from each organization became the first Cooperating Committee of the new entity. The major life insurance companies provided the funding, and the University of Pennsylvania's Wharton School was selected to provide the education. The university, in turn, named David McCahan executive director of the program. The purpose of the foundation was to provide fellowships for graduate study in a program within the Insurance Department of the Wharton School, which led to earning a PhD for those who wanted to pursue careers in college teaching of insurance.

The first year of the new decade thus brought further recognition and increased stature to The American College through the actions of several independent but related organizations. The College did not—nor did it ever—stand alone.

In 1940 the census counters raised the official United States population to 132 million people and life expectancy rose to 62.7 years. At the same time the National Chapter of graduates changed its name to the American Society of CLU, thereby focusing national attention on the valuable designation. Finally, Cooperative Fund efforts to support the College's educational programs created a solid financial base for future growth. "The number of [CLU] candidates actually taking examinations doubled in the 5 years after the establishment of the Cooperative Fund,"[19] reaching 1,735 persons from 350 cities employed by 88 life insurance companies.

Just as the 1934 Cooperative Fund program effectively stimulated study for CLU students, the Huebner Foundation emphasis on insurance teachers proved equally important to the College. Two of its graduates—Davis W. Gregg and Samuel H. Weese—later became president of the College, and numerous others joined the College as faculty and administrators. The executive director of the Huebner Foundation, David McCahan, moved quickly to organize and publicize the program to prospective scholars. Then he personally selected the candidates who he believed were committed to a career of lifetime insurance teaching. McCahan chose well. The first awards were made for 1941–1942. There were fellowships to the following five people: William T. Beadles, Dan M. McGill, Robert I. Mehr, Sterling Surrey, and Emerson Cammack. Each of them went on to have highly productive careers in insurance education.[20]

World events moved even faster at that time. President Roosevelt gave his Four Freedoms speech to Congress on January 6, 1941. Within months the United States began lend lease aid to England and the Soviet Union, occupied Iceland, and signed the Atlantic Charter with Britain before Japan attacked Pearl Harbor on December 7.

War soon affected the insurance industry in several ways. The Association of Life Agency Officers (which had been developing a sales improvement program less academic than the CLU designation) postponed its plans for the Life Underwriter Training Council (LUTC) until after the conflict. Dan McGill and other early Huebner Foundation fellows and scholars left their classrooms to enter the armed forces.

On the other hand, some forward movement continued despite the international struggle. One particular development indirectly involved The American College through the interest of its president, Solomon S. Huebner, and its dean, David McCahan, in their capacity as successive presidents of the American Association of University Teachers of Insurance, which had been organized in 1932. The association proposed the formation of an organization to help property and casualty insurance practitioners the way The American College had improved the ability and professional reputation of life insurance practitioners. Some of its members then implemented that proposal.

In 1942 the American Institute for Property and Liability Underwriters began operations in Philadelphia; in another example of "interlocking directorships" and the close relationship among a number of insurance organizations, Dr. Huebner served as chairman of the board, and his University of Pennsylvania insurance colleague, Harry J. Loman, became dean.[21]

In a sense the peripatetic president of The American College lived three lives during those hectic war years. He performed certain patriotic duties as a War Department Advisory Committee member and as insurance consultant to the Civil Aeronautics Board. As we have seen, he provided leadership for several related insurance industry organizations. He also wisely guided the destinies of the College and its CLU program.

It is interesting to note that the College's 1943 *Annual Report* placed equal emphasis on the College as an educational institution and on the total CLU program, which by its very nature had dimensions beyond the walls of Logan Hall at the University of Pennsylvania. That report gave great credit to life insurance companies, other colleges and universities, and the Society for its help to the College and "in furthering the interests of the CLU movement."[22]

Although 1942–1943 brought a one-third decline in CLU examination takers, Dr. Huebner believed the College had "seen the worst of wartime attrition, and would be able to hold to present levels for the duration."[23]

NOTES

1. Lawrence C. Woods, Jr., *The First Decade 1927–1937. A Brief History of The American College of Life Underwriters* (National Chapter, Chartered Life Underwriters, 1938), p. 26.
2. Mildred F. Stone, *A Calling and Its College* (Homewood, IL: Richard D. Irwin), 1963, p. 134.
3. Ibid., p. 121.
4. Ibid., p. 148.
5. Ibid., pp. 151–152.
6. Ibid., p. 115.
7. Ibid., p. 180.
8. Ibid., p. 168.
9. Ibid., p. 157.
10. Mildred F. Stone, *The Teacher Who Changed an Industry* (Homewood, IL: Richard D. Irwin), 1960, p 191.
11. Ibid., p. 190.
12. Woods, *The First Decade,* p. 26.
13. Stone, *A Calling,* p. 158.
14. Stone, *The Teacher Who,* p. 194.
15. Stone, *A Calling,* p. 181.
16. Ibid., p. 188.
17. Ibid., p. 187.
18. Ibid., pp. 188–190.
19. Ibid., p. 159.
20. Ibid., p. 196.
21. Ibid., p. 184.
22. *Annual Report*, The American College, 1943, p. 24.
23. Ibid., p. 15.

3

Meeting the Challenge

I wasted Time, and now doth Time waste me.

William Shakespeare

Dr. Huebner's forecast proved to be essentially correct. The College closely monitored three crucial measurements of academic activity and kept comparative records of them on an annual basis.

Matriculations, which began with only 67 persons in 1928 and rose to 1,131 people in 1939, had fallen each wartime year to reach a low of only 233 persons by 1943. The number of new students, however, started to climb again the following year.

A second computation—the number of examination takers—had peaked at 1,746 in 1939, declined gradually for several years, and dipped badly in 1943. Yet the rate of decline for 1944 was only 12 percent, and as the perceptive Huebner forecast, the number of examination takers showed a sharp rebound from then on.

The number of actual designation earners—the third basic tabulation—increased more slowly, but within 3 years would reach a new high of 200 new CLUs in 1947. It is interesting to note that the 706 wartime examinees of 1944 took their tests not only at 97 colleges and universities but also at army camps, naval bases, and even a German prison camp.[1]

Education was in the air in 1944. Congress enacted the G.I. Bill of Rights to guarantee educational opportunity for war veterans, and The American College took two steps to strengthen its own training techniques. First, it created a new Examination Board to help its own officers improve the CLU examination process. Chaired by active CLU Irvin Bendiner of the New York Life Insurance Company, and composed of other life company representatives and an outside educator, the board soon made 22 specific recommendations for better procedures and practices.

The College also established a public relations program with the American Society of CLU to improve every aspect of communication for the two organizations. The College and the Society soon published a booklet titled *CLU on the March,* which clarified their mutual objectives and in so doing "brought the two organizations into a new phase of teamwork."[2] Each strengthened the closeness of the relationship by naming several top officers to the other's respective board of directors.

The momentum of change and improvement continued into 1945, a year that on the world scene included the discovery of penicillin and the signing of the United Nations charter. Soon after the war ended, the College trustees voted to add a fifth objective to the four institutional goals stated in the original bylaws of 1927. In addition to its earlier objectives, the College (to promote research) would henceforth prepare and publish "textbooks and other materials deemed essential to the fullest realization of this College's program of study in all fields of knowledge with which a life underwriter should be acquainted."[3]

These publications would include volumes for college insurance classes, texts for agency management examinations, study supplements, refresher monographs, and a series of special brochures. Julian S. Myrick composed *Value of CLU* and Paul F. Clark wrote *Post War Challenges to CLUs.*[4]

Nineteen forty-five was a year when coffee cost 25 cents per pound, sirloin steak could be bought for 40 cents a pound, and a 4 1/2-ounce can of baby food sold for a nickel.[5] It was also a time when the nation, the business community, and the life insurance industry looked forward to an era of limitless expansion and growth.

Solomon S. Huebner, with a decade of the College presidency behind him, determined to make up for wartime restraints and expand his institution better to serve its industry by making its employees more professional. Huebner, who invariably wore red neckties and bore such nicknames as "Sunny Sol" (for his optimistic outlook) and "the Little Giant" (because of his short physical stature),[6] moved forward with two new developments in the CLU program. Both reflected his belief that the CLU designation should be considered the beginning and not the end of a life underwriter's professional education. Both were conceived with and carried out by the closely affiliated American Society. First came a publication titled the *Journal of the American Society of Chartered Life Underwriters*, which appeared in the fall of 1946. Second came a series of summer seminars called the CLU Institute. The University of Connecticut hosted the initial Institute, which gave 39 CLUs 2 weeks of instruction in the fields of estate planning, business insurance, and pension and profit-sharing plans.

The *Journal,* edited by Walter A. Craig, CLU, boasted a board of noted life insurance authorities including James Elton Bragg, CLU, a New York University professor of life insurance and a former president of the Society. Dr. Huebner contributed an article to the first issue, and he called it "New Horizons in Life Insurance."[7]

James Bragg has been described as "one of the most valuable men in the first 30 years of CLU history."[8] The College had elected him a trustee the previous year and in 1946 appointed him chairman of the new and important Examination Board to succeed Irvin Bendiner, who died suddenly of a heart attack at age 46.[9] Bragg would serve 11 years in this capacity and win praise from Dr. Huebner, who said of Bragg's efforts, "He accomplished an immense amount of good on behalf of the CLU program in his service to the College and the American Society."[10]

Joseph H. Reese, Sr., was another important person in the early years of the College. The Penn Mutual Life agency manager earned his CLU in 1930, served as a president of the American Society, and became increasingly involved with the College. He served on a number of College committees and chaired a special group created to plan the 20th anniversary observance in 1947.

That year, when Jackie Robinson broke the major league baseball color barrier and Chuck Yeager shattered the sound barrier with the first supersonic flight, The American College celebrated 2 decades of genuine accomplishment. It could point to solid achievement in spite of economic depression and world war. Every student statistic confirmed impressive gains in all aspects of the CLU program. The College reported that 2,801 men and women now held the coveted CLU designation with 4,496 others partway through the discipline. CLU chapters across the nation held special events to mark the occasion. The *Journal of the American Society of Chartered Life Underwriters* dedicated its entire March 1947 issue to this significant milestone.

The National Association of Life Underwriters, which (as we have previously noted) helped found the College, inaugurated a new award program that year to honor the life and work of John Newton Russell, one of the College's incorporators and an earlier leader of the insurance industry. In 1947 the NALU presented the John Newton Russell award to six men, retroactively to 1942, the year of Russell's death. Solomon S. Huebner received the gold watch and citation for that year as the first person to be so honored. Julian S. Myrick, 1943, and Paul F. Clark, 1945, were among the other recipients.[11]

The College had first conducted its affairs in Dr. Huebner's crowded office before a 1931 move to a somewhat larger space in a nearby building. Soon after the 20th anniversary commemoration, however, the College learned it would lose its lease in 1949. A further move loomed ahead. Joseph H. Reese, Sr., chaired a special Quarters Committee to find a permanent home to replace the rented rooms that had become quite inadequate for the burgeoning institution.

Soon the committee selected a brick and stucco residence at 3924 Walnut Street, Philadelphia, near the University of Pennsylvania campus. This building was purchased and remodeled to accommodate not only The American College but also its closely affiliated insurance compatriots: the American Society of CLU, the S.S. Huebner Foundation, the American Institute for Property and Liability Underwriters, and the Society of Chartered Property and Casualty Underwriters.[12]

Money to pay for this ambitious step came from the Edward A. Woods Foundation (the College's first endowment fund) and through a 20-year, 4 percent, $55,000 mortgage from Penn Mutual. Two hundred and fifty people attended the dedication luncheon, which featured Julian S. Myrick as toastmaster and Harold E. Stassen, University of Pennsylvania president, and Leroy A. Lincoln, Metropolitan Life president, as speakers. They praised the founding fathers and current leaders of The American College, which now occupied what an insurance reporter called "the first permanent national center of insurance education on the collegiate and professional level."[13]

There were numerous embellishments. Mutual of New York gave a portrait of Julian S. Myrick to be hung in the boardroom; Roger Hull, a Mutual Life vice president and College trustee, made the presentation. CLUs worldwide paid for a new portrait of Dr. Huebner by Alice Kent Stoddard, which soon decorated the reception area. Finally, Edward A. Woods's daughter, Marjory W. Robinson, provided a portrait of her father, together with his valuable collection of carved ivory figures. She gave the College permission to sell some of the collection if extra money was needed.

The impermanence of human life and the importance of life insurance were both underscored within a year of the College's occupancy of its new headquarters. A number of College trustees died, including George E. Lackey of Massachusetts Mutual; O.J. Arnold, president of Northwestern Life; William M. Duff, CLU, a former College official; and Walter A. Craig, editor of the Society's *Journal*.

With the passing of these old-guard stalwarts, however, came new blood in the persons of Helen L. Schmidt, who at that time began her exceptional career at the College, and a young Huebner fellow, Davis W. Gregg, from Ohio State University. A trustee commented on Gregg's appointment with these words, "From the standpoint of personality, ability, interest, and initiative, Dr. Gregg should become a real asset to the College."[14]

The 1950 census takers recorded that the U.S. population had grown to 151 million people. Life expectancy also increased from a decade earlier to a new high of 68.2 years. The College could claim legitimate gains in every phase of its program. Still, the CLU designation could not be called an unqualified success. Some industry figures felt the emphasis was too academic and not sufficiently practical for the work-a-day world. Those who did poorly on the examinations complained that they were too hard. Others were puzzled by the grading process.[15]

President Huebner put Davis Gregg to work on a study of these problems. Gregg worked with the recently appointed executive manager, Leroy G. Steinbeck, to produce a 21-page report. The document revealed that home office and field confusion between The American College and the Life Underwriter Training Council educational programs caused part of the problem.

In 1950 the two organizations formed a joint committee to clear the air. In the future, LUTC promotion would stress skill in the *use* of basic insurance knowledge, while the CLU program would emphasize the *acquisition* of knowledge, the breadth and depth of which would provide a basis of professional activity.[16]

That same year the College began a new outreach effort to high school educators across the country who came to the University of Pennsylvania for a summer session to study family financial security options, including life insurance. Initially, 33 teachers participated, but soon the program spread to other universities from coast to coast.

While the College record of higher enrollment, more graduates, and increased influence within the industry makes absorbing reading, Solomon S.

Huebner, his colleagues, and the trustees never forgot that beneath the surface of institutional achievement lay the basic goal of providing more knowledge to increase the fundamental life insurance objective of meeting human needs. Through the sponsorship of John A. Stevenson, an American College trustee and president of Penn Mutual Life, a Wharton School professor of those days prepared a printed report that confirmed the life insurance role in this regard. The study showed that in 72 percent of the cases considered, life insurance made it possible to keep family survivors together following the death of an insured person.[17]

For 24 years David McCahan had worked closely with his early mentor, then colleague, and always friend, Solomon S. Huebner. From his student days grading examination papers, through a series of promotions to the rank of dean (and later president from 1952–1954) of the College, McCahan did his share and more in carrying responsibility for the College's direct operations and as a leader in successive related undertakings. From the Huebner Foundation to the just mentioned summer workshops, McCahan invariably found himself in the thick of the action. In 1951 the mounting pressure took its toll. McCahan suffered a serious heart attack.

Julian S. Myrick, board chairman, who believed that the College had long been understaffed at the executive level, took immediate steps to alleviate the excessive workload. At his urging the trustees authorized a number of new positions. Before new people could be employed, however, McCahan staged a rapid recovery. By mid-summer he was back at work but this time as executive vice president. Young Davis Gregg became dean of the College, and within a few months two other men joined the administrative staff.[18]

David McCahan's impressive College career is just one example of Dr. Huebner's skill in finding and motivating others to help him in the struggle to being professional status to the selling of life insurance. Wharton School professor Harry J. Loman is another. One writer described Huebner and Loman as "very practical idealists" who made a good team.[19] Together Huebner, McCahan, and Loman had founded the American Institute for Property and Liability Underwriters.

The Revised Standard Version of the Bible was the best-selling book of 1952, the Atomic Energy Commission exploded the world's first hydrogen bomb, and the average American ate 42 hot dogs that year. The American College celebrated its Silver Jubilee with a panoply of events worthy of its 25 years of leadership in life insurance education. The American College of CLUs and the American Society Joint Committee put together a nationwide program that featured the College and CLUs at various industry functions. Silver predominated: One gathering was called to order by the ringing of silver bells; a silver-covered dinner program was presented at the NALU convention as part of the CLU conferment exercises.[20]

The American Society's *Journal* recognized the College by devoting its June issue entirely to the extraordinary Wharton School professor, Solomon S. Huebner. It described his contributions to the University of Pennsylvania, his role in founding The American College, his leadership in the insurance industry, and his service to the nation. Harold E. Stassen, University of Pennsylvania president, wrote the preface, and men who had been Dr. Huebner's former students contributed most of the articles. Among the contributors were David McCahan, who presented "A Collection of Huebnerian Philosophy," and Paul F. Clark, who offered "Traits—Common and Different."[21]

Two announcements accompanied these and other tributes. Dr. Huebner would retire from the chairmanship of the University of Pennsylvania's Department of Insurance after 39 years in that position. He would also retire as president of the College after 18 years in that role. He became professor emeritus at the University of Pennsylvania and continued a close association with the College as president emeritus, life trustee, and in a variety of other special positions.

The College trustees turned to the executive vice president to fill the vacancy brought about by Solomon S. Huebner's retirement. They elected David McCahan president in a move that surprised no one and that assured a smooth transition and uninterrupted institutional leadership.

Dr. McCahan became president at a time when the growth of The American College, the American Society, and the American Institute for Property and Liability Underwriters had created space problems at the 3924 Walnut Street headquarters jointly occupied by these and two other related organizations, the Insurance Institute of America and the Society of Chartered Property and Casualty Underwriters. The close proximity of the life and property insurance entities proved mutually beneficial as they shared a common approach to insurance education. Therefore the College built an addition to its Walnut Street structure and moved the S.S. Huebner Foundation, which had always been housed with the College, to a new insurance center in Dietrich Hall at the University of Pennsylvania.[22]

After 25 years the College could count 4,476 CLUs, and more than 6,350 other men and women had earned partial credit toward the respected designation. The Silver Anniversary Survey revealed the typical CLU to be a 45-year-old married male with one or two children, who owned $50,000 of life insurance, held religious convictions, and belonged to both the Society and the NALU.[23]

Nevertheless, the College continued to be concerned about recognition for those whose experience did not meet CLU eligibility requirements. The certificate of proficiency "was considered definitely second class by many."[24] The College therefore returned to a familiar concept that it first visited in 1928 with the dubious and short-lived Accredited Life Underwriter program as an alternative to the real thing.

Now in 1953, through the influence of its Registration Board, The American College introduced the CLU Associate designation in a further attempt to acknowledge the work of others within the industry. The official announcement clearly defined the difference between the two designations: The CLU designation would continue to be awarded to those persons "engaged in life insurance sales and service and those functions related thereto," while the CLU

Associate designation was intended for "persons engaged in other life insurance activities."[25]

Cumulative past success and a new academic program did not compensate for the fact that inflation and rising costs required more operating money if the College was to continue its distinctive educational leadership for the industry. To attack the problem Julian S. Myrick, board chairman, appointed a Special Committee on Financial Welfare. Led by the executive vice president of Prudential Life, Harold M. Stewart, CLU, the committee worked with the Society to produce a program that provided for a larger staff, wider services to the field, and funds to pay for them from higher examination fees and greater life company contributions to the Cooperative Fund for Underwriter Training.[26]

In 1952 two men were selected for different roles of president. The American people elected Dwight D. Eisenhower to lead the nation. The American College selected David McCahan as its president. Ike would serve 8 years, but destiny decreed McCahan a much shorter tenure. He died of heart complications on July 28, 1954. He was 56.

The trustees' memorial resolution paid tribute to their fallen associate by expressing their appreciation for his exceptional performance in many capacities over the history of the College. The resolution went beyond customary sentiments to recognize Dr. McCahan's involvement with the various other organizations with which The American College had such close connections. In a very real sense David McCahan's life epitomized the interrelation of the College with the Society, the S.S. Huebner Foundation, the American Association of University Teachers of Insurance, and the American Institute for Property and Liability Underwriters.

NOTES

 1. *Annual Report,* The American College, 1944, p. 1.
 2. Mildred F. Stone, *A Calling and Its College* (Homewood, IL: Richard D. Irwin), 1963, p. 213.
 3. Ibid., p. 207.
 4. *Annual Report,* 1946, pp. 20–21.
 5. Paul Dickson, *Time Lines* (Reading, MA: Addison-Wesley Publishing Co., Inc.), 1990, p. 5.
 6. Warren T. Hope, *The First Fifty Years* (Malvern, PA: The Institute), 1992, p. 2.
 7. Mildred F. Stone, *The Teacher Who Changed an Industry* (Homewood, IL: Richard D. Irwin), 1960, p. 220.
 8. Stone, *A Calling,* p. 211.
 9. Ibid., p. 207.
10. Ibid., p. 211.
11. Stone, *The Teacher Who,* pp. 224–226.
12. Stone, *A Calling,* pp. 222–224.
13. Ibid.
14. Ibid., p. 231.
15. Ibid., p. 232.
16. Ibid., p. 233.
17. G. Wright Hoffman, *Life Insurance at Work* (Hartford, CT: Life Insurance Management Association), 1950, p iv.

18. Stone, *A Calling,* p. 238.
19. Hope, *The First Fifty Years,* p. 5.
20. Stone, *A Calling,* p. 244.
21. Ibid., pp. 246–248.
22. *Annual Report,* 1952, pp. 1–2.
23. Stone, *A Calling,* p. 252.
24. Ibid., p. 257.
25. Ibid.
26. Ibid., p. 263.

The College's first headquarters was Solomon S. Huebner's office on the campus of the University of Pennsylvania.

The Board of Directors and members of NALU–men like Edward A. Woods, Ernest J. Clark, Paul F. Clark, and Julian S. Myrick– and Professor Solomon S. Huebner founded The American College in 1927. Huebner's vision of college-level professional distance education for life insurance agents changed the way people learned about life insurance.

Solomon S. Huebner

Edward A. Woods

Ernest J. Clark

Paul F. Clark

Julian S. Myrick

The American College Examination Board in 1945. For over 50 years students had to sit in testing centers once a year with blue books and pencils to write out examination answers.

Dr. Solomon S. Huebner and Dr. David McCahan presenting diplomas at the 1947 conferment dinner in Boston.

Davis W. Gregg joined The American College as assistant dean in 1949. He had received his PhD in 1948 as a Huebner fellow.

The College's first permanent headquarters was a mansion at 3924 Walnut Street (1948-1961) near the University of Pennsylvania.

SECTION THREE

Full Time 1954–1961
Davis W. Gregg

4

A New Era

Teach us to number our days.

Psalm 90:12

Events at The American College during the summer of 1954 seemed to confirm the view that "the history of an institution perhaps inevitably winnows down to a few prominent names tied to the dates of official events."[1] Be that as it may, the months of June through September that year proved pivotal for the College, which had just observed its 27th birthday.

David McCahan's sudden, premature death precipitated a sequence of promotions that were to have significant impact on the future of the distinctive insurance College in Philadelphia. The trustees first selected Davis Weinert Gregg to be the fifth president of the College. Then they appointed Herbert C. Graebner to the deanship. Both men deserve closer scrutiny.

Davis W. Gregg can be described as a man on the fast track. He began his relationship with the College as an S.S. Huebner Foundation fellow in 1946. Previously, he had completed college at the University of Texas at Austin, earned an MBA at the Wharton School, worked 2 years for Aetna Life, and served as a U.S. naval officer. Out of uniform and back in academia, he earned a PhD in economics at the University of Pennsylvania in 1948, where he came to know and work with Solomon Huebner, David McCahan, Julian Myrick, and others closely associated with the College.[2] They marked him as a man with future potential for the College. It came as little surprise therefore when after a short stint teaching insurance at Ohio State and Stanford Universities, he moved back to Philadelphia to be assistant dean at The American College of Life Underwriters, an institution for nontraditional education, as it was then known.

In 1951 Gregg earned the CLU designation and that same year, as we have previously noted, became dean of the College. Now, only 3 years later, and within 8 years of beginning as a Huebner fellow, he advanced to the presidency. Dr. Gregg rose quickly through the executive ranks to reach the top position, which would retain until 1982—longer than the combined tenure of his four predecessors: Edward A. Woods, 1927–1928; Ernest J. Clark, 1928–1934; Solomon S. Huebner, 1934–1952; and David McCahan, 1952–1954 (who together held that office for a total of 27 years). Gregg differed from the first four presidents in that he would be the first to serve full time.

Herbert C. Graebner, CLU, another full-time executive appointment, held degrees from Valparaiso and Northwestern Universities and had earned his PhD at Pennsylvania. He had faculty experience at Valparaiso, Westminster College, and Butler University, where he had been dean of the business college.

Nor was Graebner a stranger to The American College. He was a 1946–1947 S.S. Huebner Foundation fellow with his new boss, Davis W. Gregg. In addition, Graebner had taught CLU classes, graded CLU examinations, and been a consultant to the College. The trustees described him as a "strong and devoted educational leader to serve life insurance and collegiate insurance education."[3]

These two men set the tone for a new day at 3924 Walnut Street, Philadelphia. The trustees, in making the two appointments, recognized the need for building a full-time administrative staff at the College; further positions would be created and filled in the near future.

That same year two other men with close connections to the College—Paul F. Clark, CLU, and Dan M. McGill, CLU—assumed new roles with or related to it. Each made and would continue to make a unique and sustained contribution to life insurance and to its respected professional institution.

Paul Clark and The American College went together like the proverbial horse and carriage. He helped incorporate the institution in 1927 and had served as a board member ever since. Over the years he built an impressive career at John Hancock Mutual and became its president in 1944. Along the way he earned the CLU designation and enjoyed a leadership role at the National Association of Life Underwriters. He was NALU president in 1928, and he received that organization's John Newton Russell Memorial Award in 1945. Clark helped found the Million Dollar Round Table, and he served a term as president of the American Society of Chartered Life Underwriters. Through it all, he remained a committed American College trustee and a person well qualified for the distinction of life trustee bestowed by his colleagues in 1954. Clark's citation mentioned his influence and leadership as it praised his "devotion and special service" to the cause of life insurance professional education and its distinctive College.[4]

It is interesting to note that the board had not elected any other persons to this esteemed status since 1938–1939 when Ernest J. Clark (Paul's uncle) and three others became the first people to hold the title. Nor would there be another life trustee named until 1961.

Dan M. McGill was another person who had an extensive background with The American College and related organizations. Named executive director of the S.S. Huebner Foundation in 1954, he had begun these associations as an original Huebner fellow in 1941. After wartime service in the U.S. Army Air Corps, he returned to the University of Pennsylvania for PhD studies and earned that degree in 1947. During that time he got to know Davis Gregg. McGill was invaluable in the capacity of examination preparation for the College. He also was chairman of the Board of Graders.

After a few years on the faculty of the University of North Carolina, Dr. McGill returned to Penn as an associate professor of insurance. In this capacity he developed further relationships with the College and served it many ways. He would win many honors and be recognized as a national authority in the life insurance field. Many years later one writer described McGill as "a pension czar" for his knowledge and as "Mr. Integrity" for his character.[5]

Beyond the campus confines in 1954, Roger Bannister won fame as the first man to run a mile in less than 4 minutes. The Supreme Court ruled segregated education illegal, and the American Cancer Society reported a high heavy-smoker death rate. This specific news had personal meaning for Solomon S. Huebner. After many years of smoking more than 10 cigars per day, he developed a malignancy of the mouth. Despite an ominous prognosis and prolonged radium treatment, Huebner recovered and doggedly resumed the strenuous public speaking schedule he had maintained since his retirement from the presidency of the College a few years before.[6]

This emphasis of 1954 names in the news at the College brings life to what some people consider to be a dull business, characterized by mortality tables and the fine print on the reverse side of policy pages. Nevertheless, 27 years of successful operations produced a number of quantitative measurements worth mentioning—not only in themselves but also as the foundation for fresh initiatives undertaken at that time and in the years to follow. For example, CLU matriculations reached 1,517, the highest figure in 7 years. CLU examinations were held at 140 educational institutions in 44 states, Honolulu, and two military centers.[7] CLU designations awarded came to 378, or the second largest number since 1927. Beyond statistics, the College and the American Society of CLU started a joint publication titled *CLU Annual Review*.

There were also curriculum changes. One part of the CLU program would henceforth include the subject of accident and health insurance. In addition, the College, for greater effectiveness and control, brought the Cooperative Fund for Underwriter Training into its own organizational structure.[8]

President Davis W. Gregg took pride in The American College's past, but the new chief executive also understood that its future development depended on recognition of current happenings throughout the insurance world—stirrings in the fields of group coverage, pension plans, business insurance, and estate planning. There could be no standing still in a nation where a birth occurred every 8 seconds and a death every 22 seconds.[9]

Early in the Gregg presidency a new Council of Educational Advisers was formed. The College trustees functioned through an unusual committee structure. First, there were the traditional executive, budget, and finance groupings. Then came the large Committee for Cooperative Fund for Underwriter Training, chaired by board member Paul F. Clark (but composed largely of outside industry officials and successful agents), and finally, the Registration and Examination Boards, again chaired by trustees but made up partially of nonboard members. James Elton Bragg led the latter group, which had much to do in the mid-1950s with the College's response to these previously mentioned industry trends as the institution worked with this newborn advisers organization.

The Council of nine advisers served both The American College and the American Institute for Property and Liability Underwriters to evaluate their respective CLU and CPCU (Chartered Property and Casualty Underwriter) programs. Dr. Leslie J. Buchan, professor of accounting at Washington University, St. Louis, chaired the initial group. Among those serving with him were Laurence J. Ackerman, dean of the School of Business Administration, University of Connecticut; Edison L. Bowers, chairman of the Economics Department, Ohio State University; and Stanley F. Teele, dean of the Harvard Business School.[10]

The Council avoided generalities and tackled specific subjects such as criteria for determining professional business competency, the effect of College curricular changes on professional insurance careers, and the applicability of programmed learning to professional insurance education. This last subject commanded the College's urgent attention. The CLU diploma program based its examinations on essay-type questions. As we have already noted, several of the College pioneers helped grade these tests, including Solomon S. Huebner, David McCahan, Irvin Bendiner, Dan M. McGill, and Davis W. Gregg.

The system worked well enough in the early days when the number of examinees remained relatively low, but the passing years brought dramatic escalation in the number of examinations taken and waiting to be graded. There were 1,262 in 1945, 3,839 in 1950, and 4,521 by 1955. Clearly, something had to be done beyond trying to enlist more and more qualified graders and requiring that each one correct a larger number of papers.

The trustees retained the Educational Testing Service of Princeton, New Jersey, as educational consultants to guide the College toward a new examination system that would include both essay and objective (multiple choice) questions. ETS's Robert J. Solomon, a noted testing authority, directed this effort, which took 3 years to develop.[11]

As the College moved ahead with these and other new ventures, it remained mindful of the extraordinary contributions made to the cause and the College by the late David McCahan. The board appointed Solomon S. Huebner, James Elton Bragg, and Charles J. Zimmerman, CLU (elected a trustee in 1951), as a committee of three to plan an appropriate memorial to the recently deceased president.

Bragg and Zimmerman brought impressive credentials to this task. They also loved the College and would be included on any objective list of its most valuable persons. Bragg was at the time a manager for Guardian Life. Zimmerman, the managing director of the Life Insurance Agency Management Association, would later become board chairman of both Connecticut Mutual Life and The American College. At the time of McCahan's death, the Memorial Committee prepared affectionate and respectful resolutions and presented Dr. McCahan's portrait to the College. The committee members also proposed a more substantive recognition for their fallen friend in the form of an educational foundation, and they took the preliminary steps in that direction.

On the national scene Dwight D. Eisenhower held the first televised news conference in the history of the U.S. presidency. The AFL merged with the CIO to create a mega-union force of 15 million members, and Tennessee Williams won the Pulitzer Prize in drama for his memorable *Cat on a Hot Tin Roof.*

Solomon S. Huebner continued to be an important link between this wider world and the insurance college. Freed from direct campus responsibility, Huebner accepted a succession of invitations to be the guest of honor at various industry events and civic occasions. The Wisconsin State Association of Life Underwriters, for example, celebrated the 50th anniversary of life insurance education in 1955 and presented Dr. Huebner with a scroll signed by the presidents of four organizations, including the governor of the state.[12] The citation described the recipient as an "internationally renowned teacher, economist, author, and lecturer," who as "a great intellectual pioneer conceived the ideas and wrote the books that were needed to make insurance education possible."[13]

This award was just one example of the honors bestowed on the famous professor in those days. Another honor was awarded soon thereafter from the New York City University of Pennsylvania Club, which presented Huebner with its first Benjamin Franklin Award for "his outstanding contribution to the university."[14] These awards served a dual purpose as they simultaneously confirmed the achievements of a respected leader and brought favorable attention to The American College.

Back at the College, the trustees elected Paul F. Clark vice chairman of the board—a position that had been vacant for a number of years. In 1956 they appointed Dan M. McGill as educational consultant and added his name to the list of College officers for the first time.[15] A third action brought Thomas J. Luck from the College of William and Mary to be director of management education. He soon revived this particular program, which had languished for some time through lack of full-time professional guidance. Dr. Luck worked out a new program with the cooperation of the Life Insurance Agency Management Association and the Managers Conference of the National Association of Life Underwriters in another example of effective collaboration between the College and supportive insurance organizations.[16]

The matter of management education, however, was not the only academic area to receive attention at this time. Extensive curricular changes were put in place for the 1956 school year. The CLU program still consisted of five courses with 4-hour examinations for each, but the new curriculum gave greater emphasis to "business life insurance, pensions, group insurance, taxation, annuities, and planned and family finance."[17]

Earlier in the year, before the revised schedule actually took effect, President Davis Gregg sent the CLU headquarters staff to seven cities across the nation to explain the planned changes. The team went to Atlanta, Chicago, Cleveland, Dallas, Hartford, Philadelphia, and San Francisco and met with 219 people. These regional conference attendees came from 127 cities, represented by members of local CLU education committees. Also present were guests from life company home offices, local CLU chapter presidents, and managers and general agents. Their response was recorded as "universally favorable."[18] As a follow-up to these college gambits, the American Society sponsored staff visits to some 35 localities to bring them further information about the curriculum revisions and to stimulate formation of CLU study groups wherever possible.[19]

These efforts proved productive. In the year when Congress passed the Federal Highway System Act, the minimum wage rose to one dollar per hour, and the Lerner and Lowe musical *My Fair Lady* captured Broadway, CLU study group formation jumped to the highest level in 6 years. There were 291 groups in 1956, compared to 259 the previous year and only 202 in 1951. Individual student enrollment growth kept pace as 5,670 men and women took part in 1956, in contrast to 5,050 the year before and just 3,281 in 1951.[20]

The 1956 study groups met in 168 cities representing 42 states and the District of Columbia. The groups had different types of sponsors. The NALU and CLU chapters conducted approximately 50 groups each. Home offices and life agencies also participated. Colleges and universities, however, oversaw 46 percent of the total, and their study groups made up 55 percent of the aggregate enrollment of all 291 groups. These figures were in keeping with the original objectives of the College, which stated that the institution would "cooperate with colleges and universities in training students for the career of professional life underwriter."[21]

Each year an early page of the *Annual Report* of The American College included a paragraph that expressed the thanks of the trustees and officers of the College for the cooperation received from the American Society of Chartered Life Underwriters, from CLU chapters, and from the officials of many life companies. In 1956, as in previous years, the trustees also specifically mentioned "the very generous help of the educational authorities and the many teachers serving the College throughout the nation."[22]

Speaking of trustees, the board elected three new members in 1955–1956. Herbert C. Graebner, the College dean, became a term trustee in addition to holding the institution's number two executive position. The other two new members were Edmund L. Zalinski, CLU, PhD; and John O. Todd, CLU. Zalinski, executive vice president of the Life Insurance Company of North America, was no stranger to industry leadership. He had headed both the Life Underwriter Training Council and the National Association of Life Underwriters. Todd, a Northwestern Mutual Life special agent and Million Dollar Round Table member, had been president of the Minneapolis-St. Paul, Minnesota, CLU chapter.

In 1956 the College and the American Society formed a Joint Committee on Continuing Education, which established a College department bearing that name. The committee, chaired by Paul A. Norton and including John O. Todd, Herbert C. Graebner, and later Edmund L. Zalinski, reviewed "the whole idea and the possible avenues of Continuing Education."[23]

Through a bylaw change the board created the David McCahan Foundation in 1956 as an integral part of the College and appointed a special governing committee to direct it. Harold M. Stewart served as the first chairman of the group, soon to be succeeded by Holgar J. Johnson.

The 4th year of Davis W. Gregg's presidency brought additional people and program changes, both off and on the campus of the increasingly influential American College near the University of Pennsylvania. Out in the field, Solomon S. Huebner took two trips. The first added another honor to his long list of awards, while the second journey enabled the pioneer insurance educator to spread the gospel of the human life value concept to an ever-widening audience. Here are the details.

In 1957 Ohio State University established an Insurance Hall of Fame to recognize those who had made major contributions "to the thought and practice" of this subject in the United States and Canada.[24] Forty-five industry leaders comprised the Board of Electors, which selected three winners from among 135 nominees. Two were leaders of the past; the third recipient was a living person. Benjamin Franklin, who founded the country's first fire insurance company, and Elizur Wright, who pioneered state regulation of life insurance, were the heroes from the past. Solomon Huebner was the contemporary honoree. The citation declared, "His untiring efforts have done more to raise the professional and ethical standards of the insurance industry than the activities of any other American."[25]

A few weeks later Solomon S. Huebner and his wife began their second trip that spring. This time they covered 15,000 miles in 31 days, during which Dr. Huebner spoke in public 22 times. The Huebners attended a Japanese tea party in Hawaii as guests of the Honolulu Association of Life Underwriters.[26]

Closer to home, at the American Society of Chartered Life Underwriters, Eugene C. DeVol, CLU, former head of the Philadelphia CLU chapter, became the Society's new president. Paul S. Mills, CLU, assumed the duties of managing director, replacing Leroy G. Steinbeck, CLU, who resigned to join the Life Insurance Company of North America as vice president. Mills combined the talents of a salesperson, teacher, and manager. He had been active in the Columbus, Ohio, Life Underwriters Association and the CLU chapter there.

Within the College administration itself, Jack C. Keir, a former Kansas State University economics professor, moved up from director of educational publications to become director of educational services in a reorganization intended to give greater assistance to CLU students and teachers. Walter W. Dotterweich, Jr., who had been senior economist at Prudential Life, took Keir's place.

Both the College and the American Society had long been concerned with the need to strengthen continuing education beyond the CLU designation. Temporary attempts in this direction had not been productive. At this time therefore the two organizations formed a new Joint Committee on Continuing Education, which held its first meeting in Philadelphia on April 30, 1957. Jack C. Keir, Herbert C. Graebner, Solomon S. Huebner, and Edmund L. Zalinski represented the College.

It is interesting to note that three insurance-related educational entities observed anniversaries in 1957. The Life Underwriter Training Council was 10 years old. The American College turned 30, and the Wharton School of Finance and Commerce observed its 75th birthday. It is of even greater interest to note that these organizations enjoyed close relationships through the various services rendered to each other by past and present directors and officers of The American College. For example, Dr. Huebner and President Gregg were both ex-officio members of the American Society Board of Directors, while past and present American College directors Paul F. Clark, Roger Hull, and Charles J. Zimmerman were LUTC directors at one time or another. Solomon S. Huebner and David McCahan linked the College and the Wharton School over the years in a variety of ways too numerous to mention.

In 1957 the College and the American Society jointly held the 30th annual conferment dinner and exercises in Detroit. Stanley F. Teele, Harvard Business School dean, gave the address; 519 men and women received their CLU designations.

The College and the Wharton School came together in May that year through a 2-day International Insurance Conference sponsored by the University of Pennsylvania "in recognition of the insurance industry's long and continued interest in the affairs of the Wharton School as pioneer in the collegiate field of insurance education."[27] Davis W. Gregg and Dan M. McGill codirected the conference, which drew 400 guests to hear Dr. Huebner speak on the present and future of life and health insurance in the United States. The audience, which included people from 30 foreign countries, also heard the first McCahan Foundation lecturer, John Sloan Dickey, president of Dartmouth College.

Since the trustees had created the David McCahan Foundation the year before to "strengthen and encourage research on the nature, problems, and issues pertaining to economic security mechanisms," the governing committee appointed to oversee the operation initiated a series of annual lectures to focus on the theme of the American family. Dr. Dickey's talk, "The American Design: E Pluribus Unum," made the point "that our capacity for union in all things remains rooted in our sense of community, and this community is essentially private rather than governmental in character."[28] This emphasis echoed Huebner's long-time dictum that "the family is the philosophical heart of life insurance . . . within the family community is the constant urge to protect, to prolong."[29]

The McCahan Foundation, now off to an impressive start, would sponsor many other lectures and studies in the field of economic security during the next three decades. The International Insurance Conference had an impact beyond the Pennsylvania campus through discussion of the insurance environment of other countries with vastly different conditions of government supervision. The manager of the United States Chamber of Commerce Insurance Department, A.S. Kirkpatrick, declared that "the future of life insurance in the United States would be influenced by our international relationships."[30]

America opened its first large-scale nuclear power plant in 1957. Desegregation came to the public schools, and John F. Kennedy won the Pulitzer Prize for his *Profiles in Courage.* All in all, it had been a pretty good year for both the country and The American College.

NOTES

1. Warren T. Hope, *The First Fifty Years* (Malvern, PA: The Institute), 1992, p. 33.
2. Mildred Stone, *A Calling and Its College* (Homewood, IL: Richard D. Irwin), 1963, p. 268.
3. Ibid., p. 269.
4. Ibid.
5. John Shea, "Putting a Premium on Insurance Education," *University of Pennsylvania Gazette,* November 1988.
6. Stone, *The Teacher Who Changed an Industry* (Homewood, IL: Richard D. Irwin), 1960, pp. 279–281.
7. *Annual Report,* The American College, 1954, p. 6.
8. Stone, *A Calling,* p. 279.
9. Paul Dickson, *Timelines* (Reading, MA: Addison-Wesley Publishing Co., Inc.), 1990, p. 79.
10. Stone, *A Calling,* pp. 272–273.
11. Ibid., p. 276.
12. Ibid., pp. 283–285.
13. Stone, *The Teacher Who,* p. 285.
14. Ibid.
15. *Annual Report,* 1956, p. 31.
16. Stone, *A Calling,* pp. 284–285.
17. Ibid., p. 274.
18. *Annual Report,* 1956, p. 6.
19. Ibid.
20. Ibid., p. 3.
21. Stone, *A Calling,* p. 69.
22. *Annual Report,* 1956, p. 2.
23. Stone, *A Calling,* p. 299.
24. Stone, *The Teacher Who,* p. 286.
25. Ibid., pp. 287–288.
26. Ibid., pp. 288–290.
27. Ibid., p. 290.
28. John Sloan Dickey, "The American Design," McCahan Foundation, Reprint Series no. 1, p. 1.
29. Ibid., p. 2.
30. Stone, *The Teacher Who,* p. 292.

5

Symbol of the Future

Procrastination is the Thief of Time.

Edward Young

After 4 years as president of the College, Davis W. Gregg could proudly declare that in 1958 "an all-time record number of persons participated directly in the educational programs of the College."[1] Each of four measurement figures reached new highs. Enrollment in the CLU and Management Education study groups, for example, numbered 7,732, with another 3,300 men and women doing independent study. Examination matriculants reached 2,350, and 635 persons earned the CLU designation. Dr. Gregg's report also noted the participation of the College officers in educational conferences, field visitations, and other activities.[2]

The president did not refer to his own achievements in the *Annual Report* that year, but a review of those days reveals the broad dimension of his leadership. Gregg, before beginning his tenure, had "become acquainted with the College and the ideals of those who had been its builders over the years."[3] This depth of interest enabled the energetic executive to build well upon the work of his predecessors and then to carry the College to a position of even greater influence throughout the industry. In addition to occupying the traditional role of ex-officio member of various board committees, President Gregg personally chaired the Executive Committee and sat with a number of new planning groups, including the Special Building Committee.

Other important names to note that year include Ernest J. Clark, Jack C. Keir, and Charles J. Zimmerman. Life trustee Clark died after 31 years of unbroken service to the College, which included the roles of College president and chairman of the Board of Trustees. Clark was the only person to hold both of these positions.

Keir, who achieved his CLU designation that September, earned another promotion in 1958, this time to the rank of assistant dean, working with Dean Herbert C. Graebner. It was Keir's third title in as many years at the expanding institution.

Zimmerman, who had been an effective member of several trustee committees since his 1951 election to the board, moved into greater responsibility as chairman of the Special Committee on Financial Welfare "charged to make a thorough study of the College's present and future finances."[4]

The Zimmerman committee—which marked a turning point in College finances—included such stalwarts as Paul F. Clark, CLU, and Joseph H. Reese, CLU, as well as William H. Andrews, Jr., CLU, and Roger Hull, CLU, president of Mutual Life of New York. Up until this time the College had based its annual expense budget primarily upon student fees, which included credit certificates drawn upon the Cooperative Fund for Underwriter Training. There were precious few reserves, and greater financial burdens loomed ahead.

Zimmerman and his associates made a comprehensive review of the entire College program and convinced the trustees to create two funds designed to produce greater financial resources for the institution. The first fund sought $1 million in corporate support for permanent endowment. The second fund emphasized the need for a similar sum in annual contributions from individual CLUs and Friends of the CLU program.

Roger Hull chaired the Permanent Endowment Fund Committee. He enlisted a group of top executives from the leading companies, and they asked for specific amounts based on company size. After only 2 months, the committee counted $850,000 toward the $1 million goal with pledges to be paid in full within 5 years. More than 150 companies took part.[5]

William H. Andrews, Jr., led a Development Council created as part of the second fundraising effort, titled the Development Fund. The Andrews council involved more than 125 CLUs representing every chapter of the American Society. This program marked the beginning of organized annual gift solicitation by the College.

As new personalities guided these crucial initiatives, two veteran trustees passed personal milestones of another kind that year. Henry E. North, originally elected in 1936 and a founder of the Cooperative Fund for Underwriter Training, resigned from the board as he retired from Metropolitan Life. Julian S. Myrick, elected in 1929, celebrated 20 years' service as chairman of the board at a testimonial dinner given by his colleagues.

Solomon S. Huebner, the most durable figure in the College family, did his part, too. The peripatetic professor began another trip as ambassador to the insurance industry. This time he and Mrs. Huebner went to the Far East and Down Under at the request of the American State Department. They traveled 40,000 miles, visiting Japan, the Philippines, Australia, and New Zealand, and were away 80 days. Their 5 weeks in Japan had been arranged by insurance organizations of that country and the University of Pennsylvania Alumni Association in Japan. Gen Hirose, president of Nippon Mutual Life Company, acted as the Huebners' personal host. The Emperor of Japan decorated Dr. Huebner with the Order of the Sacred Treasure for his contribution to the welfare of the Japanese insurance industry.[6]

In addition to Huebner's well-deserved recognition, the trip was important for two other reasons: It affirmed the ongoing overseas outreach of The American College (which Huebner began with his 1927 trip to Japan), and it provided a splendid venue in all the countries (particularly New Zealand) to emphasize the value of augmenting government social programs with individual efforts toward financial security.[7]

From the beginning the College's central academic emphasis had been the CLU designation for individual salespeople. Since the early 1930s, however, the College had also offered a program for agency management people. Now, in 1958, after 25 years of indifferent results, the College introduced a revised curriculum for this subject developed by Thomas J. Luck, who had come to the College from William and Mary. He had been appointed director of management education 2 years before. Dr. Luck's new program caught on at once; 394 students in 24 study classes held in 22 cities took part the first year. There proved to be surprising demand for this program, which led to a diploma in agency management.[8]

America at this time experienced the first increase in its first-class postal rate since 1932; the price of a stamp rose from 3 cents to 4 cents in 1958. People bought more than 150 million hula hoops, creating a craze of historic magnitude, and then promptly forgot the frenzy of the fad.[9] The first U.S. satellite went into earth orbit, and President Dwight D. Eisenhower announced the formation of the National Aeronautics and Space Administration.

The College presented the second McCahan Foundation lecture, featuring an address by University of Chicago sociologist William Fielding Osburn. Dr. Osburn's lecture, "The Family in Our Changing Society," inaugurated a sequence of studies devoted to the "American Family and Life Insurance."[10]

Early in 1959 the University of Pennsylvania Press published the proceedings of the first International Insurance Conference held in Philadelphia 2 years before to commemorate the 75th anniversary of the Wharton School as the oldest collegiate school of business in the nation. Davis W. Gregg and Dan M. McGill coedited the volume titled *World Insurance Trends*. It contained articles about the impact of inflation on insurance, the regulation of insurance, and the insurance environment in 27 countries. The book offered a permanent record of the international conference, an event that Gregg and McGill described as "without precedent in the annuals of insurance."[11] The book also underscored the previously mentioned involvement of the College with insurance education far beyond its campus confines—a circumstance that brought continued satisfaction to both men.

Dr. McGill experienced further satisfaction that year through his appointment as the Frederick H. Ecker Professor of Life Insurance at the University of Pennsylvania. Metropolitan Life gave $400,000 to endow this teaching chair, which was the first of its kind in the United States.[12] Gaylord P. Harnwell, the university's president, Solomon S. Huebner, and both Frederick H. Ecker and Frederic W. Ecker hosted a luncheon in honor of Dr. McGill on March 31, 1959. The Eckers were a most unusual father-and-son pair. The elder, Frederick H., served Metropolitan Life as board chairman, while the younger, Frederic W., held the job of that company's president. Both men dressed alike in dark suits and wore black homburg hats to the luncheon. The son succumbed to a viral infection 4 years later, and his father, then aged 90, died within a month of his son's demise.[13]

People far outshine procedures and programs when it comes to reader interest, and no wonder! People bring programs to life, make them credible, give them meaning. The American College grew and gained insurance industry respect and affection because it could claim both effective people and substantive methods and systems.

The beginning of a new kind of examination for the CLU designation in 1959 highlights these dual attributes. After 3 years of preparation, the College introduced its first examinations that combined the heretofore-used essay-only questions with a number of objective (multiple choice) questions. This combination enabled the College to test candidates on a broader basis, since it had proved impossible to cover all study assignments with essay questions within the 4-hour exam period. The new plan "represented a combination of the best elements in professional examining procedures."[14] President Gregg named Albert H. Clark, a young man with two degrees from the University of Georgia, assistant director of examinations to organize and oversee these new CLU and management education examinations.[15]

The third David McCahan Lecture, which had now become a regular feature of the academic year, was another reflection of the College's capacity to create and sustain programs. James H.S. Bossard, University of Pennsylvania professor, titled his address that April "Large and Small Families—A Study in Contrasts." (Dr. Bossard, an internationally known sociologist, was commissioned to prepare a textbook in this field, but he died after writing only one chapter.[16])

Much of the College's forward momentum came from accord between its president and members of the board. The institution had been fortunate in attracting and retaining the interest of some extremely effective trustees who made the insurance College an important part of their lives. Grant L. Hill, CLU, of Northwestern Mutual Life, was one of those trustees, and his retirement from the industry and the board of The American College concluded 31 years of enthusiastic service.

Spring and summer 1959 crowded the College calendar with a series of occasions, whose significance almost surpassed the events that had marked the College's first 3 decades and served as a harbinger of even greater days to come. There would be property purchase, groundbreaking, and three new program initiatives in the period between May and September.

Thirty years of consistent growth compelled the College to think about a future home that would better serve its needs than the 3924 Walnut Street headquarters in Philadelphia. Back in 1957 Dr. Gregg had urged the trustees to form a New Building Committee to consider various options. The board named Penn Mutual's Joseph H. Reese chairman of this group, which included Eugene C. DeVol, past president of the American Society, and Charles J. Zimmerman, then president of Connecticut Mutual. Reese brought experience to the task, since he had performed a similar function as chairman of an earlier committee that had selected the Walnut Street site in the 1940s.

The committee soon realized that future plans required extensive property, which was not financially feasible within the city of Philadelphia. The College therefore sought a suburban location and finally found the 11.15-acre estate, Glenbrook, in Bryn Mawr, Pennsylvania, which had been owned by a family named McIlvaine. The College bought the land in June, demolished the old mansion on it, and proceeded with plans to build a new headquarters in September.[17]

On September 21, 1959, the College and the American Society held another of their combined endeavors that were of mutual benefit. The CLU Joint Committee on Continuing Education sponsored the first national seminar in the history of the life insurance business. More than 700 men and women attended this forum, which preceded the Philadelphia convention of the National Association of Life Underwriters. The program offered "the best thinking on vital questions concerning the meaning of life insurance in today's economy."[18]

President Emeritus Solomon S. Huebner presented a paper at the seminar and later that day took part in the ground dedication ceremony in Bryn Mawr. Dr. Huebner turned the first spade of earth for the new building designed by the architectural firm of Mitchell/Giurgola as a national center for insurance education. Participants in the ceremony included Joseph H. Reese, building committee chairman; Robert Dechert, counsel for both The American College and the Society; Edmund L. Zalinski, who presided at the festivities; and Joseph E. Boettner, CLU, chairman of the class of 1934 and president of the Philadelphia Life Insurance Company.[19]

The College held its 1959 national conferment exercises 2 days later, and as part of the September 23d event, initiated a new honor for college and university teachers of CLU classes. The College presented sterling silver replicas of the famous Philadelphia Bowl along with certificates of appreciation to three men who had taught such sessions for 25 years: Albert J. Schick of Newark, New Jersey; George L. Buck from Seattle, Washington; and Solomon S. Huebner of worldwide insurance fame.[20]

These, then, were the momentous College and American Society events of 1959, when in the world at large Alaska and Hawaii became states, Fidel Castro took over Cuba, 12 countries declared Antarctica free for science, and the United Nations reported an increase in the world population of 85 people per minute.

The incipient move to Bryn Mawr energized the entire College family. Preparations for the great event quickened the institutional pulse as President Gregg, the trustees, and the administrative staff found themselves caught up in the myriad activities of the interim period between groundbreaking and actual occupancy of the building. In addition to their ongoing operational routine, the leaders and support staff handled the endless details of planning and organizing the physical transition. Then, too, there were a number of major policy changes to prepare for and put into effect when voted by the board at the annual meeting. These actions included revising some existing programs as well as initiating several new ones that had been under study by special committees for some time.

Dr. Gregg, of course, carried the primary responsibility for the success of each area. He gladly assumed the extra burdens because they arose as a direct result of his dream for an expanded College and his vision for making that dream a reality. Gregg, as an earlier College historian commented, saw the College "as a research center with experimental laboratories for testing new teaching techniques and the development of new materials."[21] As Gregg had previously been deeply involved in the search for and purchase of the new campus, he now paid careful attention to the cultivation of both Bryn Mawr community leaders and the owners of adjacent property who would be College neighbors.

For 2 years Gregg (and his secretary, Mechthild K. Longo) had worked on a survey, *Insurance Courses in Colleges and Universities outside the United States.* Although there had been surveys of insurance education in this country on previous occasions, there had never been a comprehensive study of world insurance courses and professors.[22] In May 1960 the survey was published, and in his introductory message to the survey the president of the College distinguished between "the ancient business and science of insurance," on the one hand, and "the Twentieth Century concept of collegiate insurance education," on the other.[23]

Helen L. Schmidt became assistant to the president that year after several years in the dean's office. She made a valuable contribution to the completion of the survey, which was subsequently reviewed with favor in the *Journal of Insurance.* Schmidt had once again demonstrated her "great capacity for administrative responsibility and effective editorial work."[24]

A reporter of those days correctly declared, "The year 1960 will long be remembered in the annals of The American College."[25] He referred to bylaw changes that were to accelerate the institution's growth as a national college of both life and health insurance. The amended bylaws (1) redefined the College's basic CLU program to establish educational standards in the field of life and health insurance, (2) provided for a series of certificate courses in specialized areas (such as agency management), and (3) emphasized continuing education for CLUs through the creation with the American Society of a Joint Department of Continuing Education.

These new programs would not stand separately but were to be coordinated by a new Educational Policy Board composed of the dean, 12 other members, and (ex-officio) the chairman of the Continuing Education Committee. The trustees as a board were ultimately responsible for the entire package of decisions involved in the bylaw changes. At the annual meeting that year three of them—Julian S. Myrick, Paul F. Clark, and Charles J. Zimmerman—also attracted individual attention by exchanging leadership roles, moves that held great promise for the College.

Myrick, a trustee for 31 years and chairman for 22, celebrated his 80th birthday in 1960. He took the occasion to retire but agreed to continue as chairman emeritus. The board elected Paul F. Clark, who was a founding trustee and had served as vice chairman of the board since 1957, to succeed him. Clark was the nephew of Ernest J. Clark, the first chairman of the board and, before that, president of the College. Paul F. Clark's industry achievements as president, then chairman of John Hancock; president of NALU; Million Dollar Round Table member; and John Newton Russell Award winner made him a well-qualified successor to Julian Myrick. Charles J. Zimmerman became vice chairman, thus deepening his involvement in the life of the College that had begun as early as 1940, when as NALU president he spoke at the Solomon S. Huebner testimonial banquet.[26] Both Clark and Zimmerman would prove worthy of their new titles in the years ahead as they continued The American College board leadership tradition of energy, good judgment, and integrity, which had been its hallmarks since 1927.

In addition to these program innovations and personnel promotions, the College sponsored two one-time special events later that year. The National CLU Development Council kickoff dinner for the $1 million gift campaign for the new building and other expenses enlivened the Warwick Hotel in Philadelphia on October 21, 1960. A time capsule ceremony at the new building site the previous day brought sparkle to the Bryn Mawr campus as some 130 CLU Council members took part in both activities.[27]

Paul J. Clark presided at the time capsule ceremony, and Charles J. Zimmerman spoke at the dinner. Zimmerman closed his "We Make No Small Plans" speech with the reminder that "what happens to life insurance happens to the life of the individual, and what happens to the life of the individual happens to America."[28]

Some of the things happening in America that year include the 1960 census report, which counted 179 million persons in the U.S. population, and National Center for Health Statistics that revealed the average life expectancy in America had risen to 69.7 years—up from 68.2 years a decade earlier. The Federal Drug Administration approved the pill for birth control, and Teflon cookware made its first appearance.

The College and the nation at large came together in a dramatic moment during the NALU convention in Washington, DC, when President Dwight D. Eisenhower met with Dr. Solomon S. Huebner, Board Chairman Paul J. Clark, College President Davis W. Gregg, Julian S. Myrick, Robert Dechert, and other NALU officials including its current president, William E. North, CLU (1956).[29]

A vocation achieves professional status when it requires both formal academic training in an accepted area of knowledge and adherence to a recognized ethical standard of conduct. From the beginning all CLU designees had sworn to an oath of ethical conduct at the time their designations were awarded. The American Society of Chartered Life Underwriters, which began as an alumni association to unite graduates of the College, soon moved toward the development of a professional goal for the designation holders. It dared to be more than a trade association as it worked closely with the College to promote and support professional aims.

The Society took steps in the late 1950s to reinforce this emphasis through the appointment of a committee to develop a set of standards to which all its members would subscribe. Within 2 years the Society's Board of Directors adopted such a Code of Ethics, and a majority of the members ratified it in 1961. The Code of Ethics contained eight guides and six rules of professional conduct, including "I shall place the welfare and interests of my clients above my own interests," and "A member shall respect the agent/principal relationship existing between himself and the company he represents."[30]

The physical dramatized the philosophical during the spring of 1961 when the College effected the eagerly anticipated move from its outgrown headquarters in Philadelphia to the extensive Bryn Mawr campus on March 27. The new location combined the atmosphere of a small college town with metropolitan area accessibility.[31] As the College expanded its facilities it augmented its staff through two new appointments. It named Peter E. Camp as registrar, and Dr. Joseph M. Belth as assistant director of continuing education within the joint department set up by the College and the Society.

The College shared its new home with the four organizations that had also occupied the 3924 Walnut Street, Philadelphia, headquarters: the American Society of CLU, the American Institute for Property and Liability Underwriters, the Society of Chartered Property and Casualty Underwriters, and the Insurance Institute of America. The trustees named the new building Huebner Hall to honor the man "whose idea was the inspiration for The American College and the American Institute."[32]

Dedication day was June 1, 1961, for the distinctive brick and precast concrete 29,000-square-foot structure. The trustees met that morning in the handsome boardroom, and Byron K. Elliott, John Hancock Mutual president, presented the College with a portrait of Paul F. Clark as a gift from Elliott's company. Julian S. Myrick and Solomon S. Huebner spoke briefly on this occasion, and President Davis W. Gregg used the opportunity to praise and challenge the board by saying, "Never in history has the American public needed more the kind of security which can be given through the mechanism of insurance. Never before have those within the industry had a greater potential for service."[33]

After tours of the building, the crowd assembled under a marquee nearby to hear brief remarks by three local college and university presidents and a summation by College and Society counsel Robert Dechert, who introduced architect E.B. Mitchell to present Solomon S. Huebner with a symbolic key to the building. Dr. Huebner said he hoped the key would "unlock educational treasures and institutional progress beyond our fondest dreams and imaginations."[34]

Other events that day featured planting trees on campus and a dedication dinner at the Sheraton Hotel in Philadelphia. In the first event, representatives of three alumni classes began a custom followed by future 25-year graduates. Among the representatives were 1936 graduates Lester A. Rosen, CLU, then chairman of the Million Dollar Round Table, and Benjamin M. Gaston, CLU, who did the honors for their class by planting a Scarlet Oak on the south lawn. Former board chairman of New York Life, Devereaux C. Josephs, who spoke at the evening banquet, described Huebner Hall as "the symbol of the man who has done most in this century to shape the course of insurance by insistence upon education and research."[35]

During these exciting Philadelphia and Bryn Mawr months, the outside world saw President John F. Kennedy create the Peace Corps and Cuban refugees try to liberate their homeland with an ill-fated landing at the Bay of Pigs. New York City experienced a power blackout that paralyzed Manhattan at the start of the evening rush hour on the hottest day of the year, June 14, 1961.[36]

In September College trustees and American Society directors traveled to Denver, Colorado, for their respective annual meetings in connection with the National Association of Life Underwriters convention. At that time the NALU presented Davis W. Gregg with the John Newton Russell Award for outstanding service to the institution of life insurance.

The College board met on September 26 and elected three men as new term trustees, including William H. Andrews, Jr., of the Jefferson Standard Life Insurance Company in Greensboro, North Carolina, who led the important CLU Development Fund. For the first time since 1954, the board also designated several current members as life trustees. For "outstanding, constructive, and devoted service to the College" these four men were chosen: Robert Dechert, College counsel; Joseph H. Reese, secretary of the College; Charles J. Zimmerman, vice chairman of the board; and Earl R. Trangmar, consultant to Metropolitan Life. Trangmar enjoyed this status for less than a month. In a poignant reminder of the impermanence of life he died on October 21 after a brief illness.[37]

Trustee ex-officio Lillian G. Hogue, CLU, of New York Life in Detroit, completed her presidency of the American Society at this time and received recognition as the first woman to hold that office. Her company funded four CLU Institute fellowships in her name and honor.[38]

By the end of the year William H. Andrews, Jr., CLU Development Fund chairman, reported substantial progress in the gift campaign launched the previous October. More than 2,350 CLUs and Friends of CLU had pledged close to $750,000 for current expenses, including mortgage reduction for Huebner Hall. Better yet, 473 people had given or pledged $1,000 or more, thus becoming members of the Golden Key Society and entitled to wear the distinctive tie clasp or label pin of that select group. The ubiquitous Charles Zimmerman gets the credit for creating the imaginative "giving club" to recognize contributors of this amount or more, which they could pledge and pay over as long as a 10-year period.

Without exaggeration 1961 had been the most momentous year in the history of the College. The Huebner Hall ceremony prompted these words from a trustee: "I could feel the electric spark of the events. The dedication climaxed another era in the young life of The American College. We have a firm footing for another and larger reach in the years ahead."[39]

NOTES

1. *Annual Report,* The American College, 1958, p.1.
2. Ibid.
3. Mildred F. Stone, *A Calling and Its College* (Homewood, IL: Richard D. Irwin), 1963, p. 268.
4. Ibid., p. 309.
5. Ibid., p. 313.
6. Mildred F. Stone, *The Teacher Who Changed an Industry* (Homewood, IL: Richard D. Irwin), 1960, p. 320.
7. Ibid., p. 329.
8. Stone, *A Calling,* p. 268.
9. Paul Dickson, *Timelines* (Reading, MA: Addison-Wesley Publishing Co., Inc.), 1990, p. 97.
10. *Annual Report,* 1958, p. 2.
11. Davis W. Gregg and Dan M. McGill (editors), *World Insurance Trends* (Philadelphia: University of Pennsylvania Press), 1959, p. v.
12. Stone, *The Teacher Who,* pp. 337–338.
13. Dan M. McGill, interview with the author, October 25, 1994.
14. *CLU Annual Review,* 1959, p. 8.
15. Ibid.
16. Stone, *A Calling,* p. 288.
17. Ibid., p. 325.
18. Ibid., p. 302.
19. *CLU Annual Review,* 1959, p. 18.
20. Ibid., p. 6.
21. Stone, *A Calling,* pp. 321–322.
22. Ibid., pp. 289.
23. Davis W. Gregg, *Insurance Courses in Colleges and Universities outside the United States* (Philadelphia: The American College), 1960, p. 5.
24. Stone, *A Calling,* pp. 289–290.
25. *CLU Annual Review,* 1960, pp. 16–17.
26. *Annual Report,* 1960, p. 2.
27. *CLU Annual Review,* 1960, pp. 11, 23.
28. Charles J. Zimmerman, "We Make No Small Plans," speech at National CLU Development dinner, October 21, 1960, p. 8.
29. *CLU Annual Review,* 1960, p. 15.
30. Stone, *A Calling,* pp. 323–324.
31. *CLU Annual Review,* 1961, p. 2.
32. Stone, *A Calling,* p. 338.
33. Ibid.
34. Ibid., pp. 339–340.
35. Ibid., p. 342.
36. *New York Times,* vol. CX, no. 37,762, p. 1.
37. *CLU Annual Review,* 1961, p. 3.
38. Ibid., p. 18.
39. Stone, *A Calling,* p. 340.

The College purchased a 10-acre estate in suburban Bryn Mawr to establish a permanent campus in 1959.

Time capsule ceremony for Huebner Hall, 1960.
Left to right: Davis W. Gregg, S.S. Huebner, Paul F. Clark, and Paul S. Mills (managing director of the Society).

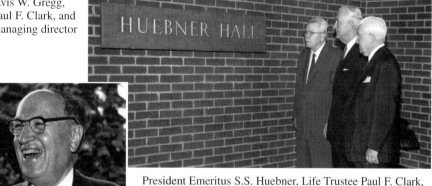

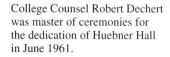

President Emeritus S.S. Huebner, Life Trustee Paul F. Clark, and Chairman Emeritus Julian S. Myrick at Huebner Hall dedication in 1961.

College Counsel Robert Dechert was master of ceremonies for the dedication of Huebner Hall in June 1961.

President Emeritus Solomon S. Huebner in his Huebner Hall office in 1961.

55

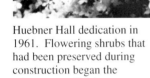

Huebner Hall dedication in 1961. Flowering shrubs that had been preserved during construction began the arboretum collection.

President Davis W. Gregg welcomes President Emeritus Solomon S. Huebner to Huebner Hall in 1961.

Life Insurance and Financial Services Research Library established in Huebner Hall in 1961.

PART TWO

Bryn Mawr
1961–1997

SECTION FOUR

Expansion 1961–1982
Davis W. Gregg

6

Great Expectations

Time, you old gypsy man, will you not stay,
Put up your caravan just one day?

Ralph Hodgson

Davis W. Gregg may not have known Robert Browning's poem proclaiming that "a man's reach should exceed his grasp,"[1] but the energetic executive lived its stimulating credo. From the beginning of his administration in 1954 the president of the College sought every opportunity to serve the insuring public by educating the insurance practitioners.

The move from Philadelphia to Bryn Mawr, Pennsylvania, afforded just such an occasion, and Dr. Gregg made the most of it. Progressing beyond the suburban campus dedication festivities into the first full year in Bryn Mawr, the College observed two important birthdays in 1962, which served as pivotal points around which the institution could sum up the past and surge toward the future: Solomon S. Huebner reached 80 on March 6, and the College itself turned 35 on March 22. Dr. Gregg maximized the impact of both events.

The College marked the octogenarian's four-score milestone with a party at the Union League Club in Philadelphia, at which the Committee of 1,000 presented him with an enormous three-tiered cake decorated with hundreds of tiny red candles. Each candle represented a new CLU candidate sponsored that year by the committee through a special effort to honor the respected patriarch of the life insurance community.

Dr. Huebner had served as chairman of the Committee of 1,000 since its organization in 1959 by a group of CLUs pledged to recruit and mentor at least one new candidate apiece for study toward the prized designation. In the first 4 years of its existence, and spurred in 1961 and 1962 by the approaching Huebner birthday observance, the committee enrolled some 1,800 new candidates.

Huebner flavored his party remarks with funny stories, but he also used the occasion to stress the symbolism of the cake and to predict that the committee's work would become increasingly important. "There is far too high a lapse rate among CLU candidates," he said. "Many candidates who are now considering dropping out would, with proper encouragement [of a committee member], continue on to get the designation."[2]

The College published a pamphlet titled *Mr. Smith Sponsors a CLU Candidate* to explain the work of the Committee of 1,000 and the responsibilities of its members. Benjamin M. Gaston, CLU, and his son, Benjamin M. Gaston, Jr., CLU, posed, respectively, as the fictional Mr. Smith and his protégé for the pictures in this illustrated story.[3]

The College commemorated its 35th anniversary with a listing of significant mileposts—dates, names, and first-time events in the steady growth of the pioneer distance education institution. It published this impressive record and circulated it among its immediate constituency and across the life insurance industry.[4]

The chronology provoked comparison of the past and present in both the academic world and the risk-protection business. Each had experienced dramatic changes during these 3 1/2 decades. Consider first the matter of education itself.

Not until the mid-20th century did general public schooling take hold. A majority of American teenagers did not graduate from high school before 1940. As one critic wrote, "The area of most people's ambition was not school but the marketplace."[5] Superimpose the College's goal of promoting higher education for insurance salespeople upon this broad base of skepticism about the value of formal study, and the inertia and obstacles the College faced in the early years become readily apparent.

Thirty years of articulate leadership and dogged effort, however, brought results (some of which have already been noted in previous chapters). The American College achieved success in every area of instruction and administration as it moved from nonexistent numbers in 1927 to these commendable figures for the 9 years ending in 1962:

Category	1953	1962
Student enrollment	3,638	10,332
Number of classes	222	528
Cities where classes were held	122	247
Matriculants	1,320	4,183
Examination takers	2,775	8,621
Examinations given	3,712	10,732
CLU designations awarded	334	785
CLU Associate designations	19	145

Life insurance industry contrasts between 1927 and 1962 were equally vivid. Company advertisements in a trade journal of the 1920s include a Fidelity Mutual of Philadelphia franchise offering that says, "For a Man's Man" to enjoy "A Wider and More Profitable Field of Service." Lincoln National in Ft. Wayne, Indiana, proclaimed, "We Write Them All—Dad, Mother, Little Sister and Baby Brother."[6]

The Insurance Yearbook for 1927 listed a total of 2,500 life companies, associations, and fraternal orders in the business of issuing policies. The 322 legal reserve life insurance companies counted premium receipts in the amount of $2,624,013,968 and claimed admitted assets of $12,939,806,809. That same publication 35 years later recorded 876 legal reserve companies with premium income of $17,582,480,183 and admitted assets of more than $126 billion.

Typical advertisements in the later edition continued to stress basic risk avoidance (in contrast to the investment-return emphasis that would characterize later years). The Union Central Life Insurance Company of Cincinnati attracted the reader's attention with these words: "Our success is measured in our two-way persistency rating: Good business that stays on the books; good agents who stay with the company." John Hancock Mutual Life put it this way: "Look to John Hancock for complete insurance service—whatever the problem. John Hancock has the modern answer to your client's life insurance needs."[7]

Regardless of the words, the figures confirmed an expanding market to a growing population with a rising standard of living, all of which offered great opportunity to The American College. The trustees and President Gregg moved forward to maintain the momentum. They did it through two board policy decisions coupled with the implementation of a new, better defined educational program that had been discussed for several years.[8]

The College cleared the academic air by announcing that it would not award multiple designations, such as Chartered Life Manager (CLM), Chartered Pension Underwriter (CPU), or Chartered Estate Planner (CEP). Furthermore, it would not permit multiple routes to the CLU designation. These decisions distinguished the CLU designation "as the professional designation for both life and health insurance personnel with the broad connotation of Chartered 'Human Life Value' Underwriter."[9]

At the September 18, 1962, board meeting the trustees spelled out the three fundamental lines for development of the College educational program: the CLU Diploma Program, Specialized Certificate Courses, and Continuing Education for CLUs.[10] The CLU Diploma Program (composed of five basic parts) made the holder eligible for membership in the American Society of Chartered Life Underwriters. The specialized certificate course in Agency Management was offered throughout the nation, while the pilot courses in Company Management and Health Insurance were to be conducted in Bryn Mawr and Philadelphia. Continuing Education for CLUs would be a joint program with the American Society, created to keep the holders of this designation up-to-date. In 1962 the Department of Continuing Education offered two Discussion Outlines to local chapters and sponsored seven one-day seminars in cities from Coral Gables, Florida, to San Mateo, California.[11]

While these important events occurred at the College, life proceeded apace on the national scene. The United States placed its first astronaut in earth orbit. America faced down the Soviet Union over the Cuban missile crisis, and 90 percent of U.S. households had at least one television set, with 13 percent having two or more. Average life expectancy continued its steady climb to pass 70 years of age, and Frank Loesser and Abe Burrows won a Pulitzer Prize for their popular musical play *How to Succeed in Business without Really Trying*. The trustees and president of The American College continued their efforts to make the institution succeed, but they knew from experience that strenuous and sustained effort would be needed for the College to grow in reputation and influence.

That year there were trustee changes. O. Sam Cummings, a former general agent of Kansas City Life in Dallas, retired from the board after 30 years' service. Frederic M. Peirce, president of General American Life in St. Louis, took his place on the governing board.[12] There were also campus promotions. Director of Educational Services Walter W. Dotterweich, Jr., became an assistant dean, joining Jack C. Keir, CLU, in that academic rank. Keir assumed broader duties.

Another 1962 initiative involved appointing educational consultants to meet the need for personal contact between the College and teachers and students in the field. The College selected four university professors, all CLUs, to visit classes and confer with pupils and their instructors: William T. Beadles, Illinois Wesleyan; David A. Ivry, University of Connecticut; Kenneth W. Herrick, Texas Christian University; and Arthur W. Mason, Jr., Washington University. These first consultants also functioned as part of the newly established American College Lecture Bureau.[13]

Wise leadership of any organization involves a blend of today and tomorrow. The trustees and the president therefore paid close attention to current operations as they looked toward the future and tried to plan accordingly. With this in mind, they created a Development Study Commission "to appraise the future extent and direction of growth of The American College."[14] They took this action better to anticipate coming requirements for money, physical plant, and staff.

Orville E. Beal, CLU, chaired the first commission, and these members served with him: William H. Andrews, Jr., Bruce Bare, Herbert C. Graebner, Davis W. Gregg, Roger Hull, Raymond C. Johnson, Ben S. McGiveran, Joseph H. Reese, Sr., Charles H. Schaaff, Edmund L. Zalinski, and Charles J. Zimmerman. All were CLUs.

*   *   *

After 35 years, the CLU abbreviation for Chartered Life Underwriter could be said to have come of age. As early as 1939 the Merriam Webster Collegiate Dictionary had listed CLU in its sixth edition. In addition to this national recognition, the College annually recorded a growing number of matriculants enrolled and a larger number of examinations taken. The College also kept count of those men and women who persevered to earn the designation. Now, in 1963, this figure exceeded 1,000 persons for the first time, bringing the grand total since 1928 to 11,410 CLUs and 212 CLU Associates.[15]

The College Registration Board also announced that over the 35-year period 46,099 candidates had met all eligibility requirements as a prerequisite to taking examinations and that more than 80,000 persons had engaged in CLU study.[16]

Reported official corporate statistics of this kind reflect not only successful program conception and administration but also enormous human effort on the part of the academic aspirants. A skeptic might ask if their labors were worth the time and money expended and if these efforts were rewarded. In other words, do field underwriters who are CLUs write more (and/or better) business and make more money than those who do not have the designation?[17]

The College decided to find out. In 1963 it turned to 32 life insurance companies for the answer, and it asked home office officials to compare the production, income, and persistency of their CLUs' business with that of their employees without the designation.

The results were overwhelmingly affirmative in favor of CLUs. CLUs had from 7 percent to 161 percent higher production than non-CLUs; the median differential was 59 percent. CLUs also enjoyed 59 percent higher earnings than non-CLUs. Finally, CLU persistency of business exceeded that of companies' non-CLUs.[18] No wonder College President Gregg and the trustees rejoiced in this objective confirmation of the College *raison d'etre* as measured by this statistical study.

The governing board, however, took action beyond mere self-congratulation. It used the good news to reaffirm policies approved in recent years, and it directed the administration to pursue them with vigor.

Curriculum is the core of an academic institution, and The American College featured a number of new courses that year—all in the Specialized Certificate category. For example, the Certificate Course in Health Insurance went national after being pilot-tested in Philadelphia the previous years. In a preliminary stage other candidates studied Company Management I and II in pilot classes held in several cities including Hartford and New York. Furthermore, the College introduced a course in Group Insurance and tested it at Huebner Hall with the intention of introducing all three courses nationally the following year if they proved to be successful on a trial basis.[19]

The American Society celebrated 35 years of existence in 1963 and formed its own Development Study Commission to determine future needs after conducting a survey of all CLUs regarding their interest in and need for improved and expanded service. Although nowhere near all CLUs had joined the Society over the years, membership had risen to 6,900 in 139 chapters by the 35th anniversary year.

The College and the Society, as we have noted previously, worked closely together from their earliest days; now a bylaw change permitted an even closer relationship by enabling the chief executive of each organization to serve on the governing board of the other. Paul S. Mills, managing director of the Society, joined the College trustees ex-officio, in counterpoint to Davis W. Gregg's similar role as a director of the Society.[20] In addition, the Society's president, vice president, and immediate past president were invited to serve as ex-officio members of the College's board.

Fresh starts, academic or otherwise, attract attention, but sustaining existing programs and fine-tuning them for greater effectiveness are equally important to a successful institution. The American College emphasized this second objective anew in 1963, with progress in both continuing education for CLUs on the one hand and in building a richer relationship with students and teachers across the country on the other. The College brought in two new executives to lead these endeavors. In May the College and Society appointed Fred J. Dopheide, CLU, as director of continuing education for both organizations. In June the College named Dr. Ronald C. Horn as director of educational services.

Dopheide, who came from the Prudential Insurance Company of America and held a Juris Doctor degree, organized three CLU Institutes that summer to continue an effort begun in 1946. The Universities of Colorado, Connecticut, and Wisconsin hosted these programs, which drew a record combined enrollment of 178 students.[21] In addition, there were eight one-day seminars cosponsored by the College-Society Joint Committee on Continuing Education, chaired by John K. Luther, CLU. These sessions were held in such cities as Pittsburgh, Atlanta, Dallas, New Orleans, and Baltimore.[22]

Ronald Horn came from Syracuse University where he had taught insurance and statistics. At The American College he became responsible for both CLU and Certificate Course programs, which together involved 700 teachers and 22,000 students. That fall his Department of Educational Services conducted a series of teacher conferences in eight cities from coast to coast.

Approximately 228 CLU and Certificate Course teachers and 47 university teachers of insurance attended these sessions, which were held on a one-day or noon-to-noon basis. The conferences gave instructors the opportunity "to exchange ideas on classroom methods and teaching problems," as well as "to learn more about the educational program of the College and to get acquainted with other teachers from their own geographic area."[23]

These College ventures took place amid inflationary economic developments and political turmoil. The first-class postal rate reached 5 cents, and for the first time in history the average American worker earned more than $100 per week. Violent death was becoming more pervasive and came to black and white leaders here at home and far away. A sniper murdered civil rights activist Medgar Evers in Mississippi. President Ngo Dinh Diem died in a Saigon military coup. John F. Kennedy was assassinated in Dallas, to be succeeded by Lyndon B. Johnson, who became the 36th president of the United States.

Within the College family a number of individuals began new relationships in 1963. The trustees established the senior officer position of executive vice president and promoted Herbert C. Graebner to fill the post as well as continuing him as dean. Two board members retired: Cecil J. North, a veteran of 24 years' service, and Hugh S. Bell, CLU, who had been a trustee for 9 years. Both men were honored with Resolutions of Appreciation and engraved Philadelphia Bowls. Bell, however, died shortly before his was to be presented, and his widow received the handsome award. Two other men were elected term trustees: Leslie J. Buchan, professor at Washington University in St. Louis, and Alexander Hutchinson, CLU, senior vice president at Metropolitan Life.[24]

Amid these personnel changes and new academic offerings the College noted with satisfaction the progress made during the year by two programs started in 1962. First, the Educational Consulting Program had gone so well that the College added two additional appointees to the original group of four. The new appointees were Dr. Grant Osburn, CLU, of Arizona State University, and Dr. John E. Stinton, CLU, of the University of Colorado.[25] Second, the College Development Study Commission increased its capacity to chart the future direction and extent of College growth through the formation of several working committees.

Roger Hull chaired the Committee on Growth Projection and Resource Needs. Orville E. Beal led the Committee on Center for Advanced Studies in Risk and Insurance. Ben S. McGiveran headed the Committee on the College's Future Role in Enforcing CLU Professional Standards. Charles J. Zimmerman took responsibility for the Committee on Graduate School for Chartered Life Underwriters. Davis W. Gregg chaired the group with the longest name: the Committee on Cooperation with the American Institute for Property and Liability Underwriters with Relation to Utilization and Acquisition of Physical Facilities.[26]

In September the trustees honored Mildred F. Stone, CLU, assistant secretary of Mutual Benefit Life, for her recently completed official history of the College, titled *A Calling and Its College*. At the board's annual dinner Chairman Emeritus Julian S. Myrick presented Stone with a pearl necklace on behalf of the appreciative board.[27]

*   *   *

Solomon S. Huebner died suddenly on July 17, 1964. The legendary insurance educator, who began life as a Wisconsin farm boy, had lived a productive 82 years, many of which were spent on the national and international scene as the highly respected articulator of his human life value concept as the true economic basis of life insurance.

The great man had influenced the lives of more than 75,000 students at the Wharton School and countless other people across the country and around the world. Saddened relatives, friends, and neighbors crowded his memorial service in Philadelphia. Among them were leaders of the life insurance industry and its numerous professional affiliate organizations.

Dr. Huebner had received many honors and had won numerous awards during his distinguished career. Yet as Joseph Conrad, the famous English writer noted, "A man's real life is that accorded to him in the thoughts of other men by reason of respect or natural love."[28] Here are some thoughts about Solomon S. Huebner by those who knew him well and felt that respect and affection.

Davis W. Gregg remembered Huebner's Pennsylvania campus lectures as "dynamic, active, inspiring, and stimulating."[29] Edmund L. Zalinski, a trustee of the College from 1954 to 1971, called Huebner "a strong educator and leader of men."[30] William B. Wallace, American College board chairman from 1991 to 1994, put it this way: "I shudder to think what would have happened to the life insurance industry if it had not been for the ideas and vision of Dr. Huebner."[31]

(Wallace, a former Columbia University football star and later president of the Home Life Insurance Company, did not shudder easily.)

In addition to such formal expressions and official tributes, there were vivid informal descriptions by those who knew first-hand of Huebner's habits, mannerisms, and personal predilections. As we mentioned earlier, some called him "Sunny Sol" to reflect his positive nature and optimistic outlook. Benjamin M. Gaston, Sr., remembered Huebner as an intense person, given to "fist shaking and teeth gritting" in persuasive conversation. Others recalled that Huebner wore red neckties, loved an office rocking chair, never learned to drive a car, and never addressed a person by his or her first name, preferring the more dignified Mr., Mrs., or Miss.[32]

Not all comments about Huebner have been laudatory. Occasional negative traits have been mentioned by those who worked with the man. For example, one American College trustee called Huebner a dictator, an insurance company president claimed that Huebner kept the board at a distance, and a University of Pennsylvania colleague described Huebner as a promoter, not a scholar.

Meanwhile, although the dynamic Dr. Huebner had passed from the scene, the College continued its practice of strengthening management and building for the future by giving greater responsibility to staff members who did well in their jobs. To illustrate, in 1964, the College promoted G. Victor Hallman, CLU, from director of educational publications to the position of assistant dean and advanced Dr. Jack C. Keir from assistant dean to the rank of associate dean.[33]

Dr. Huebner's death provided an appropriate time to review The American College's twin fundraising efforts begun in 1960. The Permanent Endowment Fund for $1 million from life insurance companies (chaired by Roger Hull) achieved early success, as we have noted in a previous chapter. The Development Fund for a similar sum from CLUs and Friends of CLUs (headed by William H. Andrews, Jr.) had scored slower but still sure progress; now in 1964 it reached—and even surpassed—its ambitious goal, with 3,255 contributors giving $1,090,659 in cash and pledges.[34]

The trustees had organized the Development Fund to raise money for Huebner Hall, the first building on the Bryn Mawr campus. Campaign receipts freed other College funds to expand Continuing Education and other programs. Interestingly enough, 751 persons pledged $1,000 or more, thereby becoming eligible for membership in the Golden Key Society. Even better, many donors who had made modest initial commitments later agreed to increase their pledges to the $1,000 Golden Key Society qualification level.[35]

The Development Fund Committee praised Andrews for his "remarkable leadership" and "creative and energetic efforts" but acceded to his request that another person serve as national chairman in the future. The trustees selected Walter L. Downing, CLU, for this position. Downing vowed to strive to reach Dr. Huebner's dream "when the professional designation CLU will lead to an enlightened institution, working as a whole, toward an enlightened insurance service to the public."[36]

The trustees, increasingly conscious of their growing responsibilities for the expanding institution and perhaps urged by President Davis Gregg, who sensed the potential for wider industry involvement, revised the bylaws once again to permit three additional term members and to bring the authorized total to 24. Three life insurance company presidents, all CLUs, joined the board at this time: Earl Clark, Occidental Life of California; W.D. Grant, Business Men's Assurance of America; and J. Harry Wood, Home Life of New York City.[37] Coy G. Eklund, CLU, senior agency vice president of Equitable Life, filled the vacancy created by the retirement of Clarence B. Metzger, CLU, an Equitable senior executive who had served 15 years. Metzger, who had ably chaired the Registration Board for more than a decade, received an engraved Philadelphia Bowl from his appreciative colleagues.[38] The College presented another prestigious Philadelphia Bowl (which by this time had become a traditional part of recognition at retirement or for longevity of service) to professor and CLU, William T. Beadles, of Bloomington, Illinois, for 25 years as a CLU teacher.[39]

During the goings and comings that year, two of the five College Development Study Commission working committees made their final reports. Roger Hull's group on growth projection and resource needs and Orville E. Beal's task force to look into the formation of a facilitative research organization under College sponsorship completed their work. The other three subcommittees would make their final reports a year later.

Growth projection took concrete form as the College acquired a former carriage house and approximately one acre of land adjacent to Huebner Hall. The College announced that it would remodel the structure for dining, meeting, and classroom use as the Julian S. Myrick Pavilion.[40]

The College's commitment to research was in keeping with Davis W. Gregg's vision for the College. Gregg saw the value of experimental laboratories for testing teaching techniques and new materials. He looked beyond specialized courses to opportunities for broader business education. In this vein the trustees approved expansion of existing College research activities to function under the Governing Committee of the David McCahan Foundation.[41]

These existing research efforts had begun in the late 1950s with a series of foundation-sponsored annual lectures emphasizing the American family. After a few years, the foundation decided to work toward preparation of a textbook on the American family, often considered "the philosophical heart of life and health insurance."[42] Dr. John W. Riley, Jr., of Equitable Life collaborated in this undertaking. Essentially, this was a continuation of the work begun by Dr. James H.S. Bossard, who had died before he could complete the book (see chapter 5).

Now, in 1964, with the Development Commission's recommendation for program enlargement, the College would employ "an able research director" to head the task. If McCahan Foundation funds (initially contributed by CLUs across the country) were insufficient to cover the cost, the College would augment the funds from its annual operating budget. The director was to develop a complete index of all research done in this field that could be shared with other interested groups and interpret the meaning of this information to life and health insurance.[43] Both new undertakings helped to move the College forward and equip it for greater service to an expanding constituency and nation.

The College held its 37th annual conferment exercises in Cincinnati, Ohio, on September 23, 1964. Dean Graebner presented the candidates and President Gregg awarded diplomas to more than 1,100 new CLUs and CLU Associates following a dignified ceremony that introduced many distinguished guests and recognized the class of 1939, which was celebrating its 25th anniversary. Dr. Huebner's portrait photograph on the front page of the program set the tone for the occasion.

*   *   *

In the world and nation of the mid-1960s certain events were widely reported and considered significant. The Kremlin ousted Nikita Khrushchev as Soviet premier; France withdrew from NATO; and Panama suspended relations with the United States. Here at home California surpassed New York as the most populous state, *My Fair Lady* won an Academy Award, and bell-bottom trousers and mini-skirts came into vogue. Two national events of particular interest to the life insurance industry involved cigarette smoking. A survey revealed that Americans smoked 524 billion cigarettes per year—215 packs for each man and woman over the age of 18.[44] Soon thereafter President Lyndon Johnson signed a new law requiring cigarette packages and advertisements to carry a printed health warning.[45]

These cigarette smoking developments illustrated the close connection between society at large, the human-life-value-protection industry, and the educational institution founded to serve that undertaking by providing advanced professional study for the men and women in life and health insurance. As new needs arose, the College continued to seek wider opportunities to reach out to its constituency and better prepare it to cope with emerging challenges.

President Davis W. Gregg's determination and drive powered the College's ongoing growth in size and influence. Gregg participated personally in these efforts and led the College to expand the programs of its different departments. For example, he gave the readers of a national magazine a veritable life insurance education through a nine-page interview that featured his answers to questions posed by the publication's staff reporters.[46]

In 1965 Gregg chaired the committee to administer a new Program for Creative Excellence approved that year by the Board of Trustees. The program was designed to accelerate the growth and development of the College as an institution of higher learning "through the stimulation of the creative endeavor of its career personnel" as it aided the "career and professional development of these persons."[47] The program had a fivefold emphasis: seminars for creative excellence, teaching for creative excellence, courses for creative excellence, publications for creative excellence, and research for creative excellence.

As its professional staff moved toward this standard, the College increased its capacity to do a better job both on campus and in the field. In 1965, often with the cosponsorship of the American Society, it organized a growing number of educational activities that had started on a smaller scale in previous years. For instance, the Department of Education planned and conducted a series of regional teacher conferences for CLU and Certificate Course instructors. These were held in Bryn Mawr, Columbus, Milwaukee, Hartford, Houston, San Francisco, and Tampa. There were also five CLU Institutes. Winter programs were held at Arizona State University and at Stetson University in Deland, Florida. The three summer CLU Institutes enrolled a total of 220 CLUs in the Universities of Connecticut, Wisconsin, and Colorado.[48]

Chairman John K. Luther and his Joint Committee on Continuing Education were responsible for 24 one-day seminars in cooperation with local CLU chapters—up from eight such seminars 2 years before. More than 4,100 people attended, an increase of 1,566 over the previous year's enrollment. Finally, Continuing Education added a fifth Discussion Outline titled "Pension Planning for Small Businesses" to the other four titles offered to CLU chapters: "Stock Redemption," "The Case of Mr. Smith," "Split-Dollar Life Insurance," and "Nonqualified Deferred Compensation."[49]

In the spring that year the campus was enriched through ornamentation of one building, dedication of another, and acquisition of a third structure as The American College extended its physical facilities in conjunction with the increased scope of its nationwide academic program. The details merit our attention.

The trustees dramatized Solomon S. Huebner's contribution to the College by commissioning local sculptor Edward Fenno Hoffman, III, to create a bust of the deceased insurance guru. Massachusetts Mutual home office and field personnel contributed the funds for this memorial, which was placed in the lobby of Huebner Hall.[50]

In May 1965 the Myrick Pavilion was dedicated. The renovated former carriage house contained three main rooms named for friends and associates of Julian S. Myrick: the Hoover Room for Herbert C. Hoover; the Ives Room for Charles Ives, both a business partner and noted composer of classical music; and the Woods Room for Edward A. Woods, Myrick's close friend and the first president of the College.

Purchase of a 10-acre parcel of land containing a wood-and-shingle residence increased the size of the campus to 22 acres and provided office space for College research facilities. The former dwelling—now known as McCahan Hall in honor of the late David McCahan, fourth president of the College—would appropriately house the foundation that already bore his name.

Personnel growth kept up with property expansion in the College's 38th year when both administrative and governing board changes placed incoming and incumbent employees in new positions of responsibility. G. Victor Hallman advanced from assistant to associate dean, joining Jack C. Keir, who was already at that organizational level, to make two officers of that academic rank. John E. Stinton and Glenn L. Wood began their College careers as assistant deans to serve with Walter W. Dotterweich, already an assistant dean—which gave the

College three persons in this position. All in all, including Vice President and Dean Herbert C. Graebner, The American College now had six deans. These appointments, together with a number of other staff additions and changes, provided the increased manpower needed to give impetus to the College's expanding educational programs, and they promised to give the existing overworked staff some measure of well-deserved relief, according to the *Annual Report* that year.[51]

Dr. Jerry S. Rosenbloom, CLU, replaced Dr. Robert M. Crowe as director of examinations, and Dr. Vane B. Lucas replaced Dr. Ronald C. Horn as director of educational services, the department that constituted the College's direct link with CLU teachers, students, and teachers of insurance in colleges and universities. Lucas later rose to a high administrative position and would render significant service to the College.

For their part, the trustees focused on changes at the top in 1965, as three men acquired new roles in the leadership of the board. First, Paul F. Clark retired after 6 years as chairman and an extraordinary 38 years as trustee. Clark had established a record of longevity of tenure unequaled in the history of the College to that time. He had worked with five presidents, beginning with Edward A. Woods, and continuing with Clark's uncle, Ernest J. Clark, then Solomon S. Huebner, David McCahan, and the first decade of the Davis W. Gregg administration. No wonder the board elected him honorary chairman!

In the second new leadership role in 1965, Charles J. Zimmerman, Connecticut Mutual Life president and a man who had made increasingly crucial contributions to the College since he joined the board in 1941, was named chairman. He had served on the board until 1944 when he left for military service. He then had to wait to return to the board until there was a vacancy, which occurred in 1951. Roger Hull, president of Mutual of New York, moved into the vice chairmanship.

The trustees expressed their enthusiasm for Zimmerman with a testimonial dinner in Philadelphia on September 24. Dr. John Sloan Dickey, president of Dartmouth College, chaired a committee to plan a program of accolades from community and industry leaders who knew Zimmerman. They called it "The Several Lives of Charlie Zimmerman." Connecticut Mutual executives unveiled a portrait of the guest of honor by Martin Kellogg and presented it to the College for display in Huebner Hall. The board also gave Mr. and Mrs. Zimmerman a handsome Steuben glass creation titled "Excalibur," which symbolically linked the noted executive with the legendary King Arthur. Davis Gregg described Zimmerman as "a friend and inspiration to all," and added, "We all stand a little taller and a little prouder because of his leadership."[52]

An event of even greater lasting significance also took place that fall. The College began a pilot program to separate its CLU national conferment from the annual convention of the National Association of Life Underwriters of which that exercise had been a part since 1928. Over the years the total undertaking had grown with the inclusion of one new activity after another. The American Society added its annual meeting in 1929, and 30 years later expanded this program to include an Educational Forum. The total College and Society effort had become too big to be accommodated within the framework of the NALU meeting.

Through 1964 the College National Conferment exercises were held as part of the NALU conclave. Beginning in 1965, however, there were three conferments—one in St. Louis, a second in Philadelphia, and another in Los Angeles. The College and the Society then formed a joint committee to evaluate these sessions and to make plans for the following year. This group met in Washington, DC, on November 10, 1965, reviewed hundreds of questionnaires returned from people who had attended these meetings, and by unanimous vote recommended that there be three conferments again in 1966. The first would be held in Boston with the cooperation of the Society's area chapters; it would include an Educational Forum. The second (with no forum) would be part of the NALU convention in New Orleans. The third was scheduled for San Francisco, and it, too, would be presented with area chapter assistance as both a forum and conferment.[53] The committee believed that these extra Boston and San Francisco meetings would make the CLU designation more meaningful, enhance its image, and contribute to greater professional competence of CLUs.[54]

*   *   *

The College Development Study Commission, appointed in 1962, functioned at a deliberate pace, reflecting the complexity of its task. Despite a versifier's warning, "Walk through all the towns and cities, you will find no monuments to committees," the Commission had formed five working committees in 1963. Two reported the following year, and in 1965 the remaining three groups made their recommendations.

The CLU Professional Standards Committee proposed implementing a College Code of Ethics to go beyond the Society's 1960 guide to professional conduct, and the committee was discharged from further responsibility.

The Committee on Cooperation with the American Institute for Property and Liability Underwriters (regarding the acquisition and best use of campus physical facilities) reviewed such possibilities as an addition to Huebner Hall or purchasing adjacent land to erect another building. Since the Institute did not need additional Huebner Hall space that year, the group recommended appointing a joint American College-American Institute Building Committee to study the matter in greater detail. The Committee on Cooperation was also discharged for its diligent work.

Charles J. Zimmerman's Committee on Graduate School for CLUs presented an interim report and beginning in 1966 would consider a proposed resident study facility as well as an educational laboratory project. In summer, then, after 4 years the College had examined five areas of present interest and future potential that would receive careful attention in 1966 and the years ahead.

The College began 1966 with a ceremony to honor Julian S. Myrick, board chairman emeritus, who at age 86, had been described earlier by a *Time* reporter as "the grand old man of life insurance." On January 26 the College unveiled a bust of the greatly admired Myrick created by sculptor Edward Fenno Hoffman, III, and presented as a gift from the CLU Association of Mutual of New York. Speakers at the ceremony and luncheon included CLU Harry K. Gutmann, representing the field representatives and employees who contributed to the sculpture fund, Board Chairman Charles J. Zimmerman, President Davis W. Gregg, and Vice Chairman Roger Hull. Hull's remarks included these words: "Life insurance should be an unending process of education, of a striving to do better, to gain wisdom, to pursue and achieve excellence."[55]

In February these three men continued to make news at The American College. Gregg began a 6-month sabbatical that took him and his family around the world to study the field of security, risk, and insurance. Zimmerman presented the 1966 Philadelphia Life Underwriter's President's Cup to Dr. Gregg in a ceremony at which Frederick R. Griffin, Jr., CLU, president of the Philadelphia Association of Life Underwriters, presided. Hull became a life trustee of the College he had served so capably since 1944. We'll look at each event in greater detail.

In a sense the Greggs' trip echoed the College's international outreach begun years before with Solomon Huebner's overseas journeys. Furthermore, this trip would be connected with the planned second edition of the multilingual survey, *Insurance Courses in Colleges and Universities outside the United States*. Originally published by Gregg and Longo in 1960, the second edition would be compiled by Joseph J. Melone and Helen L. Schmidt in 1968. Finally, the projected travel would provide an opportunity to lecture on insurance, to repay visits of insurance dignitaries who had called on The American College since World War II, and particularly in Australia and New Zealand, to study the relationships between private and government insurance. Vice President and Dean Herbert C. Graebner served as acting president during Gregg's absence, but ill health en route would bring the travelers home 2 months earlier than planned.

Dr. Gregg's President's Cup, which was presented in absentia since he had already started his trip, recognized "enthusiastic support toward the progress of the Philadelphia Association of Life Underwriters in expression of the true spirit and ideals of the institution of life insurance."[56]

Hull's election to a life trusteeship continued an honor originating in 1938 when Ernest J. Clark, Franklin W. Ganse, and Solomon S. Huebner were the first to achieve this rank.[57] Except for Julian S. Myrick (1939) and Paul F. Clark (1954), there were no additional life trustee appointments until 1961, at which time Robert Dechert, Joseph H. Reese, Sr., Earl R. Trangmar, and Charles J. Zimmerman achieved this status. Roger Hull brought impressive credentials and extensive experience to his life trusteeship. As president of Mutual of New York, a director of the Institute of Life Insurance, and chairman of the Life Insurance Association of America, he clearly kept good company with those already enjoying this position. Hull complemented his corporate ability with church and community leadership as president of the Presbyterian Lay Committee and director of the Protestant Council of New York City.

Turmoil set the tone for many national and world events in 1966, the year when 52,500 Americans would die on the roads and 9 million would be injured in traffic accidents.[58] The spring months saw the beginning of the Chinese cultural revolution to drive out bourgeois ideology, and there were rallies against the Vietnam War in both the United States and Europe.

Tranquillity, on the other hand, was the keynote at The American College as two administrators earned promotions and four new executives began work on the Bryn Mawr campus to advance the College's steady growth as recommended by committees of the College Development Study Commission. Greater size called for more staff. We have previously noted the increase in the number of deans, and the 1966 promotions of Walter W. Dotterweich from assistant to associate dean and Vane B. Lucas from director of educational services to assistant deanship further increased the total.

The new appointees included Joseph J. Melone, CLU, insurance professor at the University of Pennsylvania. Dr. Melone's association with The American College, however, began years before as a Huebner fellow, continued as a grader of examination papers, and included his marriage to a College employee, Marie DeGeorge. The College named Melone research director of the McCahan Foundation for Basic Research in Risk, Security, and Insurance, thus giving that entity full-time leadership for the first time since its creation in 1955.

President Davis W. Gregg dreamed of a McCahan program that would capture the imagination of the life insurance industry as the College developed a National Information Center to "collect, analyze, and catalogue all recorded knowledge pertaining to the general field of economic security, including all aspects of risk and insurance."[59] Gregg believed that Melone had the capacity to bring the College to that position and in so doing to secure life insurance industry financial support to endow the McCahan Foundation, which heretofore had been funded by annual allocations from the operating budget.

The three CLU national conferments later that year were highly successful. Building on the experience gained in the pilot programs of the previous year, the 1966 multiple events were well attended, and both the College and the Society—which had pooled ideas and shared costs for these events—were satisfied with the results.

Members of the 1941 CLU 25th anniversary class were honored at conferment dinners. A survey of the 25-year alumni revealed a high level of achievement among its members. For example, their ranks included three people who became both American College trustees and presidents of their companies: Orville E. Beal of the Prudential, Massachusetts Mutual's Charles J. Schaaff, and Edmund L. Zalinski of the Life Insurance Company of North America. There were 33 teachers of CLU classes; 80 college graduates, a number of whom held more than one degree; and 68 graduates who had served the American Society as local chapter officers. This class also claimed a substantial number of Million Dollar Round Table members.[60]

Enthusiastic about the Mitchell/Giurgola design of Huebner Hall, the College trustees commissioned the Philadelphia architects to prepare a master plan for future development of the entire campus, and the firm began this task in 1966. Mitchell/Giurgola would prepare a phased implementation program with initial emphasis on construction of a Life Learning Laboratory with additional buildings to follow.[61]

Great things lay ahead for The American College.

NOTES

1. Robert Browning, "Andrea del Sarto," 1.97.
2. *CLU Annual Review,* 1962, p. 2.
3. Benjamin M. Gaston, Sr., interview with the author, August 7, 1995.
4. *CLU Annual Review,* 1962, pp. 28–29.
5. Nicholas Lehman, "The Structure of Success in America," *Atlantic Monthly,* vol. 276, no. 2, August 1995, p. 53.
6. *The Insurance Yearbook,* 1927.
7. Ibid., 1962.
8. *Annual Report,* The American College, 1962, p. 1.
9. Ibid.
10. Ibid.
11. *CLU Annual Review,* 1962, p 7.
12. *Annual Report,* 1963, p. 2.
13. Ibid.
14. Ibid.
15. Ibid., p. 12.
16. Ibid., p. 13.
17. *CLU Annual Review,* 1963, p. 14.
18. Ibid.
19. Ibid., pp. 25–26.
20. *Annual Report,* 1963, p. 2.
21. Ibid., p. 20.
22. *CLU Annual Review,* 1963, p. 27.
23. Ibid., pp. 13–14.
24. *Annual Report,* 1963, p. 2.
25. Ibid.
26. Ibid.
27. *CLU Annual Review,* 1963, pp. 13, 28.
28. Joseph Conrad, *Under Western Eyes,* 1911, part 1.
29. Davis W. Gregg, Oral History interview, July 28, 1983.
30. Edmund L. Zalinski, interview with the author, October 10, 1994.
31. William B. Wallace, interview with the author, December 12, 1994.
32. Benjamin M. Gaston, Sr., interview with the author, August 7, 1995.
33. *The American College Catalog,* 1964–1965, p. 87.
34. The American College Development Fund Report, 1964, p. 6.
35. Ibid., p. 7.
36. Ibid.
37. *Annual Report,* 1964, p. 2.
38. Ibid., p. 3.
39. Ibid., p. 7.

40. Ibid., p. 2.
41. Ibid., p. 14.
42. Ibid., p. 15.
43. Ibid.
44. Paul Dickson, *Timelines* (Reading, MA: Addison-Wesley Publishing Co., Inc.), 1990, p. 140.
45. Ibid.
46. "What You Should Know about Buying Life Insurance," *U.S. News and World Report,* October 7, 1963, pp. 94–102.
47. *Annual Report,* 1965, pp. 1–2.
48. Ibid., p. 21.
49. Ibid., pp. 21–22.
50. Ibid., p. 3.
51. Ibid., p. 2.
52. "The Several Lives of Charlie Zimmerman," dinner program transcript, September 24, 1965.
53. "Confidential Memorandums," American Society, November 15, 1965, to its Board of Directors, p. 1.
54. American Society minutes of National Planning Committee, December 15, 1965, p. 1.
55. David A. Partridge, director, Joint Department of Public Relations, The American College-American Society press release, January 27, 1966., p. 2.
56. Press release, February 8, 1966, p. 2.
57. *Annual Report,* 1966, p. 2.
58. Dickson, *Timelines,* p. 152.
59. *Society Page,* American Society of CLU, vol. 5, no. 5, July 1966, p. 3.
60. Press release, September 2, 1966, pp. 1–3.
61. "Center for Advanced Studies in Insurance," Mitchell/Giurgola Associates Architects, 1966.

7

A Longer Reach

Time, the devourer of all things

Ovid

In a 1967 report to The American College constituency its president, Davis W. Gregg, reminded his readers that while "insurance as a science is almost as old as modern civilization [and] insurance as a business is also of ancient vintage . . . collegiate insurance education is a product of the twentieth century."[1]

The College's 40th anniversary observance provided the opportunity for the academic executive to note the College's consistent growth in both size and reputation. The College "seems proof," Dr. Gregg said on another occasion that year, "that life insurance, one of the nation's greatest financial institutions, has fully embraced the concept and attaches great value to trained intelligence."[2]

Educational enterprise in this country offers no guarantee of success; as many as 700 colleges were founded and failed before 1861.[3] Two factors, however, were crucial to The American College's success: (1) The trustees paid careful attention to voluntary financial support from individuals and organizations, and (2) they kept a close eye on the basic academic emphasis of the College. In this anniversary year they authorized the administration to make a thorough review of the entire Chartered Life Underwriter program since its inception in 1927. First, however, let us examine the development picture.

The use of part-time employees in the early years kept costs low and operations within the income from budgeted registration fees. Expanded programs and the enlarged payrolls required to administer them called for more money, which led to the fundraising activity of the later 1950s. The Permanent Endowment Fund campaign generated $1 million from 126 life insurance companies. On the heels of this program came the 1960 American College Development Fund to secure gifts from individuals "to further the creative force of the College and to provide funds for the expansion of physical facilities on the Bryn Mawr campus."[4] The first year 2,398 persons pledged $750,157 and paid $133,832 in cash. The Golden Key Society was launched; individuals who contributed or pledged $1,000 or more became members.

The trustees had created a Development Fund Committee to oversee operations of a National Development Council composed of representatives from various Society chapters across the country. The Development Fund Committee, under the successive leadership of William H. Andrews, Jr., and Walter L.

Downing, garnered gifts from a growing number of enthusiastic supporters. Now, by December 31 of the 40th anniversary year, pledges came to $2,209,061 with payments of $734,335.[5]

An examination of the 4,486 contributors revealed a total of 1,804 donors of $1,000 or more to qualify for Golden Key Society membership. These special givers, in a sense, represented the backbone of the Development Fund outreach. Their 10-year pledge commitments of $1,000 or more were a significant portion of total gift income. Moreover, their largesse lifted the sights of all potential participants and thereby energized the entire effort.

This widespread response from CLUs from Alabama to Wyoming and eight foreign countries prompted nine life companies to include the College in their lists of educational institutions eligible for their matching gift programs. Connecticut Mutual Life, Mutual of New York, and the Insurance Company of North America were among those generous and cooperative corporations.[6]

Davis W. Gregg knew from experience the value of keeping in contact with the College's alumni. The 1952 CLU survey of graduates had proved helpful to the trustees and president as they planned the academic innovations of the next 15 years. In 1967 therefore Dr. Gregg decreed a reprise of that earlier opinion sampling. He designated Dean Vane B. Lucas; Helen L. Schmidt, assistant to the president; and John S. White, systems consultant, as a committee of three to do the work and present a comprehensive report of their findings.

This *CLU Profile,* based on 50 questions mailed to 4,471 persons, revealed some interesting comparisons and contrasts to the information gathered in 1952. For example, in the 1952 survey the typical CLU emerged as a 45-year-old married male with one or two children. The new questionnaire disclosed that the typical life underwriter was now slightly younger and had more formal education than his predecessor of the 1950s. He also had more children and carried considerably more life insurance ($127,735 in 1967 versus $50,000 in 1952).[7]

The 1967 prototype CLU was a member of the American Society of Chartered Life Underwriters, belonged to several service organizations, and spoke in public on at least two occasions each year.[8] In fact, according to a business writer of those days, "The American life insurance business has become one of the most respected fields of endeavor in the country."[9]

The College's cumulative student enrollment and graduation totals for the 40-year period, during which the College had contributed to higher industry standards through better education of its employees, support that statement. A total of 68,947 men and women had complied with all eligibility requirements prerequisite to taking the examinations, and 17,229 had actually earned the respected CLU designation. Many others had completed some courses and would, after an average study period of 5 years, receive their diplomas.[10]

Interesting national and world events that winter furnished an ever-changing backdrop for campus innovation. The United States Constitution added its 25th amendment, which dealt with the disability and succession of the president. Los Angeles hosted the first Super Bowl as the Green Bay Packers beat the Kansas

City Stars 35 to 10. Joseph Stalin's daughter, Svetland Alliluyeva, defected from the USSR and came to New York City.[11]

The American College announced five staff promotions, which President Gregg promised would "bring further leadership strength to the College at a time of major demands upon its services." The trustees named Herbert C. Graebner executive vice president and treasurer. Drs. Walter W. Dotterweich, G. Victor Hallman, and Vane B. Lucas became full deans, and Dr. Jerry S. Rosenbloom was named assistant dean.[12]

Graebner moved from academic oversight to policy and financial management. Each new dean would now lead a division in the reorganized educational program: Dotterweich in charge of Instruction, Hallman responsible for Curriculum and Examinations, and Lucas leading the Administration section.[13]

The College made these changes to carry forward its educational and research responsibilities more effectively. The Program for Creative Excellence, organized in 1965, awarded grants to College personnel for special work involving courses, publications, research, seminars, and teaching, and to personally evaluate textbooks, teaching materials, and classroom procedures. The deans of the newly formed divisions and some of their associates taught classes in such places as the University of Pennsylvania, Penn Mutual Life Insurance Company, and Villanova University. It was clearly understood, though, that "assigned and implied College responsibilities take precedence over teaching activities."[14]

Soon after the College purchased the 11.15-acre McIlvaine estate in Bryn Mawr, Pennsylvania, and moved there in 1961, the expanding institution sought more land to extend its campus. As we mentioned in an earlier chapter, in 1963 the College acquired an adjacent acre that contained the former McIlvaine carriage house, which it transformed into the Myrick Pavilion in 1965. The trustees realized that the area was rapidly being developed and urged the administration to be alert to the availability of other contiguous property. Within a year the College bought an additional 10 acres, once part of the Vauclain estate, which contained a usable residence that before long became known as McCahan Hall.

In the 40th anniversary year there was another real estate opportunity as the Seiler property next to the northeast edge of the campus came on the market. The College bought these four acres, which contained two buildings—a handsome house, which became the curriculum building, named Dechert Hall; and a barn, which served as print shop, storage space, and mail facilities until it was replaced by the General Services Building in 1979. In the aggregate these acquisitions amounted to more than 26 acres and formed the basis for the Mitchell/Giurgola master plan for the development of the entire parcel of land.

Three CLUs made trustee news that June. Carroll Walker, secretary of the American Society, and Joseph E. Boettner, president of the Philadelphia Life Insurance Company, joined the board at the annual meeting. Wm. Eugene Hays was elected life trustee. Chairman Charles J. Zimmerman lauded Boettner's "strong support" of the College's "goals and objectives." President Davis W. Gregg noted Boettner's "highly creative" earlier service on various College committees and predicted that Boettner's "counsel as a trustee will be invaluable."[15]

Hays became the 12th person in College history to be honored with life trusteeship for "outstanding, constructive, and devoted service."[16] Hays had graduated from Stanford University in 1926, where he began selling life insurance as a student. He then built a successful career with New England Mutual Life, where he earned a reputation as "one of the outstanding general agents in the history of life insurance."[17] Later he went on to provide industry leadership in management education. He had been an American College trustee since 1946.

Toward the end of the anniversary year Pennsylvania Governor Raymond P. Shafer proclaimed "Chartered Life Underwriter Day" throughout the Commonwealth as part of the Society's diploma presentation ceremony on September 29, 1967, at the Barclay Hotel in Philadelphia. The proclamation commended the College and the Society for their respective efforts "to produce professionally trained insurance counselors" and "to raise the standards of the industry and to improve the quality of life insurance to the public."[18]

*   *   *

A year later the editor of a business publication echoed these sentiments when he discussed the Society's national forum and the College's diploma exercises of September 5–6, 1968. The journalist extolled the efforts to raise the educational level of the risk-protection industry. "Had it not been for the CLU movement," he asserted, "life insurance marketing would be back in the Dark Ages. In those days there were office building signs which warned, 'No beggars, peddlers, or life insurance salesmen allowed.' "[19]

After 4 decades of struggle, the College and the Society had earned the approbation of both government and industry. For their joint contribution to better careers for underwriters and superior service to society, they confirmed anew Benjamin Franklin's adage in *Poor Richard's Almanac,* "An investment in knowledge pays the best interest."

There would be no slackening of effort as the College continued to improve existing programs and to consider other offerings. President Gregg proudly reported in 1968, "New records were attained on most scales of activity. New CLU diplomas awarded exceeded 2,000 for the first time, and active candidates reached a new high of 35,618."[20]

Overall, dramas of life and death had marked the early months of 1968. In January, Dr. Christian Barnard performed a successful heart transplant operation in Capetown, South Africa. A few months later an assassin shot civil rights leader Martin Luther King, Jr., in Memphis, Tennessee. King's violent death offered a vivid reminder of the value of life insurance. Earlier, Martin England, a life insurance salesman, had discovered that the clergyman had little or no death protection. He pursued Dr. King for weeks and finally sold him adequate coverage not long before the minister met his sudden death.[21]

At the College, the McCahan Foundation began a publication program that year. Organized in 1955, the foundation sponsored a number of annual lectures in the mid-1950s before entering a period of reduced activity. Inadequate funding and lack of full-time leadership kept the foundation from achieving its potential. Successive annual reports conveyed the entity's underlying objective "to enhance understanding regarding the nature, problems, and issues pertaining to economic security systems,"[22] but deeds fell far short of dreams until 1966 and the appointment of Joseph J. Melone as research director.

Expanding upon its commitment eventually to establish a mechanized information retrieval system to cope with an "ever-mounting volume of literature pertaining to insurance and related fields,"[23] the McCahan Foundation undertook a comprehensive summary of worldwide insurance education to begin this new program. Dr. Melone and Helen L. Schmidt published this survey in 1968, which listed courses and teachers in 369 colleges and universities in 63 countries as far apart alphabetically as Algeria and Yugoslavia and as geographically distant as Argentina and China. President Davis Gregg believed the study "would afford increased opportunities for the exchange of scientific information among insurance educators of the world" and open the channels of communication and fellowship among insurance educators in many lands.[24]

Another 1968 McCahan Foundation publication began a series of Occasional Papers. It was titled "The Conjugal Family and Consumption Behavior" by Dr. John Scanozi, a sociology professor at Indiana University. Dr. Scanozi asserted that "the family, rather than individuals *per se,* is the most appropriate unit of observation" for a study of this subject. "Aspiration and expectations of husband and wife are the two key variables basic to family consumption decisions."[25] Melone introduced the thesis with a forward to the text in which he said, "This research should be of considerable interest to persons in the life insurance business . . . and general area of family planning."[26]

These two offerings in the 1968 publication program carried the McCahan Foundation official logotype emblazoned upon their respective front covers. The logo depicted the silhouette of two human figures standing side by side with outer hands raised to the shining sun above and between them, and inner hands clasped together over these words: "In Search of Truth about Man's Quest for Security."[27] This imaginative trademark would identify all future McCahan Foundation projects, including four research papers in 1970.

Despite this auspicious event and the general revitalization of the McCahan Foundation, hoped-for grants to endow the program were hard to find. Before the year's end, Dr. Melone resigned to become an officer of Prudential Life. President Gregg named Dr. Jerry S. Rosenbloom as acting research director of the McCahan Foundation in addition to his new duties as dean of the College's Curriculum and Examinations Division.[28]

Melone's departure was only one of a number of staff resignations in the late 1960s. Not long after the president's return from his 1966 sabbatical, Davis W.

Gregg faced the loss of other young administrators who left The American College for what an earlier College historian called "the more familiar culture of traditional colleges and universities."[29] Associate Dean Jack C. Keir departed in 1967 for Temple University. Dean Walter W. Dotterweich went to the University of Tennessee in 1968. Dotterweich, however, continued to serve the College as an educational consultant.

President Gregg moved Dean Vane B. Lucas from the Administrative to the Instruction Division to replace Walter W. Dotterweich as head of that group. He also promoted Richard T. McFalls, business manager, and gave him broader administrative responsibilities. In addition, Gregg announced the promotion of three other men to the position of associate dean, effective September 1, 1968: Dr. Barnie E. Abelle, CLU, would be responsible in the Instruction Division for class development; Dr. James M. Daily, also of the Instruction Division, would concentrate on life insurance companies' greater use of The American College in their overall human resource development plans; Robert V. Nally, Esq., would function in the Curriculum and Examinations Division.

At this time the energetic chief executive welcomed three more people to the College staff: Everett T. Allen, Jr., as associate dean; Dr. Kenneth C. Huntley to serve as director of educational services; and Richard J. Morith, as director of examinations. "It is with a great deal of pleasure that I announce these appointments," the president said. "Each person assuming these responsibilities is a highly capable educator, dedicated to the growth of professional education in insurance."[30]

On the world scene 1968 would be remembered as the year the Soviets invaded Czechoslovakia, and the year that America buried Robert Kennedy, elected Richard M. Nixon president, and signed a treaty with 59 nations prohibiting the proliferation of nuclear weapons. The American College and the American Society welcomed John T. Fey, president of the National Life Insurance Company of Montpelier, Vermont, to their diploma exercises and forum at the Bellevue-Stratford Hotel in Philadelphia on September 6, 1968.

Dr. Fey challenged the crowd with a call to plan for the future. The magnetic speaker declared, "Techniques of the last decade are already obsolete, and the sales methods of today will have to be adapted and modified to serve the needs of our new markets tomorrow."[31] Fey's experience and ability, together with then unforeseen future events, would soon propel the dynamic educator-executive into a crucial leadership role at the College.

People and places within an institution enjoy a dynamic relationship. People bring life to places, and places shape the way people perform. The College trustees had been mindful of this synergy when in 1966 they retained Mitchell/Giurgola Associates to prepare a master plan for the Bryn Mawr campus. A year later the board approved the plan and accepted the architects' concepts for two new buildings: a life learning laboratory and a general services facility. By 1968 the board took still another step and approved the preliminary plans for the learning laboratory, which would become the award-winning MDRT Foundation Hall.

Ehrman Mitchell and Aldo Giurgola did more than design new College buildings and renovate existing structures. They also enlarged an existing pond in the center of the College property to make it the focal point of the campus. The trustees named it Reese Lake to honor Joseph H. Reese, who had served the College for 30 years as ex-officio, term, and life trustee. He had been on many board committees and since 1949 had held the position of corporate secretary.

In anticipation of Reese's impending retirement the College proceeded with plans for the dedication of a bronze plaque at the site and commissioned sculptor Edward Fenno Hoffman, III, to execute an appropriate commemorative tablet. Reese posed repeatedly for it, but when he became ill, the unveiling event had to be postponed.

The College rescheduled the ceremony for October 31, 1968. President Gregg mailed invitations on October 4, but Joseph H. Reese died 2 days later. Board Chairman Charles J. Zimmerman, Dr. Gregg, and other College leaders took part in a poignant ceremony with Reese family members to unveil the plaque. Chairman Emeritus Julian S. Myrick expressed the feelings of those who gathered there that day as he described what Joseph H. Reese "meant to the building of our institution." Myrick said, "Few men in history have been so dedicated to the common purpose and so unselfish in sharing their energy and imagination. Joe has fought the good fight, has run the good race, and has kept the faith. I know that he is safe in the hands of God."[32]

*   *   *

Seventy days later death claimed the man who had written those words; Julian S. Myrick died on January 9, 1969, in his 89th year. A down-to-earth man, Myrick once remarked, "Nobody consults you about insurance. You have to go out and consult them."[33] Myrick followed his own advice and after "retiring" several times, qualified for the Million Dollar Round Table at 80 years of age.[34] Individuals and companies had long expressed their admiration for his many achievements through awards, honors, and accolades. The following are just a few representative tributes: "He pioneered important changes in the business," one man said. Another person proclaimed Myrick to be "one of the best salesmen in the business." A third individual called him "one of the greats in the history of The American College."[35] The College concurred.

The new year would be marked by the first men on the moon and the first flight of the Boeing 747 jumbo jet, which inaugurated a new era of commercial aviation. The year 1969 was a time when inflation became a major recognized international phenomenon, and the rate of the world's population growth reached 2 percent. The Woodstock rock music festival reflected the turbulent, counterculture morality, taste, and values of America's disaffected youth, which would affect the nation into the mid-1970s.[36]

The new year on campus proved to be equally forward looking as The American College made two major policy decisions, which reflected the trustees' determination to keep up with the times and to position the College to take full advantage of these national and world developments through fresh educational offerings.

In February the board voted to modernize and restructure its basic CLU program in an effort, according to President Davis W. Gregg, "to initiate instructional design plans and policies" that would make the College programs "richer and more meaningful to individual career growth and fulfillment."[37] At the same meeting the trustees approved construction of the $3.5 million Adult Learning Laboratory for the Bryn Mawr campus in a move that Dr. Gregg applauded as enabling the College "to assemble the pieces of the educational revolution in the coming years." Gregg went on to point out, "Instructional technology holds great promise for all education but is of particular significance to the adult professional."[38]

The CLU designation had always been more than one uppercase letter after another. Solomon S. Huebner had insisted that the College stress the breadth and depth of knowledge required to earn the diploma. In the beginning the five-part curriculum had consisted of these subjects: (1) Life Insurance Fundamentals, (2) Life Insurance Salesmanship, (3) General Education (including English), (4) Commercial and Insurance Law, and (5) Finance.

For an extended period of time the College made minor adjustments and tinkered with the nomenclature and juxtaposition of the offerings. It added Taxation and Business Insurance to Commercial and Insurance Law during the first decade (1930–1940). In the 1940s General Education moved up from third to second position in the curriculum; Life Insurance Salesmanship moved down from second to fifth and was called Life Underwriting (Comprehensive). In the 1950s the name of a section in Life Insurance Fundamentals—"Economics of Life Insurance"—was changed to "Economics and Social Problems." A few years later the College added Annuities to the overall description of Life Insurance Fundamentals, which had been called that since 1930. General Education changed names to the more comprehensive Business Life Insurance, Accident and Sickness Insurance, Group Insurance, and Pensions.

This curriculum remained essentially unchanged in content and description through the 1960s, but by the end of 1968 various task forces and committees of the board's Long-range Planning Commission had the whole CLU diploma program under scrutiny as they prepared the recommendations to the trustees that the board approved the following February. The changes would take effect with the 1970–1971 school year. Although they proved to be significant for the future of the College, the dramatic announcement of the projected on-campus building tended to somewhat overshadow these academic changes.

Trustee confidence in and enthusiasm for Mitchell/Giurgola Associates began with Huebner Hall, which won a gold medal and widespread professional approval. One architectural journal said that its "appearance and substance stem from the observance of the order of the building's operation, from the architectural identity of the component parts expressed also in their hierarchy, and from the appropriate employment of precast-concrete technology."[39]

Board commitment to the renovations had increased with conversion of the carriage house into the Myrick Pavilion and adaptation of a farmer's house on the Vauclain estate to become McCahan Hall. In 1967 the trustees endorsed the Mitchell/Giurgola long-range master plan for the entire campus and the preliminary plans for the learning laboratory. The projected structure had four different names between its conception and construction. In 1967 it first appeared as a Life Learning Laboratory to provide computer-assisted instruction, closed-circuit television, and video. The next year College publications called it the Research Facility for Adult Learning-Teaching. In 1969 it was named the first Adult Learning Research Center and finally the Adult Learning Laboratory, which became its official name.[40]

The Turner Construction Company was to begin work in January 1970; completion was projected for the following year. Broad policy would be set by a Learning Research Committee chaired by trustee John T. Fey, who had been elected to the board July 10. Since he had rapidly moved through a sequence of leadership positions at the College, Fey warrants a closer look.

Prior to becoming president of National Life Insurance Company of Vermont, this extraordinary man had been a lawyer and one-time member of the Maryland legislature before serving successively as president of the University of Vermont and the University of Wyoming. Fey could claim what a journalist of those days described as an "unusual background of the legal, academic, and business worlds."[41]

The new trustee and his committee began work at once. In response President Gregg started filling staff positions for a structure still in the blueprint stage. He selected Associate Dean James M. Daily of the Instruction Division to be director of learning systems.[42] Danny G. Langdon would serve as director of instructional design, and David Joslow of Chester Electronics, Inc., would function as technical consultant.

College publicity described the building design in these words: "The five-floor facility will consist of lower-level laboratory facilities including classrooms, a television studio, a learning sciences laboratory, individual study carrels, and other supporting spaces for instructional technology. The upper levels will house the educators and other professional staff."[43]

Trustee John O. Todd credited Davis W. Gregg with the vision to imagine the project and the persuasive power to convince the board to move ahead. "We voted to approve spending $3.5 million that we didn't have for a building that was to be an adult learning center," Todd said, adding, "It was one of the most courageous things I ever saw anybody do."[44]

Todd and Gregg were directors of the Million Dollar Round Table organization. They and James B. Irvine, Jr., CLU, former MDRT president, and by 1969 also an American College board member, were later successful in securing from the Round Table Foundation a $1.5 million grant commitment to the College for the building. In return, the College agreed to recognize the gift by naming the learning laboratory MDRT Foundation Hall.[45]

Todd and Irvine were not the only trustees who deserve individual attention that year. Charles J. Zimmerman resigned as board chairman to become chairman emeritus. Roger Hull succeeded him as chairman. Hull, president of Mutual of New York and a trustee since 1944, had held a series of committee chairmanships and other responsible positions. He was well qualified for the role as chairman.

Furthermore, that year Davis W. Gregg completed 20 years as an employee of the College, dating back to October 1949 when he began as assistant dean. Dr. Gregg's leadership had been and would continue to be a blend of personal performance and a ceaseless search for alumni and others in the industry who might help the College in one capacity or another. Another of Dr. Gregg's management strategies was to promote from within, and two people who benefited from this policy were Vane B. Lucas and Helen L. Schmidt.

Dr. Lucas had enjoyed a new title for each of 5 successive years since joining the College staff in 1965 as director of educational services. The next year he rose to an assistant deanship; in 1967 he moved up to a deanship in charge of the Administrative Division. Twelve months later Lucas was dean of the Instruction Division. Now in 1969 Vane B. Lucas achieved the vice presidency of the College, and the trustees elected him to the board as well.

Helen L. Schmidt continued to expand her influence at the College through advancement to corporate secretary. She had been assistant to the president for 9 years, during which she coauthored the 1967 *CLU Profile* with Vane B. Lucas and John S. White. She had also shared the honors with Dr. Joseph J. Melone in the compilation of the 1968 McCahan Foundation survey of worldwide insurance education. Schmidt's conscientious efforts under three presidents— Huebner, McCahan, and Gregg—confirmed the value of loyal, long-term employees to any successful organization.

Not long before the College rewarded Schmidt for her extended service, it welcomed another talented woman to the administrative staff. Marjorie A. Fletcher began work as research librarian and director of the campus library. Fletcher, a Bryn Mawr College alumna, was destined to occupy a number of important positions at the College over the next 2 decades.

*   *   *

As The American College entered the 1970s, President Davis W. Gregg declared, "It does so strongly in step with the emerging forces and trends of American education." Dr. Gregg noted that "all education is under immense economic pressure," and that most of it "is undergoing a pedagogical crisis." Gregg also believed, however, that the College was "at the leading edge of learning as efficiency, relevancy, and humanity are the key areas of concern."[46]

The trends and forces to which Davis W. Gregg alluded sprang from the vitality and restlessness of the nation in those days. Ambitious citizens and hard-working men and women in many occupations felt greater stress and sensed that they lacked time to reach their goals amid the quickening pace of contemporary life. The 1970 census count came to 203 million people, and the federal government that year issued U.S. passports to 2.2 million of them for foreign travel.[47] Average life expectancy at birth continued its steady climb to reach 70.8 years.[48] The larger population and increased longevity, however, brought dissatisfaction to many young people caught up in the hippie culture that continued throughout the country. *Newsweek* described the year as one in which "drug-age Bedouins roam the land."[49]

Young professionals were better educated than those of any previous generation. In the life insurance field, for example, by 1970, eight out of 10 Connecticut Mutual full-time agents had attended college.[50] This meant that CLU matriculants began their studies with broader academic experience and greater sophistication than those who had sought the designation in the early years of the program.

The Adult Learning Laboratory and the curriculum revision decisions of the previous year moved from concept to reality as the new decade began. The College's foresight and follow-through enabled it not only to maintain its momentum but also to increase its capacity and reputation for better service to the industry. In a sense these decisions reflected the thought of the early American poet James Russell Lowell, who wrote, "New occasions teach new duties, Time makes ancient truth uncouth; They must upward and onward, Who would keep abreast of truth."

The Adult Learning Laboratory went from drawing board to groundbreaking on April 21, 1970. Trustees, staff, and guests gathered that day to dedicate the site with a ceremonial digging of the dirt. It would be difficult to exaggerate the exhilaration of the moment that fulfilled Dr. Gregg's dream of such a pioneering facility. As another architect observed, "Buildings tell us who and what we are, not only as individuals but as a community."[51]

Davis W. Gregg announced that the Adult Learning Laboratory would "serve as a national resource center dedicated to the improvement of learning efficiency and productivity for persons engaged in life insurance careers and related professions."[52] The president and trustees therefore would have understood the further architectural insight that "buildings have always provided images of status and accomplishment for the clients who commissioned them."[53]

Trustee Chairman Roger Hull presided at the ceremony. Davis W. Gregg and John T. Fey, who headed the board's Learning Research Committee, stressed the significance of the anticipated structure. Iram H. Brewster, president of the Million Dollar Round Table Foundation, and Edmund L. Zalinski, chairman of The American College's trustee development board, talked about funding for the audacious undertaking. The program included planting a Sophora Japonica or "scholar tree" in a hole refilled with soil from all 50 states, which was presented in packets mailed from CLUs across the country.[54] The Turner Construction Company planned to begin work in June.

The curriculum revision counterpart to this architectural adventure was less dramatic but equally important to the College. That fall the CLU Diploma Program effected a cluster of changes to begin the new academic year. The explanatory paragraph in the 1971–1972 *Catalog,* which introduced the offerings, remained as before, but the specifics that followed were quite different. The program would "provide the candidate with (1) a broad understanding of the general fields of knowledge with which he should be acquainted, (2) a thorough knowledge of life and health insurance, and (3) a capacity for applying this knowledge to actual family and business situations."[55]

The aggregate of courses changed nomenclature as Parts gave way to Courses and increased from five to 10; each former Part became two Courses. The changes went beyond mere multiplication, however, to involve broader subject matter and deeper analysis. All examinations would henceforth be given in June for even-numbered courses and in January for odd-numbered courses. Examination questions for courses 1, 3, 5, 7, and 9 would be entirely objective (multiple choice). Examination questions for courses 2, 4, 6, and 8 were to be part objective, part essay. Questions for course 10 would be entirely essay. All exams would be 2 hours in duration and require a minimum grade of 70 to pass. People already in the program were delighted to learn that credit would be given for examinations previously passed under the former Parts schedule.[56] The College believed that these changes would create a closer time relationship between study, testing, and feedback of learning results.[57]

The CLU designation emphasized education for life insurance sales and service. The College awarded diplomas to persons "managing, training, or supervising" men and women in these fields. As we discussed earlier, in 1953 the trustees had broadened the program by creating a CLU Associate designation for "persons engaged in all other life insurance activities" and had awarded it to 19 successful candidates that year. However, the CLU Associate option had never really caught on. Although the number of CLU designations awarded had increased since 1953 by 18,684, only 174 people had earned the Associate diploma. In the late 1960s therefore the board voted to discontinue the CLU Associate diploma in 1970. CLU Associates could apply their credentials toward becoming a CLU.

The CLU program flourished because of its intrinsic merit and demonstrated value to sales agents. But it also benefited over the years through the efforts of the Committee of 1,000, which the College and the Society had started in 1959, appointing Solomon S. Huebner as chairman. The Committee sought 1,000 CLUs to recruit at least one new candidate apiece for CLU study. Within 4 years the members had sponsored some 1,800 candidates. Thus in 1968 the College introduced a special Sponsorship Award to recognize the efforts of committee members in encouraging new candidates to pursue and obtain the CLU designation. By 1970 the College had presented handsome award plaques to more than 300 veterans who had successfully sponsored candidates.[58]

In addition to revising its curriculum and examination methodology, the College made administrative changes to match. President Gregg named Dr. Barnie E. Abelle to head a new Education Division formed from the earlier Instruction and Curriculum-Examinations Divisions, which were discontinued. There were fewer deans (the number dropped from eight in 1967–1968 to two in

1969–1970) but more directors (the number of people with this title rose from five in 1968–1969 to 10 in 1969–1970).[59]

The McCahan Foundation showed increased vitality. Its research director Jerry S. Rosenbloom published an *Information Series* of annotated bibliographies featuring such topics as "Operations Research and Insurance Applications," "Variable Annuities and Separate Accounts," and "Demand for Life Insurance."

In contrast to the subjective emphasis of most life insurance industry research, the McCahan Foundation emphasized objectivity. Dr. Rosenbloom's topic selection for these papers reflected this stance. The research director found fulfillment in this work, but he discovered life at the College involved considerable administrative duties, which placed a poor second to his first love of teaching. Before 1970 was over therefore he resigned to return to Temple University, where within a few years he became chairman of the Insurance Department.[60]

In addition, Robert Dechert resigned as individual counsel for The American College that summer after 34 years in that pioneering role. Dechert, who had joined the board in 1937, became a life trustee in 1961. Mildred F. Stone, an earlier College historian, praised Dechert's "sound judgment and broad experience," which "led the College safely through the mazes of many problems."[61] The board did not appoint an individual successor to Dechert but opted for future legal representation by his firm, Dechert Price and Rhoads.[62]

A third departee was Herbert C. Graebner, executive vice president and treasurer, who retired that fall. He had been a trustee since 1955. Graebner's ability and forthright manner had given the College strong financial and administrative direction.

With changing times and the promotion of young executives including Vane B. Lucas, new faces appeared in nonacademic leadership roles at the College. In 1970, for example, four people began their work on the Bryn Mawr campus, although one of them—the new vice president, Leroy G. Steinbeck from The Insurance Company of North America—had served the Society as full-time executive vice president from 1950–1957. Other arrivals were Charles S. DiLullo, CPA, with both academic and business accounting experience, who became controller; David H. Kidder from Beloit College in Wisconsin, who headed Communication and Development; and Harold F. Rahmlow, who was appointed executive director of the Adult Learning Laboratory. Steinbeck, DiLullo, and Rahmlow were destined for outstanding long-term relationships with the College.

The trustees elected five new members to the board for 3-year terms. They included Donald S. MacNaughton, Prudential chairman; Richard R. Shinn, CLU, president of Metropolitan Life; and Dr. Clarence C. Walton, president of Catholic University of America in Washington, DC.

Amid the goings and comings, President Davis W. Gregg announced the receipt of the largest single gift from an individual in the 43-year history of The American College. Charles Lamont Post, CLU, gave a major grant to further higher education and research in insurance. Post, a former Penn Mutual Life, Guardian Life, and Travelers veteran who later formed the insurance brokerage firm Post & Kurtz, Inc., believed in the College and in Dr. Solomon S. Huebner's dream. Post credited the College with helping him get his career started. In giving the gift, Post hoped to inspire others to further philanthropic giving in the future.

Post's benefaction would indeed have that effect in the future, but it also served to dramatize the ongoing importance of voluntary financial support for the College, which had grown steadily since the establishment of the Development Fund in 1960. After a decade of effort, which produced cash and pledges in excess of $2.6 million from more than 4,800 donors, the College Development Fund's board convened a meeting of local chairpersons from across the country in October 1970. More than 100 people came to the national conference in Bryn Mawr, Pennsylvania, to meet College officials, hear inspirational talks, and participate in work groups.

James B. Irvine, Jr., from Chattanooga, Tennessee, chairman of the Development Fund board, chaired the colloquy. The College trustee chairman, Roger Hull, spoke at the dinner. President Davis W. Gregg and his top officers led a presentation titled "At the Leading Edge of Learning." Three directors of the American Society, all CLUs and chairmen of local development fund committees—Joseph H. Baynard, Baton Rouge, Louisiana; Robert D. Griewahn, Northwestern Pennsylvania; and Bernard H. Zais, Vermont[63]—conducted a how-to session.

For the American nation 1971 brought a lowering of the legal voting age from 21 to 18, a ban on radio and television tobacco advertising, and the introduction of the first hand-held calculator, which sold for $249. The cost of mailing a first-class letter rose from 6 to 8 cents.[64] For The American College 1971 was also a year of significant firsts. The first mid-winter CLU examinations and the first CLU conferment exercise as an independent ceremony were held, a new Long-range Planning Commission was appointed, and the College's Development Fund set a one-year record. Dr. John T. Fey, with only 2 years of College board experience, accepted greater responsibility and assumed a wider role in the life of the College. Finally, the College inaugurated a named-lecture series.

On January 29, 15,942 candidates took 19,726 examinations for Courses 1, 3, 5, 7, and 9 at 262 educational institutions across the country.[65] A smaller number of candidates took somewhat fewer examinations in June—proving the popularity of the new schedule, which offered greater flexibility than the previous June-only dates. The overall passing ratio for these tests was 72 percent.

Trustees at their July board meeting received good news from the development board and authorized the formation of a special commission on long-range plans. The fundraising group reported continuing success toward reaching its goals for the Golden Anniversary Decade ending in 1977. The board formed the commission "to study the aims and objectives of the College's education and research development."[66]

Two previous Long-range Planning Commissions had done much to guide the College's growth and development, but the trustees believed that new perspectives were needed for the decade ahead. They therefore appointed Dr. John T. Fey, recently elected vice chairman of the board, to head the commission that would apportion its work among four task groups and report to the whole board the following summer.[67]

James B. Irvine, Jr., announced that the College had passed two significant milestones. "Pledges since the establishment of the fund in 1960 now exceed $3 million," Irvine said, "and Golden Key Society membership totals more than 2,500. Cash income for 1970–71 of $289,726 sets a one-year record for the Development Fund."[68] The fund board had emphasized enrollment of Golden Key patrons who pledged their annual giving for a second 10 years.

Irvine also reported other plans for reaching the Golden Anniversary Decade goals, including seeking foundation grants, securing major gifts and bequests from individual donors, and soliciting corporate contributions. He concluded his report by saying, "We have the capacity, and I believe the wisdom, to see that this momentum is not only sustained but accelerated. Together we can demonstrate our confidence in the positive contribution that The American College can make to the quality of life through the advancement of adult learning and professionalism."[69]

That advancement took a new turn on September 14, 1971, when the College introduced the first in a series of lectures named for a distinguished life insurance educator, to be given over a period of years by a succession of eminent guest speakers. The College inaugurated the William T. Beadles Lectures named for the noted Illinois Wesleyan University professor of insurance, emeritus, CLU, who also served as national insurance education adviser for State Farm Insurance Companies. Beadles had been a long-time CLU teacher and in 1971 served as the senior educational consultant to the College.[70] The Beadles Lecture was funded by gifts from members of the Central Illinois Chapter of the Society who wished to honor Dr. Beadles—another dramatic illustration of the College and the Society cooperating in a joint effort for their common cause.

Peter F. Drucker delivered the first Beadles Lecture as Clarke Professor of Social Science at Claremont Graduate School, Claremont, California. Born in Austria and educated in Europe, Dr. Drucker was a renowned management consultant to business, governments, hospitals, and universities.[71] Drucker saluted the College in his talk titled "What We Already Know about American Education Tomorrow" as he asserted, "The most important learning is the continuing education of adults."[72]

That same month the College conducted its CLU national conferment exercises in a new format, which represented a further refinement of the changes begun in 1965 when the College and the Society first separated their yearly national activities from the NALU annual meeting. In Chicago on September 24, 1971, the conferment exercise became a separate ceremony as an afternoon commencement without the preliminary banquet that had previously prefaced the event. Trustees Charles J. Zimmerman, Roger Hull, and John T. Fey joined President Davis W. Gregg as platform speakers on this occasion.[73]

NOTES

1. Joseph J. Melone and Helen L. Schmidt, *Insurance Courses in Colleges and Universities outside the United States* (Bryn Mawr, PA: McCahan Foundation), 1968, p. vi.
2. *Annual Report,* The American College, 1967, p. 2.
3. James W. Hall, *Access through Innovation* (New York: National University of Continuing Education), 1991, p. 19.
4. *Annual Report,* 1967, p. 16.
5. Development Fund Report, 1967, p. 2.
6. Ibid., p. 16.
7. *CLU Profile: A Report on the 40th Anniversary Survey of Chartered Life Underwriters, 1927–1967,* p. 3.
8. Ibid.
9. Holgar J. Johnson with Croswell Bowen, *Speaking with One Voice* (New York: Appleton-Century-Crofts), 1967, p. 2.
10. *Annual Report,* 1967, p. 11.
11. Paul Dickson, *Timelines* (Reading, MA: Addison-Wesley Publishing Co., Inc.) 1990, pp. 156–157.
12. The American College news release, February 10, 1967.
13. *The American College Catalog,* 1967–1968, p, 88.
14. Program for Creative Excellence, 1966, pp. 4–5.
15. The American College news release, June 9, 1967.
16. Ibid., June 2, 1967.
17. Ibid.
18. Ibid., September 25, 1967.
19. *United States Review,* September 14, 1968.
20. *Annual Report,* 1968, p. 5.
21. Tony Campolo, *Everything You've Heard Is Wrong* (Dallas: World Publishing), 1992, p. 17.
22. Melone and Schmidt, *Insurance Courses in Colleges and Universities outside the United States,* 1968, p. v.
23. Ibid.
24. Ibid., p. vi.
25. John Scanozi, "The Conjugal Family and Consumption Behavior" (Bryn Mawr, PA: McCahan Foundation), 1968.
26. Ibid.
27. *Society Page* (Bryn Mawr, PA: American Society of CLU), May 1968, p. 5.
28. Ibid., September 1968, p. 7.
29. Mildred F. Stone, unpublished manuscript, chapter vi, p. 9.
30. *Society Page,* September 1968, p. 7.
31. *United States Review,* September 14, 1968.
32. Script for Reese Lake dedication ceremony, October 31, 1968.
33. Mildred F. Stone, *A Calling and Its College* (Homewood, IL: Richard D. Irwin), 1963, pp. 181–183.
34. *Society Page,* March 1963, p. 3.
35. Stone, *A Calling,* p. 184.
36. Dickson, *Timelines,* pp. 171–175.
37. *Annual Report,* 1969, p. 5.

38. Ibid.
39. "Offices Near Philadelphia," *Professional Architecture,* December 1961, p. 123.
40 *Annual Report,* 1969, p. 14.
41. *Insurance Advocate* (New York: Roberts Publishing Corp.), July 6, 1968.
42. *Society Page,* July 1969, p. 9.
43. *Annual Report,* 1969, p. 14.
44. Oral History interview, 1979.
45. Stone, unpublished manuscript, chapter vi, p. 9.
46. *Annual Report,* 1970, p. 3.
47. Dickson, *Timelines,* p. 180.
48. *World Almanac and Book of Facts* (Mahwah, NJ: World Almanac Books), 1994, p. 972.
49. Dickson, *Timelines,* p. 180.
50. William Cahn, *A Matter of Life and Death, the Connecticut Mutual Story* (New York: Random House), 1970, p. 255.
51. Witold Rybczynski, *Looking Around, a Journey through Architecture* (New York: Penguin Books), 1992, p. 191.
52. *Annual Report,* 1970, p. 10.
53. Rybczynski, *Looking Around,* p. 206.
54. Stone, unpublished manuscript, chapter vii, pp. 13–14.
55. *The American College Catalog,* 1971–1972, p. 24.
56. Ibid., p. 19.
57. *Annual Report,* 1971, p. 3.
58. Ibid., 1970, p. 5.
59. *The American College Catalog,* 1969–1970, p. 92.
60. Jerry S. Rosenbloom, interview with the author, November 14, 1995.
61. Stone, *A Calling,* p. 317.
62. Marjorie A. Fletcher, memorandum, October 17, 1995.
63. *Society Page,* February 1971, p. 4.
64. Dickson, *Timelines,* pp. 186–189.
65. *Statistical Analysis,* The American College, 1970–1971, p. 5.
66. Ibid., p.14.
67. Ibid.
68. Development Fund Tenth Annual Report, 1970–1971, p. 3.
69. "Report of the Development Board to the Board of Trustees of The American College," July 13–14, 1971, pp. 3–4.
70. *The American College Today,* vol. 1, no. 1, pp. 1, 4.
71. Peter F. Drucker, "What We Already Know about American Education Tomorrow," Beadles Lecture, 1971, p. 1.
72. Ibid., p. 11.
73. *Society Page,* August 1971, p. 3.

8

Looking Ahead

Time like an ever-rolling stream
Bears all its sons away.

Isaac Watts

Successful organizations avoid attachment to old ways, dependence upon organizational forms, and self-congratulation and reverence for established procedures. John W. Gardner, for 10 years president of the Carnegie Foundation for the Advancement of Teaching, addressed the challenge of leadership renewal in his perceptive essay, "The Life and Death of Institutions." Dr. Gardner stressed the need to emphasize "ideas, ideals, and goals" that contribute to "unsparing standards of performance."[1]

The American College had followed this lodestar for four decades. Beginning in 1927, a succession of board chairmen from Ernest J. Clark through Roger Hull had worked with a progression of presidents from Edward A. Woods through Davis W. Gregg to maintain a forward-looking vision and the vitality to implement goals on a continuing basis. After 45 years, the College showed no lessening of vigor as it moved into 1972, which would bring new trustee leadership, a larger campus, and the most modern of educational facilities.

Early in the year, the death of Board Chairman Roger Hull necessitated a change in leadership. Hull, who died on February 6 after a short illness, was also board chairman of Mutual of New York and had spent his entire business career of 42 years with that company. He began his involvement with the College as a CLU in 1934. The board elected him a trustee within a decade and chairman in 1969. One colleague called Hull a "giant,"[2] while another lauded him as an "outstanding leader of men."[3]

The Green Mountain State's John T. Fey succeeded Hull as chairman of the board. Fey had been a trustee less than 3 years and vice chairman for all of 7 months, but he was clearly the man for the job. The president of the National Life Insurance Company of Vermont, with previous experience in government, the law, and education, he had held high positions in the American Life Convention and the Life Insurance Association of America.[4] Furthermore, Dr. Fey's intense experience in heading the College's Long-range Education and Research Development Commission made him knowledgeable about the College's current capacity and future potential.

97

Approximately 80 people served the Commission in four task forces that considered, respectively, learning experiences, research and development, education and special services, and organization and financial resources. Amid their deliberations a challenge arose from the Boston Chapter of the American Society to limit the CLU designation to field people in life insurance selling and management and to offer a different designation to all others. The trustees carefully considered the option, but they reaffirmed the College's position to have only one designation with specific standards of acceptable experience in life, health, and related fields.[5]

The Commission Steering Committee summarized the task force reports with 20 conclusions and proposals that gave both long- and short-term guidelines for the College. One recommendation called for a "more intensive study of the College's mission and scope as a nontraditional professional education institution, particularly as it may respond to forces of change taking place both in the business of life insurance and in American institutions of higher learning."[6]

When the trustees named John T. Fey chairman, they also elected W.D. Grant, CLU, as vice chairman of the board. Grant, CEO of Business Men's Assurance Company of America, had served 8 years as a College trustee and was widely known for his work in numerous insurance associations.[7]

Soon after the announcement of these promotions, Mutual of New York created the Roger Hull Foundation for Creative Leadership, to be located on The American College campus. Initially funded by members of the MONY family, the foundation would now seek broader support as it honored Hull by identifying "what makes a man a creative leader and how this quality can be nurtured in others."[8]

Hull died a short time later, and the foundation became a memorial. The first Hull Memorial Lecture was given on June 22, 1972. United States Commissioner of Education Sidney P. Marland, Jr., spoke at a campus dinner where he paid tribute to Hull's personal leadership and stressed the need for educators to respond to the pressures of social problems afflicting the nation. MONY Chairman J. McCall Hughes unveiled a portrait of Hull presented by MONY and contributed a grant check to the foundation.

In early 1972 by purchasing 8.60 acres (the Wister property), the College acquired additional land for the fourth time since moving to Bryn Mawr, Pennsylvania, 13 years before.[*] The 1972 acquisition had been the site of Longhouse, home of the popular novelist Owen Wister, who wrote *The Virginian*. President Davis W. Gregg had ceaselessly sought opportunities to expand the campus beyond its original core holding, and in this he had been successful as the summary on the next page reveals.

---

[*] Note: In 1963 the board's purchase from the Vauclain family of a 50-foot strip of land connecting Bryn Mawr Avenue and Vauclain Lane assured that the campus would remain one parcel.

Year	Property	Dedicated As	Acres
1959	McIlvaine	Huebner Hall*	11.15
1963	Carriage house	Myrick Pavilion	1.00
1964	Vauclain	MDRT Foundation Hall* McCahan Hall	10.00
1967	Seiler	Dechert Hall	4.00
1972	Wister	Gregg Conference Center*	8.60

*New construction

The Wister property purchase did more than merely add acreage to the College campus. Because the Wister parcel was bounded on three sides by College land, it could easily be integrated into the existing grounds through the construction of a campus roadway and additional parking space. A College spokesman explained, "The acquisition will permit the master campus plan study to proceed with the possibility of the construction of . . . another educational facility within the next few years."[9]

Besides increasing campus size, the College made astute use of its existing property. Mitchell/Giurgola Associates designed the five-story MDRT Foundation Hall into the hillside in a way that minimized its height and made it aesthetically pleasing in the College's residential area. The imposing glass and tile structure, which the College dedicated at a ribbon-cutting ceremony on July 29, 1972, easily met three classical requirements for a building: "that it stand on the right spot; that it be securely founded; that it be successfully executed."[10]

The dedication program also included a banquet held the night before at the Marriott Motor Hotel on nearby City Line. Board Chairman Emeritus Charles J. Zimmerman presided at the banquet, which featured short statements by five men: Davis W. Gregg, College president; James B. Irvine, Jr., College trustee; Donald Shepherd, president of the MDRT Foundation; John T. Fey, chairman of the board; and life trustee John O. Todd. Both Irvine and Todd were former presidents of the Million Dollar Round Table and the MDRT Foundation.

The presentation included a time capsule ceremony. Representatives of more than 20 organizations that had been helpful to The American College came forward to deposit documents and artifacts in the capsule, which would be placed in a cavity under the stone floor of the reception area of the new building. After the presentations from dignitaries from such industry associations as the Insurance Institute of America, the Life Underwriter Training Council, and the General Agents and Managers Conference, Cindy Gregg (Davis and Mille Gregg's daughter) placed a copy of Mildred F. Stone's history of the College's early years, *A Calling and Its College,* in the capsule. Cindy Gregg had also participated in the 1960 time capsule ceremony for Huebner Hall

The next morning a smaller group of people gathered for breakfast in the Myrick Pavilion, then walked the short distance to the new building, where they assembled before the main entrance to MDRT Foundation Hall. Board Chairman

John T. Fey presided, speaking briefly about the common interests and pursuits of the College and the Million Dollar Round Table. Donald Shepherd, MDRT Foundation president, thanked all who had contributed money for the project. The two men were then joined by Charles Zimmerman, Davis Gregg, James Irvine, John Todd, and James Longley, president of the Round Table. Each of the seven held a pair of scissors and at a given signal simultaneously cut the ribbon stretched before the doorway. Along with the ribbon, there was an equal length of video tape to symbolize the new technology of adult learning that would emanate from "the little red schoolhouse of the twenty-first century."[11]

These 1972 College events took place during several national and world incidents worth noting. The United States concluded its manned lunar landing program with Apollo 17, *Life* magazine ceased publication, and the Dow Jones stock average reached 1,000 for the first time.[12] On the international scene Richard Nixon went to China, Munich hosted the Olympic Games, and airlines began mandatory baggage and passenger inspection.

Before the year ended, the College named part of MDRT Foundation Hall the Charles J. Zimmerman Adult Learning Laboratory and dedicated it on November 10 with a luncheon; an address by Clarence C. Walton, Catholic University president and College trustee; and the unveiling of a bust of the honoree. The learning laboratory was now dedicated to an individual. The ceremony followed a "Mustangs and Edsels" seminar on the successes and failures of instructional technology.[13]

Last but not least, the College marked 1972 with a change in one institutional publication and the introduction of two new informational pieces. *The American College Catalog*, for the first time, separately listed members of the administration and the faculty (established by the Board of Trustees in 1972). The College began publication of a *Resume of Activities* for internal consumption and started *The American College Today,* which would be mailed on a regular basis to the entire institutional mailing list.

*   *   *

Paul F. Clark, the last surviving member of the College's original board of incorporators, died on January 11, 1973, at age 80. Davis W. Gregg called him "an outstanding figure in the history of the school."[14] The Society hailed Clark as one of the "extremely dedicated protagonists in the history of the life insurance profession"[15] and praised him for taking "a personal interest in the training of insurance agents, in recruiting women to sell insurance, and in promoting ethical standards."[16]

That same month, as former colleagues mourned Clark's death, the board adopted the recommendations of the Special Committee on Mission and Scope, which the College had formed the previous year as a result of the findings of the Long-range Education and Research Development Commission. Charles J. Zimmerman headed the mission and scope group, which presented its findings on January 30. Zimmerman observed that the five conclusions of the committee reflected the belief that life insurance men and women would need more specialized knowledge in their increasingly complex field of life insurance and estate planning.

The committee recommended that the College should (1) stress the CLU curriculum, diploma, and designation, (2) include continuing education activities, (3) not embrace the learning needs and professional certification of other financial services persons substantially distinct from the process of protection, accumulation, conservation, and distribution of economic values associated with human life, (4) include courses of study aimed at the learning needs of persons engaged in other financial services to the extent that these persons can gain a greater understanding of insuring human life values, and (5) expand its program of advanced career education with a masters-level program.

Board members received another special report on January 30, 1973, when trustee Clarence C. Walton published his report, *Nontraditional Education in Contemporary America.* A year before the board had commissioned the Catholic University of America president to undertake this study, which accomplished two things: It examined emerging modes of nontraditional education, and it assessed "the potentialities and problems of accreditation for The American College."[17]

Dr. Walton brought impressive credentials to his task. He held three academic degrees and had done postdoctoral work at the University of Geneva and Harvard Business School. Before becoming president of Catholic University of America, he served as dean of Columbia University's School of General Studies. Walton compared The American College with the Open University of Great Britain and the external degree granted by the University of London, noting that the College had become "a prestigious front-runner in nontraditional higher education on approximately the graduate level."[18]

Trustee Walton concluded the first part of his report with the following six recommendations: The College should (1) experiment with computer-assisted instruction, (2) consider a one- or 2-week residential period on campus for CLUs seeking additional work, (3) develop specialized training packages, (4) continue its no-tenure policy for faculty appointments, (5) create a permanent task force to monitor new developments in American education and report to the board, and (6) work toward a masters-level degree supportive of the CLU diploma.[19]

Dr. Walton also urged the College carefully to consider seeking academic accreditation because of what it would mean for both the College and the students. As a final thought, Walton added that the accrediting agencies themselves might well gain much from the College's singular success and experience.[20] The publication of this study and the trustee response to its recommendations proved to be a determining factor in the College's future.

In the wide world that spring and summer of 1973, East and West Germany established diplomatic relations and the British left the Bahamas after 300 years of colonial governance. In Washington, DC, Watergate scandal reverberations put pressure on the Nixon presidency. At The American College one of its tenants and close associates, the American Institute for Property and Liability Underwriters, moved to Malvern, Pennsylvania, to establish its own campus. It was not an unexpected decision.

Reasons for the departure had been building for some time. As previously noted, the American Institute (and its alumni affiliate—the Society of Chartered Property and Casualty Underwriters—and the Insurance Institute of America) had moved from Philadelphia to Bryn Mawr in 1961 and occupied space in Huebner Hall. After 3 months, cramped conditions there forced the Society of Chartered Property and Casualty Underwriters to leave for larger quarters in nearby Media, Pennsylvania.[21]

The American Institute, for its part, soon began thinking about the possibility of erecting its own building "on separate but nearby grounds."[22] When the adjacent Wister property first became available in 1970, the Institute sought to acquire it. The College, however, was less than enthusiastic because, it reasoned, if the Institute bought the land and applied for real estate tax exemption in its own name, it would jeopardize the expansion the College had planned for the existing campus.

The College prevailed; the Institute purchased property in Malvern, Pennsylvania, and moved there in June 1973. The American Institute settled into its own attractive 23-acre campus, naming its main building in honor of past president Harry J. Loman and dedicating it on June 15. Dr. Loman and David McCahan had both been protégés of Solomon S. Huebner, who turned to McCahan for help in developing the CLU concept in the 1920s and to Loman for help in developing its property/casualty counterpart somewhat later.

In addition to planning for the future, College trustees and the administration were involved in a variety of here-and-now events during the autumn months of 1973. September, for instance, brought the annual CLU conferment exercise held in conjunction with the Society's annual meeting and forum. This yearly collaborative effort symbolized the close connection between two separately incorporated, nonprofit organizations. They had "one overriding concept they share totally; that is a dedication to professionalism in life underwriting."[23]

The main sessions took place at the Philadelphia Marriott Motor Inn, but the total program included "Breakfast in Bryn Mawr" and a campus program and tour for more than 600 attendees who came to the College on Saturday morning. Festivities included planting the 25th anniversary class tree by Ben Feldman, CLU, to continue a custom that began years ago "to protect and enhance the natural beauty of the campus by developing it in harmony with nature and the neighboring environment."[24] The class of 1948 planted a Japanese White Pine; the 40th anniversary class also dedicated a tree. In addition, the College, which planted "dedicated" trees from time to time, planted a Copper Beech in 1973 to recognize Margaret F. Carlsen, CLU, of the CLU Associates of Equitable Life.[25]

That year College librarian Marjorie A. Fletcher developed a new method for storing and cataloging insurance-related audio-visual materials through an extension of a Library of Congress classification. The Insurance Library Division of the Special Libraries Association endorsed Fletcher's system.[26] A national system for computer retrieval of all cataloged materials through OCLC became standard.

Leo R. Futia, CLU, took pride in announcing that Development Fund pledges passed the $4 million mark for the first time since the program began in 1960. Futia, who had recently succeeded James B. Irvine, Jr., as Development board chairman, also reported cash gifts and pledge payments amounting to $1,991,451.[27]

The College not only counted more dollars at this time, but more people as well. The opening of MDRT Foundation Hall added some 30 new employees to the campus administration, faculty, and staff. John A. Bajtelsmit, who came from Villanova University and began as a research associate, was one of them. Dr. Bajtelsmit has continued his research career with the College and is currently the director of course evaluation and research administration.

In the year when Henry Kissinger won the Nobel Peace Prize, Walter Cronkite earned the title of most trusted American, the Sears Tower in Chicago—at 1,454 feet—became the world's tallest building, and the 1973 median price of a family home in the United States stood at $28,900,[28] the College joined the University City Science Center on October 17 and became the 28th member of that Delaware Valley nonprofit corporation sponsored by academic institutions of the area. The Center strove to apply "scientific and technical knowledge to help solve the problems of society and to improve the quality of life"[29]—a mission with which the College could readily relate.

Finally, to close out another crowded year in the life of the expanding CLU institution, the College began a 12-month study program with the Greensboro, North Carolina, Center for Creative Leadership. The two organizations would work with 24 life insurance company executives "to foster increased knowledge and practical application of creativity in leadership skills"[30]—another example of the College's cooperation with other educational entities.

*   *   *

Davis W. Gregg described the 1973–1974 academic year as "one of the most meaningful periods in the history of The American College."[31] The president referred to the reorganization of study programs and student population figures that reached all-time highs. It was also a significant time for two members of the administration, Vane B. Lucas and Helen L. Schmidt, who were recognized for exceptional work. In January 1974 the trustees promoted Dr. Lucas and saluted Ms. Schmidt.

Vane B. Lucas thereby earned his fifth promotion in 8 years. In 1972 he had become senior vice president and now moved up to the position of executive vice president on the recommendation of Dr. Gregg. The president described Lucas as "one of the nation's most knowledgeable and experienced persons in professional education and innovative learning systems. For the College and those it serves he is the right person in the right place at the right time."[32]

A good many other people enthusiastically agreed, and over a period of the next 4 months sent Lucas congratulations for his achievement. Letters came from across the country and all sectors of the life insurance industry. Edward B. Bates, president of Connecticut Mutual Life, for example, spoke of "well-deserved recognition."[33] President Armand C. Stalnaker of General American Life, St. Louis, expressed his pleasure.[34] General agents and other insurance professionals joined in the congratulations. A CLU from Prudential Life exclaimed, "Highly deserved,"[35] and another from State Farm Insurance Companies opined, "The trustees could not have made a wiser choice."[36] College and university deans were similarly impressed.

Helen L. Schmidt, for her part, attended a special luncheon in honor of her 25th anniversary and accepted a unanimous trustee resolution, expressing board "admiration and affection" for her "loyal and creative service to The American College."[37] In making the award, Chairman John T. Fey joined President Davis W. Gregg in extolling both Schmidt's accomplishments and her friendship. Later that year the board presented Schmidt with a bronze sculptured bird by artist Edward Fenno Hoffman, III, whose other work already adorned a number of College buildings.[38]

The trustee meeting that brought attention to these two College "stars" was also the occasion for board approval of a realignment of the academic program within the College's organizational structure. Henceforth there would be three separate schools of instruction. Not long after that epochal meeting President Gregg announced the details of the new plan, which identified distinct dimensions of faculty and administrative responsibility to provide for meeting learning needs through quality teaching.

First, there would be the Solomon S. Huebner School of CLU Studies named in honor of the founder of the College and long-time University of Pennsylvania distinguished professor of insurance. The Huebner School would have complete charge of the CLU curriculum, awarding diplomas, and conferring designations. Dr. Gregg explained that the status of some 45,000 students already engaged in the program would not change. Examinations that year would be given in June and January under the same conditions as previously announced.[39]

Second, the School of Advanced Career Studies would offer "a variety of courses and other programs" designed to further the career development of CLUs and to be of interest to other students, including bank trust officers, certified public accountants, and lawyers. This school would emphasize courses in advanced estate planning, advanced pension planning, financial planning, and management.[40]

Third, the College would include a Graduate School of Financial Sciences, which for the first time in the history of the College would provide courses leading to a Master of Science in Financial Services. This MSFS would be a degree distinct from the CLU designation.[41]

Dr. Gregg gave four reasons for the creation of the three schools. First, it clarified the exact nature of the different programs about which there had been some uncertainty in the past. Second, it outlined faculty and academic obligations. Third, it delegated responsibility within the academic operation. Finally, it strengthened financial accountability and planning. The College soon moved the newly formed schools of instruction from the conceptual to the concrete through the appointment of individual deans to head the now clearly defined organizational units.

Later that spring, Executive Vice President Vane B. Lucas announced the names of the people who would administer these academic departments. Barnie E. Abelle would lead the Solomon S. Huebner School of CLU Studies. Herbert Chasman, JD, CLU, would be responsible for the School of Advanced Career Studies. Dr. Denis T. Raihall would guide the Graduate School of Financial Sciences.[42]

None of these educators was new to the College. All had been members of the faculty before becoming deans. Furthermore, each had been doing work closely related to his new assignment but with a lesser title. Abelle, for example, had chaired the CLU Curriculum Department, Chasman had been chairman of Advanced Underwriting Education, and Raihall had chaired the Department for Financial Education.[43]

Dr. Lucas gave each a glowing introduction to the alumni and broader College constituency, noting that "Dr. Abelle has an excellent background for the position." Lucas described Chasman as "eminently qualified," and he stressed Raihall's combined "academic experience and practical investment management background."[44]

Frank Newman, president of the University of Rhode Island, gave the second William T. Beadles Lecture on May 8, 1974. The former Stanford University official and noted author and lecturer addressed a group of Delaware Valley educators and business leaders in a talk on "Higher Education in Tension and Transition." The question-and-lecture format reviewed these four tensions: a growing conflict between egalitarianism and merit, earlier maturation of students, higher education as a less certain path to upward social mobility as more people attend college, and the need for more diversity of institutions as students become more diverse.[45]

As the College made these important academic decisions and maintained the momentum of the Beadles Lecture Series, much was happening overseas and throughout the country. The United States evacuated its civilians from Saigon on April 29, 1974. Later, the British House of Commons outlawed the Irish Republican Army. National news highlighted Richard Nixon's resignation and the beginning of the Gerald R. Ford presidency. Hank Aaron's 715 home runs topped Babe Ruth's long-standing record. Unemployment climbed past 7 percent, while consumer prices rose by 12 percent in the largest yearly increase since 1946.[46]

On two occasions in 1974 the College made its presence known off campus in a special way. One, the American Institute of Architects selected MDRT Foundation Hall to receive its respected Honor Award. The AIA picked the tile-and-glass structure as one of only eight so recognized out of a total of 414 submitted for consideration that had been completed anywhere in the world during the previous decade.[47] Two, the Greater Philadelphia Chamber of Commerce and the Pennsylvania Horticultural Society presented the College with a leadership horticultural award to recognize the scope and beauty of the approximately 35-acre campus.[48]

The trustees continued to be busy throughout 1974. At the annual meeting in June they increased the authorized size of the board from 27 to 30 members to serve in classes of 10 each for a 3-year period. They also elected four new trustees: Earl Clark, CLU, CEO, Occidental Life; Sidney P. Marland, Jr., College entrance examination board chairman; J. Edwin Matz, president of John Hancock Mutual Life; and Harris L. Wofford, Jr., president of Bryn Mawr College. In July the trustees revised the bylaws to contain only the essentials of organization, policy, and operation. They then issued separate "Rules of Governance" to cover operational areas subject to more frequent change.[49] Finally, they elected Davis W. Gregg a life trustee in recognition of his 25 years of American College leadership.

This honor was only one of several that the College accorded its forceful and influential president to commemorate his silver anniversary of service. The College honored Dr. and Mrs. Gregg at a special dinner on June 27, when more than 100 guests—trustees, their spouses, and the Greggs' friends—gathered in Foundation Hall. After dinner, a nostalgic audio-visual presentation emphasized the 25 years of Dr. Gregg's tenure and his many contributions. Three months later, faculty and staff held a campus reception in the Greggs' honor.[50]

Soon thereafter the Bryn Mawr campus was the setting for another anniversary celebration for an American College V.I.P. On November 1 the College hosted a dinner to help Charles J. Zimmerman, honorary board chairman, commemorate 50 years in the life insurance business. President Davis W. Gregg presided on this happy occasion when business leaders and educators across the nation saluted Zimmerman for his half-century of service to the industry, a large percentage of which included involvement with The American College.[51]

In addition to observing noteworthy anniversaries in 1974, the College played host to important visitors. Pennsylvanians comprised the first group. The second delegation came from the USSR. Each was important but for far different reasons. Five educators arrived from within the Commonwealth to inspect and evaluate the College's application to confer a masters degree through the recently formed Graduate School of Financial Sciences. Four Soviets included the College in their 15-day United States tour of business and management schools connected to various universities.

Among the Commonwealth group evaluating the College for degree-granting status, Dr. Dan M. McGill represented the University of Pennsylvania's Wharton School. Dr. Ralph E. Hughes, president emeritus of Shippensburg State College, chaired the committee; three other educators rounded out the roster. A favorable report from the Evaluation Committee and the Pennsylvania

Department of Education would move the College closer to possible academic accreditation.[52]

The Soviets came to America as part of an agreement between the two countries to cooperate in the application of computers to management. President Gregg, Executive Vice President Lucas, and Dr. Harold F. Rahmlow, vice president of learning systems and testing, met with the Soviet delegates to explain The American College methodology of education and the new technological developments in adult education. The College had long displayed international life insurance influence dating back to Solomon S. Huebner's world tours. Now it enjoyed the satisfaction of outreach in the field of technology.[53]

*   *   *

The American agenda for 1975 seemed to accentuate the negative; the country digested such bad news as higher unemployment and a rising cancer death rate. There were more than one million divorces for the first time in United States history.[54] The American College, however, would press ahead with plans for enriching both its academic palette and its financial resources. Better yet, it would be successful in both areas.

Against a background of record CLU statistics—for example, reaching a combined January and June examination enrollment total of more than 50,000 for the first time[55]—the Department of Education of the Commonwealth of Pennsylvania authorized the College to confer the Master of Science in Financial Services degree. Secretary John C. Pittenger said, "I am particularly pleased to make this authorization in that your organization was founded as one of the original nontraditional or 'open university' approaches to learning."[56] Pointing out the College's intent, Pittenger added, "To provide an opportunity for those in or aspiring to enter the financial science professions to undertake a masters-level curriculum . . . is most certainly important."[57] The College would next seek accreditation.

The mid-1970s were also a time of fulfillment for Davis W. Gregg. In 1974 he spoke on a *Voice of America* program beamed throughout the world in 26 languages.[58] In 1975 he won an American Academy of Achievement Golden Plate Award as an outstanding American who typified "the traditions of personal achievement in all fields that have made this country the strongest and most progressive on earth."[59]

After 48 years of operations, the College had a fiscal 1975 balance sheet and income-expense statement showing these figures:

Total assets	$14,171,874
Fiscal 1975 income	5,131,401
Excess of 1975 fiscal revenues over expenditures	318,354
Mortgage payable	3,494,739 [60]

Total assets and income, impressive as they were—particularly when compared to the modest figures of the early years—would not suffice for the future. The College needed to liquidate the mortgage debt, build up the endowment, and provide for future campus development. The trustees had been reviewing these circumstances for some time, and as early as June 1974, they authorized a major fundraising program to seek cash gifts and pledges amounting to $20 million by the 50th anniversary year of 1977–1978.

The capital campaign originated with a trustee standing committee known as the Development Board, and chaired at that time by Leo R. Futia. Thirteen men comprised this group, which included such fundraising stalwarts as James B. Irvine, Jr.; John O. Todd; and Charles J. Zimmerman. The Development Board proceeded to expand this cadre into a 45-member Golden Anniversary Fund National Committee, which included representatives from coast to coast. These participants in turn widened the organizational circle to include more than 180 Chapter Development Program chairmen from the Society's local chapters across the nation.[61] As Board Chairman John T. Fey explained, their overriding objective would be "to insure the ability of the College to serve in the future."[62]

More than 150 of these leaders attended a May 8–9, 1975, meeting on the Bryn Mawr campus at which time Zimmerman and his cohorts, Futia and Irvine, publicly announced the campaign and thereby launched the Golden Anniversary Fund. Half of the money raised would be used to retire the mortgage and add to endowment. One-quarter would be earmarked for research, development, and funding faculty chairs. The remaining quarter would be put toward campus development, including the construction of a proposed graduate study center.[63]

Plans called for $13 million to be raised through annual pledges from individuals and corporate matching gifts, and $7 million from major gifts by individuals and foundation grants. The College would jump-start the campaign by counting $4 million in pledges payable from individuals, corporations, and foundations on commitments made before 1975.[64]

At their annual meeting the following month the trustees elected four new board members: Walter L. Downing, New England Mutual Life; John H. Filer, CEO of Aetna Life and Casualty of Hartford; Dan M. McGill, chairman of the Insurance Department at the University of Pennsylvania's Wharton School; and Lester A. Rosen, an agent in Memphis for Union Central Life. Downing and Rosen were already members of the Golden Anniversary Fund National Committee.[65]

Concurrently, the trustees authorized the creation of the Solomon S. Huebner Gold Medal as a special award to those persons "whose outstanding support and contributions have been of particular meaning to the mission and program of the College." Edward Fenno Hoffman, III, whose sculptured portrait busts of important College leaders already decorated the interiors of various campus buildings, created a 3 ¼" gold-plated disc with Dr. Huebner's likeness embossed on one side and these words inscribed on the other: "In recognition of distinguished service to education and professionalism."[66] The board selected Charles Lamont Post as the first recipient of the medal.

That fall President Davis W. Gregg presented the medal to Post at the annual conferment luncheon of the New York Chapter of CLUs. In so doing Dr. Gregg remarked that Post was one of the nation's first CLUs, one of the first leaders in the New York Chapter, and one of the first officers of the American Society.[67]

Soon after presenting the first Huebner Gold Medal to Charles Lamont Post, Dr. Gregg was back in action at the College's Woodland Garden dedication in late October. Former trustee Joseph E. Boettner and his wife, Ruth, gave money to create the garden along the stream that runs through the campus. Landscape architect W. Terrence McDonnell and horticulturist Stevenson W. Fletcher landscaped an area approximately 200 feet by 1,000 feet on the hillside below MDRT Foundation Hall. The garden contained 21 trees, 784 shrubs, 4,290 ground-cover plants, and 3,850 bulbs in an endeavor that represented still another significant step in the long-range development of campus beauty.[68]

Amid the satisfaction of participating in these positive events, the president was somewhat disappointed in his portrait, which was painted by the noted American artist Clifford Hamilton Schule. The portrait had been commissioned by the trustees and paid for by contributions, and although everyone admired the quality of the work and its striking likeness of the subject, Dr. Gregg felt uncomfortable with the painting's life-size dimensions. He was also a person who preferred to recognize others and was uncomfortable with having the portrait hung while he was still active at the College. Furthermore, he could think of no suitable place to hang it.[69] Consequently, it was not displayed until 1990 when he agreed to its installation in Gregg Hall.

The College experienced both loss and gain during the last 2 months of 1975. Robert Dechert died on November 8 at age 79. The Commission on Higher Education of the Middle States Association of Colleges and Schools accepted The American College as a "Candidate for Accreditation." Each event deserves closer attention.

Robert Dechert had enjoyed a long relationship with the College, beginning in 1936 when he became counsel to the College. Elected a trustee a year later, he achieved life status in 1961. The institution recognized his distinguished service by naming a campus building Dechert Hall. Davis W. Gregg called Dechert, whose career spanned the fields of law, education, and insurance, "a moving force behind many of Philadelphia's leading philanthropic and community groups."[70]

For its first 48 years the College had not sought accreditation because the faculty and trustees "viewed the restrictions of certain traditional accreditation criteria as outweighing the possible advantages" of that status.[71] However, as the institution grew in size, formed distinct schools of instruction, and earned authorization to grant a graduate degree, the College began the process of seeking this academic credential. By then, too, the accrediting bodies had become more receptive to acknowledging nontraditional education. Candidate status for accreditation indicated that an institution was progressing toward but was not assured of accreditation. The designation confirmed evidence of sound planning and the institution's potential for reaching its goals within a reasonable time.[72]

The process of seeking accreditation was an arduous one, starting with formal application by the College and campus visits by authorities. After acceptance of the College as a candidate, the faculty would conduct an in-depth self-study, and there would be a final report by an evaluation team, which would visit the campus for several days.

*   *   *

Regularly scheduled flights of the Concorde Super Sonic Transport began on January 21, 1976, to herald a new era of air travel. This was also the year when Tandy Corporation introduced the first personal computer and a Pulitzer Prize went to the musical comedy *A Chorus Line*. According to statistics, the "average American" of those days was 28.7 years of age, had 12.4 years of formal schooling and 2.3 children, and lived in a house with 5.3 rooms.[73]

Big changes were afoot at The American College. In 1976 the College began printing a "Notice of Nondiscriminatory Policy as to Students" as a part of its *Annual Report*.[74] It also moved its fiscal year from the more academic September 1–August 31 schedule to the more businesslike July 1–June 30 calendar, which meant that the annual financial reports issued that summer were for 10 months only to reflect the new plan. More important, the College shortened its name from the original and somewhat awkward American College of Life Underwriters to the more succinct The American College, which had been the actual working name for several years. The change came with the supplementary provision that the statement "An Institution for the Advancement of Learning and Professionalism in Life Insurance and Related Financial Services" would also be used where appropriate.[75] (This addendum, however, did not suffice for some alumni and others in the industry who were opposed to the ambiguity of the new name.)

The decision to change the College's name was not made lightly. There was an extensive and involved procedure for the name change: CLUs were surveyed and committees held several meetings. The College effected the name change through a sequence of three events, beginning with legal reincorporation in Pennsylvania as a nonprofit educational corporation on March 22, 1976.[76] The trustees unveiled a new Charter Resolution scroll—bearing signatures of all trustees serving at that time—at its annual dinner on May 13, held at the First Bank of the United States, erected in the 1790s near Independence Hall in Philadelphia. Finally, the College completed a merger with the original American College of Life Underwriters, a District of Columbia nonprofit educational institution on July 4, 1976, to coincide with the national bicentennial celebration.

As Dr. Gregg observed, the name change would accomplish three things: "sharpen the school's role as a collegiate educational institution in contrast to a membership body, clarify the distinction between the College and the Society membership organization of CLUs, and enhance the opportunity for broad national recognition of the unique College with an undergraduate and graduate curriculum."[77] Board Chairman John T. Fey and Honorary Chairman Charles J. Zimmerman were equally sanguine about the change. They believed it was in the best long-term interests of the College.

During the intense activity surrounding the name change, campus academic activity flourished. The Hull Foundation for Creative Leadership, which became a memorial tribute to Roger Hull's enormous contribution to the College after his 1972 death, sponsored a leadership seminar on April 14, 1976. It featured a presentation by Professor Eugene E. Jennings of Michigan State University Graduate School of Business. Dr. Jennings, author of such books as *The Executive in Crisis*, addressed a group of business leaders and educators who then had the opportunity to respond with comments and questions. The proceedings were recorded to be published for distribution to a wider audience.[78] (An earlier Hull Foundation seminar had featured Dr. Edward de Bono of the Department of Investigative Medicine, Cambridge University, England, who had come to the campus the previous fall.)

In May 1976 three other educators came to Bryn Mawr as part of the Visiting Faculty Program organized the previous spring: Dr. Frank E. Ranelli, chairman of marketing and economics at the University of Florida; Dr. Benjamin M. Perles, dean of Old Dominion University's School of Business Administration; and James Van Dyke, dean of the Social Science/ Communication Division of Portland, Oregon, Community College. They came primarily to familiarize themselves with The American College's learning systems and testing procedures, although their presence obviously stimulated a worthwhile exchange of ideas with the College faculty and staff, as well as a visit with officers of the Society.[79]

These were not the only special academic developments announced at this time. Two others—interestingly enough, both involving Marjorie A. Fletcher, assistant professor of education and research librarian—also warrant discussion. In the first, the Philadelphia Chapter of the Special Libraries Association named Fletcher president and made her responsible for all the bicentennial year programs of the association.[80] In the second, Fletcher assumed accountability for a newly established Oral History Center as part of the College library. The center would be funded by the CLU class of 1951 as part of its 25th anniversary commemoration. Over succeeding years the Oral History Center would record and preserve interviews with men and women who, as President Davis Gregg expressed, "had seen the College grow from a struggling newcomer to a position of international prominence in higher education for adults."[81]

The College scored another first in July when 14 resident students spent 2 weeks on campus as part of their work toward the Master of Science in Financial Services degree. (Actually, the students slept in a nearby Bryn Mawr College dormitory, but they did their coursework and had their meals on The American College campus.)

Growing enrollment, experimental courses, and the graduate degree program called for more teachers and administrators. Consequently, the College added seven faculty members and two staffers during the 1975–1976 academic year, bringing the total employee count to 170 persons.[82] William H. Rabel, CLU, PhD, won promotion to the deanship of the Solomon S. Huebner School after serving as acting dean the previous year.

Most successful organizational growth also necessitates some selective retrenchment. Certain initiatives are mounted to meet specific needs, which after a time are no longer a high priority. The Creative Excellence Program illustrates this point. Organized to encourage faculty development and effective for a number of years, the program became less important when the College achieved degree-granting status. As a result, the College ended the program that summer.[83]

Board member James S. Bingay died on July 30, 1976, at age 56. Mutual of New York's CEO had been a College trustee since 1972, and as was typical of many College board members, he headed a major corporation, was a director of other companies, and exercised charitable and community leadership as well. Another important quality was his interest in adult education, specifically, insurance. He became one of the first in a series of College leaders whose demise created the opportunity to increase the College's endowment by establishing memorial funds for lectureships or teaching chairs. In this case, Bingay's successor as president of Mutual of New York soon announced plans for his company to fund the James S. Bingay Chair of Creative Leadership. MONY planned to raise $300,000 to supplement the $200,000 already given or pledged to the Hull Foundation and thereby reach the $500,000 needed to fund the effort.

Not all institutional endowment funds come into existence as memorials to the dead. Living persons, with the conviction and capital to commit substantial money for such a purpose, can also establish permanent named funds. Frank M. Engle of Tulsa, Oklahoma, was the first person to so endow a lectureship for The American College. In mid-1976 he gave $100,000 to make possible the Lectureship in Economic Security bearing his name.[84]

As Board Chairman John T. Fey applauded the gift, he noted the change in the nature of economic security mechanisms brought about by government programs that did not exist when the College began in 1927. "It is critically important," Dr. Fey asserted, "that the impact of this growing public system be understood and that the impact of both the public and private systems on the American family be realized."[85]

Engle's leadership gift was only part of the development good news that season. Golden Anniversary Fund cochairmen James B. Irvine, Jr., and Charles J. Zimmerman reported genuine progress after the first 12 months of the constituency-wide endeavor. The enthusiastic leaders counted a total of $8.9 million secured in cash gifts, pledges, and bequests; $4.7 million came from Golden Key Society participants and $4.2 million from foundations, individuals' major gifts, and bequests.[86]

The College punctuated the general campus mood of achievement and enthusiasm of those days by recognizing two men with Huebner Gold Medals. As part of the 49th annual conferment exercises in September 1976, Executive Vice President Vane B. Lucas presented the award to William T. Beadles, professor of insurance emeritus at Illinois Wesleyan University and senior consultant to the College. Board Chairman John T. Fey then presented the Huebner Gold Medal to none other than the ubiquitous Charles J. Zimmerman, who, over a period of 35 years, had served on every major committee and board of the College.

NOTES

1. John W. Gardner, *No Easy Victories* (New York: Harper & Row), 1968, pp. 40–45.
2. *Annual Report,* The American College, 1972, p. 1.
3. John T. Fey, *The American College Today,* spring 1972, p. 3.
4. *The American College Today,* summer 1972, pp. 2–4.
5. Mildred F. Stone manuscript, chapter 8, p. 5.
6. *Annual Report,* 1972, p. 1.
7. *The American College Today,* summer 1972, pp. 1–2.
8. Ibid., spring 1972, p. 1.
9. Letter to Radnor Township Commissioners, September 1972, p. 1.
10. John Wolfgan von Goether, *Elective Affinities,* 1808, book I, chapter 9.
11. Ribbon-cutting ceremony program notes, July 29, 1972.
12. Paul Dickson, *Timelines* (Reading MA: Addison-Wesley Publishing Co., Inc.), 1990, pp. 193–198.
13. William C. Lewis, letter to William Hanford, dean, Wisconsin State University, October 5, 1972.
14. *The American College Today,* spring 1973, p. 3.
15. *Society Page* (Bryn Mawr, PA: American Society of CLU), February 1973, p. 3.
16. Ibid.
17. *The American College Today,* summer 1973, pp. 1–2.
18. Ibid.
19. Ibid.
20. Clarence C. Walton, *Nontraditional Education in Contemporary America* (Bryn Mawr, PA: The American College), 1973, pp. 33–37.
21. Edwin S. Overman, interview with the author, November 11, 1995.
22. *President's Report,* AIPLU, 1961–1962, p. 2.
23. *Society Page,* December 1973/January 1974, p. 2.
24. *Horticultural Guide to The American College Campus.*
25. *The American College Today,* summer 1973, p. 3.
26. Ibid., autumn 1973, pp. 1–4.
27. *Annual Giving Report,* The American College, 1972–1973.
28. Dickson, *Timelines,* pp. 200–207.
29. *Review of Activities,* The American College, 1973–1974, p. 4.
30. Ibid., p. 5.
31. *Annual Report,* 1974, p. 1.
32. *The American College Today,* March 1974, p. 1.
33. Letter to Vane B. Lucas from Edward B. Bates, February 20, 1974.
34. Letter to Vane B. Lucas from Armand C. Stalnaker, February 19, 1974.
35. Congratulatory message from William L. Olson, March 3, 1974.

36. Congratulatory message from Loren L. Andrews, March 3, 1974.
37. *The American College Today,* March 1974, p. 4.
38. Ibid., October 1974, p. 3.
39. Ibid., March 1974, p. 1.
40. Ibid.
41. Ibid.
42. Ibid., July 1974, pp. 1–2.
43. *The American College Catalog,* 1973–1974, p. 66.
44. *The American College Today,* July 1974, pp. 1–2.
45. Ibid., p. 1.
46. Dickson, *Timelines,* pp. 209–210.
47. *Review of Activities,* 1973–1974, p. 11.
48. *The American College Today,* October 1974, p. 4.
49. *Review of Activities,* 1973–1974, p. 10.
50. *The American College Today,* October 1974, p. 1.
51. Ibid., January 1975, p. 1.
52. Ibid., p. 2.
53. Ibid.
54. Dickson, *Timelines,* p. 216.
55. *Annual Report,* 1975, p. 1.
56. *The American College Today,* September 1975, p. 1.
57. Ibid.
58. Ibid., July 1974, p. 2.
59. Ibid., September 1975, p. 2.
60. Auditors' Statement—1975, Coopers & Lybrand.
61. Golden Anniversary Fund Report, 1975–1976, pp. 44–47.
62. Ibid., p. 3.
63. *Annual Report,* 1975, p. 1.
64. *Review of Activities,* 1974–1975, p. 13.
65. *The American College Today,* September 1975, p. 1.
66. Ibid., January 1976, p. 1.
67. Ibid.
68. *Review of Activities,* 1974–1975, p. 12.
69. Davis W. Gregg, letter to Vane B. Lucas, Leroy G. Steinbeck, and Richard T. McFalls, March 10, 1975.
70. *The American College Today,* January 1976, p. 4.
71. *Annual Report,* 1975, p. 1.
72. Ibid.
73. Dickson, *Timelines,* p. 223.
74. *Annual Report,* 1976, p. 4.
75. *The American College Today,* spring 1976, p. 3.
76. *Review of Activities,* 1975–1976, p. 12.
77. Ibid.
78. *The American College Today,* spring 1976, p. 2.
79. *Review of Activities,* 1975–1976, p. 7.
80. *The American College Today,* spring 1976, p. 3.
81. Ibid., p. 1.
82. *Review of Activities,* 1975–1976, p. 13.
83. Ibid., p. 7.
84. *The American College Today,* fall 1976, p. 1.

85. Ibid., p. 4.
86. Golden Anniversary Fund Report, 1975–1976, p. 4.

9

Bittersweet

*Boast not thyself of tomorrow: for thou
knowest not what a day may bring forth.*

Proverbs 27:1

American higher education in the mid-1970s presented a pastiche of teaching patterns ranging from the traditional 4-year, full-time educational environment for late-teen, resident students to the experimental, innovative systems being developed for part-time, older, nonresident scholars. As a pioneer in nontraditional education, The American College found itself in the forefront of these new concepts and techniques.

The College built its credo of "Education for Performance" on five decades of greater emphasis on student need and less concern for institutional convenience. From the start the College stressed diversity of opportunity over time and space requirements. As a result, by 1977 it had accepted more than 145,000 CLU matriculants and had awarded the respected CLU designation to 39,651 of them.[1]

For Davis W. Gregg and the College therefore the 50th birthday observance was a time to savor a half-century of genuine achievement and simultaneously to confront the challenge of the future. Both president and institution accomplished this with dignity and flair as the drama of those days unfolded.

In early 1977 the nation was suffering from high inflation and had an unemployment rate near 8 percent.[2] President Jimmy Carter pardoned most Vietnam-era draft resisters, and the Episcopal church ordained its first woman priest in this country.[3] Important news at the College included the announcement that the Charles Lamont Post Fund for Advanced Studies had been established on the basis of gifts valued at $170,000. Post's gifts began with $60,000 in 1970 and would increase to a total of more than $2 million.

President Davis W. Gregg indicated that the Post Fund would enable the College to conduct research into social responsibilities and ethical challenges faced by business and the professions. Post Fund money would permit stronger curricular offerings and provide honoraria to visiting authorities for consultation with the faculty and teaching in the residency program of the Graduate School of Financial Sciences.[4]

In March the first two in a series of College Golden Anniversary events occurred, although the entire celebration had been planned far in advance by a

117

committee led by Charles J. Zimmerman. President and Mrs. Gregg hosted a luncheon in Myrick Pavilion on the 22nd to commemorate the issuance of the charter 50 years before. People who were related to the founders and early officers of the College were the guests of honor. Dr. Solomon S. Huebner's son, John H. Huebner, who had recently retired as a senior vice president of Penn Mutual Life, was there, along with his wife. Mrs. David McCahan came, too, as did a niece of the College's first president, Edward A. Woods. Helen L. Schmidt helped to round out the party.[5] Three days later the entire campus family of College and American Society employees and their spouses attended a birthday dinner in MDRT Foundation Hall, which featured dancing and entertainment in a happy evening enjoyed by "everybody from the president to the mail boy."[6]

The trustees held their annual meeting in May and used the occasion for two more Golden Anniversary events on the 12th and 13th of that month. They began with a reception and dinner at the University of Pennsylvania Museum for some 450 friends and supporters from the academic and insurance communities. Board Chairman John T. Fey presided and introduced many of the distinguished guests. Fey paid special attention to the National Association of Life Underwriters and the University of Pennsylvania, which were both honored for their respective roles in founding The American College. Fey presented a framed Resolution of Appreciation to Penn's president, Martin Meyerson.

The board also awarded Huebner Gold Medals that night. It posthumously honored David McCahan and presented this medal to his widow, Rebecca. The board then recognized the contribution to the College made by the Wharton School's distinguished professor of insurance, Dan M. McGill, who had served the College in a variety of capacities for the past 25 years.[7] The program also included a multimedia presentation with congratulations from Robert W. Forker, NALU president; William J. Braun, Society president; Alexander F. Tambouras from Athens, Greece; and Gen Hirose, chairman of the Life Insurance Association of Japan.[8]

The next day, May 13, the College convened a campus "Confrontation at Infinite Life" seminar written and directed by new England Mutual CEO Abram T. Collier expressly for this occasion. The seminar included a case study that dramatized the management decisions made by a hypothetical life insurance company when broadening its base of financial services.[9]

Executive Vice President Vane B. Lucas took an active part in these early Golden Anniversary happenings and participated in planning others to come later that year. Tragically, however, Lucas died suddenly on May 29, 1977, after his daily, early-morning, cross-country run. He was 42.

His death stunned the College family. It brought tears to Davis W. Gregg, who had counted on Lucas to succeed him as president of the institution. Dr. Gregg described the situation with these words: "A giant of a person has fallen. Much of the past, most of the present, and about all of the future leadership of the College was in Vane Lucas. He is and will be sorely missed."[10]

The supportive relationship between the two men was reciprocal. The president nurtured and encouraged his protégé. Dr. Lucas adopted many of his boss's philosophies. Both men belonged to the Merion Golf Club and the Bryn Mawr Presbyterian Church. Lucas did reflect his own individuality and talent as he rapidly assumed greater responsibility and demonstrated exceptional capacity as a rising young executive.

Nevertheless, no one is indispensable and life went on at the distance education College in suburban Philadelphia. That summer Denis T. Raihall, vice president of academic affairs, announced two new faculty appointments and the promotion of C. Bruce Worsham, CLU, to the rank of assistant professor. Worsham had come to the College in 1969 as director of curriculum development. He first heard about the College from law school friends with whom he played touch football. In 1994, 25 years after joining the College, Worsham was still "excited about where this place is going."[11] By that time he had become associate vice president and director of the Huebner School.

William E. Jaynes, Oklahoma State University psychology professor, joined the faculty as the first James S. Bingay visiting professor of creative leadership. For a 4-month period, beginning September 1, 1977, Dr. Jaynes would explore the future direction of both the Bingay Chair program and the Hull Foundation in developing objectives within the College mission.

Fiftieth anniversary activities dominated the autumn agenda, starting with a sequence of September events connected with the Society's annual meeting and forum, the fall meeting of the Board of Trustees, and the annual CLU conferment exercises. The Society held its functions at the Philadelphia Marriott Hotel where the College and the Society hosted a "The Way We Were" banquet on September 17 for more than 700 CLUs and their spouses from across the country.

Hostmaster Charles J. Zimmerman reminisced about the early days of CLU and presented a Huebner Gold Medal to former trustee William H. Andrews, Jr. Two other American College greats—Paul F. Clark and Julian S. Myrick— received the award posthumously, bringing the number of people so honored to eight since the medal's inception in 1975.

The trustees, who had adopted Resolutions of Appreciation for six institutional groups at their May meeting, then proceeded to present these documents that evening. The Society, ACLI, LIMRA, LUTC, MDRT, and NALU were the recipient organizations. Robert W. Forker, president of the NALU, responded in kind by presenting Davis W. Gregg with a Resolution of Appreciation to the College from his organization.[12]

Other events followed in swift succession—a Golden Anniversary Fund campaign conference for 175 leaders of that effort, a Sunday worship service and "Bryn Mawr Brunch" for some 800 CLUs and their families, and finally, the 50th annual conferment exercises. Equitable Life Assurance Society CEO Coy G. Eklund addressed more than 700 members of the College's class of 1977. The College conferred 2,353 CLU designations at that time; actual diploma presentations were scheduled later by local CLU chapters across the country.

October rounded out the anniversary year with a campus art exhibit for community friends and neighbors and the first Master of Science in Financial

Services commencement program. Thirty-three people received MSFS degrees and heard a perceptive address by trustee Clarence C. Walton, president of Catholic University of America.[13]

Behind the ceremonial events and public occasions the trustees continued to prepare The American College for an even more influential future. In 1977, for example, the board voted to purchase an adjacent parcel of land from Mr. and Mrs. William T. Carter, which would increase the campus by more than nine acres. The board also decided to move ahead with plans for the long-discussed Graduate Studies Center.

*   *   *

December ended the most memorable year in the first five decades of American College history. A half-century of consistent achievement certainly warranted celebration. Increases in building count, campus growth, endowments, faculty stature, gift support, and student enrollment all contributed to one of the most remarkable success stories in modern American distance higher education. No wonder victory in the struggle for academic respect brought a certain campus euphoria to those caught up in the theatricality of those exciting days. After all, as the highly respected Wharton School insurance professor Dan M. McGill later declared, "Through its innovative and high-quality educational programs, The American College made an enormous contribution to the financial security of American families and to the stability of family life."[14]

Notwithstanding the accolades, awards, and resolutions, two specific problems lurked beneath the surface. CLU matriculations were off and cumulative debt burdened the balance sheet. The number of new Huebner School students had dropped for 3 consecutive years beginning in 1975[15]—not cataclysmic but a cause for concern. Lack of money posed a more serious threat. Despite the aggressive and successful fundraising efforts of the Golden Anniversary Fund volunteers (and their predecessors of earlier days), College financial statements listed assets of $4,877,871 in gift pledges, while liabilities included a $2,447,871 mortgage payable.[16]

However, Davis W. Gregg, ever the optimist, faced these problems with confidence based on the belief that the life insurance industry would continue to support the College in appreciation for its boost to the industry.[17] This conviction was not mere commercial self-interest; the College continued to command respect as "An Institution for the Advancement of Learning and Professionalism in Life Insurance and Related Financial Services,"[18] as it lived its credo of "Education for Performance Since 1927."

President Gregg enjoyed both personal and institutional recognition in early 1978. Dow Jones & Co., Inc., publisher of the *Wall Street Journal* and other business newspapers, elected him a director that year. More significantly, the Commission on Higher Education of the Middle States Association of Colleges and Schools granted the College full accreditation on March 25. The good news culminated a process dating back to the Long-range Planning Commission report of 1972, which had recommended continuing evaluation of the possibility.

Professors and board members alike celebrated the achievement. Vice President for Academic Affairs Denis T. Raihall called accreditation a "seal of approval."[19] Board Chairman John T. Fey went even further, saying the new status would "facilitate the College's sharing with the academic world its pioneering work in nontraditional, adult professional education, thereby benefiting not only the educational community but society in general."[20]

The College made another meaningful announcement early in 1978 when it reported the establishment of the Charles Lamont Post Chair in Ethics and the Professions, which had been made possible by gifts totaling $500,000. The College's first endowed teaching chair represented a deepening of Post's interest following his contribution to create the C. Lamont Post Fund for Advanced Studies the previous year. As an early CLU and later an exceptionally successful life underwriter, Post proudly explained, "I have always seen The American College as my college, my alma mater."[21]

A third major event that spring happened on April 13. University of Pennsylvania Professor Sidney Weintraub delivered the first Frank M. Engle Lecture in Economic Security at The Union League in downtown Philadelphia. The noted economist addressed a major problem of those days when he titled his remarks "TIP: To Stop Inflation."[22] This was the first of 19 consecutive annual lectures, whose success led A. Gilbert Heebner, PhD, economist and Eastern College professor, to applaud the Engle Lectures. "They have become," he said in 1994, "a major vehicle for bringing to the Philadelphia area outstanding scholars in economic security, public policy, international economic affairs, and the private enterprise system."[23] Internationally renowned economist John Kenneth Galbraith will deliver the 20th annual Engle Lecture, which is scheduled for May 19, 1997.

The trustees' annual meeting that May emphasized campus development. The board members approved plans for the hoped-for Graduate Studies Center to permit for the first time short-term, on-campus resident students. The projected $7.5 million structure would include academic facilities, a dining and commons area, and a 50-room residence building known as the Hall of States. Each room would be named for one of the United States and funded by or in honor of an insurance leader with ties to that state.[24]

Simultaneously, the board also approved construction of a less glamorous but necessary General Services Building to accommodate certain housekeeping activities heretofore conducted in Huebner and McCahan Halls. Third, the trustees honored the late Vane B. Lucas by dedicating the College library in MDRT Foundation Hall in his memory to recognize his contribution to the College and to professionalism. They presented a posthumous portrait of Dr. Lucas by Slayton Underhill at the May 28 dedication ceremony.

Three new trustees joined the board that month: George J. Hauptfuhrer, Jr., Esq., of Dechert Price and Rhoads; Harold S. Hood, CLU, president of American General Insurance Company; and William B. Wallace, CLU, general agent of Home Life, Washington, DC.[25] Wallace is of particular interest for two reasons. First, he later became chairman of the College Board of Trustees. Second, at the time of his election to the board Wallace was a spokesperson for a group of insurance industry leaders who believed that field management training lagged too far behind sales agent education. He served on a committee of GAMC, LIMRA, and LUTC representatives, which began meeting to discuss ways to study the problem. These industry leaders soon reached an agreement that The American College be asked to do more in the basic education of field management.[26]

By the end of 1978, the inflation rate had risen to 12.4 percent, the cost of mailing a first-class letter had reached 15 cents, and California voters had approved Proposition 13 to reduce property taxes by 57 percent, spotlighting the national revolt against high taxes.[27] Amidst it all, E.F. Hutton introduced a new insurance product called *universal life.*

Summer at the College provided time to prepare for a dramatic September. Trustee Clarence C. Walton retired from the presidency of Catholic University of America and became an academic consultant to The American College, effective the first day of that month. The College sponsored a series of events on September 28 and 29 as an initial Founders Day program to honor people who had pledged $10,000 or more to become Founders of the Golden Key Society. Festivities included an opening dinner at the Historical Society of Pennsylvania, followed by breakfast at Myrick Pavilion the next morning. Guests then attended a seminar led by former Deputy Secretary of the Treasury Charls E. Walker before lunching in MDRT Foundation Hall.

Board Chairman John T. Fey opened the actual on-site dedication ceremonies for the Graduate Studies Center by posthumously awarding the Huebner Gold Medal to the College's first president, Edward A. Woods. Charles J. Zimmerman, master of ceremonies *par excellence,* discussed financial support for the College. He first announced gift commitments for eight rooms in the Hall of States residence facility and then introduced Mr. and Mrs. Richard D. Irwin of Flossmoor, Illinois, identifying them as having been the donors of the $2.5 million anonymous gift to the College in 1976. Zimmerman and five other trustees, including Chairman Fey and President Gregg, closed the program by wielding shovels in an earth-turning exercise.[28]

Commencement exercises for the Graduate School of Financial Sciences concluded the cluster of September events. Board Chairman John T. Fey addressed the 46 recipients of degrees, reminding them, "Dr. Huebner's concept, coupled with hard work, great commitment and careful planning," had made possible the development of a program that "is unlike any program that exists anywhere in the U.S."[29]

In October 1978 the State Insurance Corporation of Zambia sent three of its employees—Domenick M. Lizebete, Frederick Kanga Knonde, and Whippy Aston Nsama—to the College for 3 months' study to improve their understanding of life insurance and related financial services. Freddy Moses Chabaya, also from Zambia, had visited the College the year before. These visits illustrate the College's ongoing international outreach initiatives, which had begun with Solomon S. Huebner's world trips and continued with Davis W. Gregg's overseas journey and visits to the Bryn Mawr campus by foreign students and executives.[30]

*   *   *

William Shakespeare's memorable "Double, double, toil and trouble; Fire burn and cauldron bubble," written in 1606 could readily apply to 1979 as world events early that year featured the overthrow of the Shah of Iran and the kidnapping of the American ambassador to Afghanistan. Back home, the U.S. Surgeon General issued a less dramatic but equally somber message when he warned the public that smoking was the "most important environmental factor contributing to early death."[31]

At the same time, The American College continued its less sensational but substantive progress toward greater recognition and influence, which had been its hallmark for 5 decades. Both the good reputation of professorial newcomers and the solid performance of existing faculty members propelled the institutional advances of those days. Yung-Ping Chen, PhD, came to the College from the University of California to be professor of economics after spending a year at Bryn Mawr College as a visiting professor, and Robert W. Cooper, PhD, a former Solomon S. Huebner Foundation fellow, joined the faculty as professor of insurance. Worthy of note among those already on campus were Danny G. Langdon, associate professor of education, who edited a 20-volume *Instructional Design Library,* and John A. Bajtelsmit, who by this time had earned promotion from assistant to associate professor of psychology.[32]

The College did not ignore the distaff side in its appointments and promotions. Susan M. Harmon, JD, led the list of women making academic news at that time. A former assistant U.S. attorney for the eastern district of Pennsylvania, she came to the College as assistant professor of taxation in the School of Advanced Career Studies.[33] Other appointees included Rosemary Selby, research psychologist and assistant professor of psychology, and Maureen E. Strazdon, librarian and academic associate. Helen L. Schmidt, corporate secretary and CLU, however, was clearly the star of the group. That January the College honored her 30 years of loyal and creative service with a dinner and the gift of an illuminated terrestrial globe.[34]

As the College continued to recognize personnel achievements, its dependence on office technology in both administration and teaching was steadily growing. The College's use of data processing began in 1952 and accelerated after the move to Bryn Mawr a decade later. The College and the Society leased IBM equipment of increasing capacity and sophistication and employed a succession of specialists to operate the systems. Dennis R. Meyers began this task in 1965 and by 1979 held the title of director of computer services. At that time IBM upgraded the memory of the College's system and installed a more sophisticated computer with a business planning system to provide cost-effective means to increase capabilities and productivity.[35]

Meanwhile, The American College's School of Advanced Career Studies, more popularly known as SACS, continued its special workshops for graduate students under the direction of Dean Herbert Chasman. Early in 1979 there was a 5-day workshop on Human Relations and Management, followed by a 2-day session devoted to Estate Planning for the Closely Held Corporation. As Dr. Chasman observed, the workshops showed "great potential and the important indirect benefit of acquainting more people with the College and its achievements."[36]

The Daniel J. Keating Company began construction of the Graduate Studies Center in April to climax a series of governing board actions that began 2 years before when the trustees first approved the program. With the new general services facility nearing completion across the campus, the College now experienced the excitement and stimulation of two simultaneous building projects.

Maintaining the forward momentum of the annual Frank M. Engle Lectures, Eli Shapiro, professor of management at MIT, came to the campus in May to deliver the second address in this thought-provoking series. In discussing "Policies for Productivity Growth," Dr. Shapiro called for a realistic rethinking of public policy to deal with the problems of inflation and declining productivity. "The expectations of many people about the future of inflation have to be proven incorrect," Shapiro said.[37] Frank M. Engle traveled from Tulsa, Oklahoma, to meet the distinguished educator, who had been a vice chairman of the Travelers Insurance Company and economic consultant to both John F. Kennedy and Richard M. Nixon.

The College's semi-annual board meetings were typically times of both decision making and human interest. The June 1979 session reflected plenty of each. The trustees acted upon important reports, opened a new building, approved an official's retirement after long service, authorized a new capital funds gift campaign, and elected new members to the governing body.

James B. Irvine, Jr., cochairman of the Golden Anniversary Fund for $20 million, reported that 97 percent of the ambitious goal had been met. "It is heartwarming," he said, "to know that the mission of the College means so much to so many."[38]

The previous year the trustees had awarded the contract for the General Services Building to the J.R. Farrell Construction Company. Now the structure was ready for occupancy and would house the mailroom, printshop, and shipping and storage activities that had previously been scattered among several other buildings. Mitchell/Giurgola Associates had designed the two-story, brick facility as part of their campus master plan. Interestingly enough, a number of the men who had been involved in the planning and construction of Huebner Hall 20 years before were still on the job and again shared responsibility for this latest campus improvement. Aside from architect and builder, they include LeRoy E. Varner, a Penn Mutual Life engineer, College consultant, and chairman of the building and grounds committee; and Richard T. McFalls, the College's director of property management.[39]

Institutional life is marked with continual comings and goings of men and women who serve for awhile and then are either asked to leave or voluntarily resign to accept a position elsewhere. A third group of people, however, dedicate themselves to their careers and remain with their employer until retirement. The College has had more than a few of these committed employees and has been the better for it. Walter B. Wheeler, CLU, is one of them, retiring in 1979 after almost three decades at the College. During that time, he served successively as director of field services, director of company relations, and finally as certification officer with responsibility for supervising matriculation, certification, and examination center activities.[40]

In June 1979 the trustees promoted one of their own and welcomed several newcomers to the governing fraternity. The board designated Chairman John T. Fey a life trustee and elected six business and life insurance executives as term trustees. Through this action Fey became the 14th person to achieve life status and the fifth of that number still active. The term trustees also included Robert A. Beck, CLU, CEO of the Prudential Insurance Company of America, who would later succeed Fey as chairman. Five of the six term trustees were CLUs, attesting to the growing significance of the designation throughout the industry.

The board put Beck right to work by naming him chairman of a new Capital Gifts Campaign Committee formed to seek $5.5 million to help pay for the now-under-construction Graduate Studies Center. Coming right on top of the $20 million Golden Anniversary Fund, this fundraising effort would demand the best efforts of all concerned. Beck's committee included veteran Charles J. Zimmerman, who would direct the Hall of States solicitation; Joseph C. Ladd, CLU, president of Fidelity Mutual Life, who would head the academic/commons money raising; and William B. Wallace, elected a trustee only a year before but already successfully involved in the Golden Key Society Charter Founders program, which began as part of the Golden Anniversary Fund.[41]

This new campaign, which started on July 1 and was scheduled to last 18 months, got off to an impressive start. After only 4 months, Beck reported over $2.6 million secured in cash and pledges—47 percent of the goal. "The leaders of the life insurance business are well aware both of the service provided by The American College and the desirability of supporting the College's creative growth," Beck said. "This is one of the most appealing programs of which I have been a part."[42]

While the trustees were raising money for the future of the institution, the administration announced the appointment of Dr. Rodger D. Collens of Drexel University as the second Hull Foundation visiting professor of creative leadership.[43]

The College and the American Society continued their cooperative efforts, an annual example of which was combining the Society's annual meeting and forum with the College's conferment exercises. In New Orleans, on October 16, 1979, the College conferred 2,461 designations and presented Solomon S.

Huebner Gold Medals to Davis W. Gregg and Raymond C. Johnson, retired board chairman of New York Life.[44] Dynamic trustee William B. Wallace addressed the designees.

*   *   *

January introduced a new year that would be memorable for the nation, the life insurance industry, and The American College. Census takers would count 226 million people, and average life expectancy continued its reliable rise to 73.7 years (compared to under 60 years when the College began in 1927).[45] Within the first 2 weeks of 1980 the U.S. bailed out the almost bankrupt Chrysler Corporation with a controversial $1.5 billion loan, and the Surgeon General warned that lung cancer in women would soon overtake breast cancer as a cause of death. The report raised the question of "whether one cost of women's economic equality might be reduced life expectancy."[46]

January also began a decade of disturbance for the financial protection industry. Media headlines, such as "The coming crunch in life insurance,"[47] sounded the alarm. Industry association studies set the tone for an era of turmoil when "life insurance [was] being judged by standards more stringent than in the past."[48]

College president Davis W. Gregg responded with his habitual optimism. Moving into his 26th year in office, the buoyant CEO recognized the looming perils. However, with long experience in facing challenge, abetted by an innate positive outlook, he elected to stress opportunities over problems. When he reported to the trustees at their New York City meeting that month, Gregg presented his recommendations for addressing three major challenges.

He pointed to what he called "the College's 'fuzzy' image, the inadequacy of fees, and increased competition in our kind of education."[49] The articulate Gregg reviewed current trends in financial security affecting the national economy. He then pushed for greater awareness of what the College "is, does, whom it serves, who supports it, what it should be, where it is going."[50] He also urged the board to adopt a realistic schedule of student fees to balance the 1980–1981 budget. Finally, the president called for a long-range committee to study the College's mission and goals for the 1980s.[51]

The trustees responded with alacrity. They authorized formation of a Special Planning Commission and appointed board member Robert M. Best, CLU, chairman of Security Mutual Life of Binghamton, New York, to head it. Best, elected a trustee in 1972, with experience as chairman of the College's Educational Policy Committee, apportioned the Special Planning Commission's tasks among four committees to set objectives, carry out discussions, and recommend courses of action.

At that time the trustees also announced the appointment of Clarence C. Walton as Charles Lamont Post Distinguished Professor of Ethics and the Professions. As the incumbent of the first endowed teaching chair, Dr. Walton enjoyed a third distinct relationship with the College in as many years. He had retired from the board in 1978, had served as a paid consultant in 1979, and then joined the faculty in 1980—a record without equal in the history of the institution. Board Chairman John T. Fey affirmed the appointment with these words, "Clarence Walton has opened the minds of American business to the importance of maintaining high standards of ethical conduct."[52]

Meanwhile, the Graduate Studies Center was rising dramatically on the campus adjacent to Myrick Pavilion. As we mentioned earlier, the complex would contain a Hall of States residence facility of 50 dormitory rooms named for life insurance greats through corporate or individual contributions of $60,000 each. It would also feature a Hall of Nations area to symbolize the College's global outreach. On May 19, 1980, trustees, faculty, and friends honored Mr. and Mrs. Alexander F. Tambouras of Athens, Greece, at a campus dinner. Tambouras was responsible for his country's being the first to participate in this global part of the campaign. In addition, the Tambourases made it possible for a sculpted symbol of global unity, executed by Robert Engman of the University of Pennsylvania, to decorate the Hall of Nations upon its completion.[53]

Lindley H. Clark, Jr., editor of the *Wall Street Journal,* delivered the 1980 Frank M. Engle Lecture in Economic Security. The noted journalist's talk, "Inflation Expectations," pointed to government's inconsistency in "announcing that inflation is the number one problem and that they are going to do something about it . . . followed by an inflationary program of economic stimulus."[54]

In summer that year Board Chairman John T. Fey made the surprising announcement of the formation of a presidential search committee to seek a successor to Davis W. Gregg, who planned to retire from that position in 1982. Fey indicated that Prudential Insurance Company CEO Robert A. Beck would chair the committee, which would be composed of Fey; Jarrett L. Davis, Society president; Joseph C. Ladd, president of Fidelity Mutual Life; former U.S. Assistant Secretary of Education Sidney P. Marland; Louis B. Perry, president of Standard Insurance Company; Harris L. Wofford, Jr., former Bryn Mawr College president; and Charles J. Zimmerman, retired chairman of Connecticut Mutual and former chairman of the College Board of Trustees.[55]

The announcement of the president's intention to retire came concurrently with word of his latest achievement. In Paris, France, on July 7, International Insurance Seminars, Incorporate, awarded Davis W. Gregg its John S. Bickley Founders Gold Medal for Excellence, citing his "singularly creative and innovative contribution to insurance thought, practice, and education."[56]

Dr. Gregg, aged 62, had been a College officer half his life and president for 26 of those years. He may have mentioned the possibility of impending retirement to close associates on the board, but the official announcement startled many in the College constituency at large. It would be difficult to exaggerate Gregg's total contribution to the College. His energy, enthusiasm, and vision were unequaled aspects of a unique and enduring leadership. According to the current director of the Graduate School of Financial Sciences, M. Donald Wright, "He had tremendous conceptual vision." Edwin S. Overman, president emeritus of the American Institute for Chartered Property and Casualty

Underwriters/Insurance Institutes of America and president of the Institutes at the time of Gregg's retirement, described Gregg as "a true futurist." Charles J. Zimmerman put it this way: "For over 30 years he made a habit of biting off more than the rest of us could or would chew."

Educational ritual provides the continuum of life for colleges and universities, and this proved to be particularly true for the life insurance institution in suburban Philadelphia. Lacking the entrenched traditions that result from longevity, the College made the most of every opportunity to dignify and enhance each award ceremony, building dedication, commencement program, conferment exercise, and even tree-planting occasion. The 1980 conferment exercises at the Chicago Marriott Hotel on September 30 were a case in point. The College reinforced the collaborative nature of the annual event by presenting the Huebner Gold Medal to Paul S. Mills, executive vice president of the American Society of CLU. Charles J. Zimmerman ranked Mills "among the giants who have toiled on behalf of The American College and the Society." [57] President Gregg conferred the designation on 2,614 CLUs—the largest class in the history of the College—and led some 700 men and women actually present in the recitation of the CLU Pledge, which committed them to evince good moral character and to practice high ethical standards. Clarence C. Walton, the newly installed C. Lamont Post distinguished professor of ethics, challenged the graduates to recognize an "obligation to restore trust through competent professional performance." [58]

At the dignified MSFS commencement in Bryn Mawr a month later, 63 of the 138 members of the class of 1980 received their diplomas and heard Pulitzer Prize-winning financial columnist Joseph A. Livingston's critique of the nation's economic condition. Livingston told the graduates to "diligently and conscientiously fight inflation as they guide people in these difficult and untrustworthy times." [59] After 4 years of this newest College program, 302 men and women had earned the Master of Science in Financial Services degree; a total of approximately 1,800 persons had been admitted to the program.

Board Chairman John T. Fey ended the College calendar year by announcing the establishment of the Joseph E. Boettner Distinguished Professorship in Financial Counseling. President Davis W. Gregg explained that the Boettner teaching chair endowment would emphasize a research program "to understand the public's needs for financial counseling at various stages of life." [60]

"Inflation will continue to beset us," Boettner explained. "There is a great need for informed, lifelong guidance to help people establish rational financial goals. It is up to the private sector to improve and increase its ability to serve public needs. I believe The American College must lead the way." [61] Dr. Gregg added a personal note by saying, "The Boettners have been very generous to the College with their resources, their friendship, and their spirit." [62]

*   *   *

"History is likely to mark 1981 as a watershed year for The American College." That's what President Davis W. Gregg told the trustees in his next-to-last report as president.[63] Dr. Gregg was obviously thinking about the curricular enrichment and physical plant expansion of that calendar period—and for good reason. Academically, the institution expanded its Graduate School of Financial Sciences and introduced a new designation, the ChFC, to stand beside the CLU. Simultaneously, the College opened the imposing new Graduate Center building, which would be named the Davis W. Gregg Educational Conference Center. These changes did not occur in a vacuum. One represented the fulfillment of a long-held dream, while others reflected the College's response to recent developments within the life insurance industry. All bore some relationship to the economic state of the country.

The national debt, for example, reached $1 trillion with inflation at the 14 percent level. The price of a first-class postage stamp rose twice in 12 months—first to 18 cents, then to 20 cents per ounce.[64] Closer to home, the College experienced continued CLU enrollment decline. Matriculants dropped from 10,330 to 7,567 in the 4 years beginning in 1978. A total of 45,162 examinations were administered in 1981, down from 49,422 the previous year. The number of CLU classes and students enrolled also went down. Ten years earlier there were 1,307 classes with 21,835 enrollments, compared to 1,069 classes with only 13,578 enrollments in 1980–1981.[65]

The nation reacted to the broader challenges by electing Ronald Reagan as president of the United States that January. The American College also made it a meaningful month through a key faculty appointment and bold board decisions.

Robert M. Crowe, CLU, PhD, director of examinations 2 decades before, returned to the campus as senior vice president. Within 3 months he moved Charles E. Hughes, CLU, to the position of vice president for academic affairs. Hughes had previously served in other faculty positions.

The trustees, for their part, approved an early recommendation of the Planning Commission to initiate a new program leading to "a professional designation in the broad area of financial counseling." The decision came in response to the changes of a decade in life insurance and other financial services institutions. Increased competition, higher consumer expectations, and the growing emphasis on financial planning in the marketplace underscored the need for new educational opportunities.[66]

The new designation was not named until the College had surveyed some 4,300 people about possible titles and conducted legal and professional inquiries regarding the rights and risks of using certain combinations of letters to correspond with the already established Chartered Life Underwriter (CLU). The College sent questionnaires concerning a name for the new designation to financial services professionals, current College students, and Main Line area neighbors. By late April, Rosemary Selby, research project director, reported Chartered Financial Consultant was the clear favorite.

At the June board meeting the trustees took action to approve the specific courses required for the new designation. Chairman John T. Fey said, "The curriculum is equally appropriate for CLUs, CPAs, attorneys, trust officers, and others."[67] The board postponed a decision regarding the name of the new program, however, pending further advice from counsel Dechert Price & Rhoads. In July president Gregg polled the trustees on their preference for either "a name tied to the institution or tied to the profession."[68] In August, after 6 months of painstaking research, the board selected Chartered Financial Consultant (CFC).[69]

On October 26, however, the College received legal notification that its use of the initials CFC in connection with the Chartered Financial Consultant designation infringed upon the rights of Capital Formation Counselors, Inc., in its service mark, CFC. The College denied any such infringement existed and filed a court action seeking a declaratory judgment to that effect,[70] thereby placing the figurative fat in the proverbial fire.

The new designation initials imbroglio worsened as Capital Formation Counselors, Inc., filed counterclaims against The American College, seeking injunctive relief and monetary damages. Eight months and 19 affidavits later, however, both parties (by and through the stipulation of their counsel of record) agreed to "voluntarily dismiss all claims and counterclaims."[71] The College would henceforth use the letters ChFC for its Chartered Financial Consultant designation. Case closed.

Meanwhile in 1981, the College presented the fourth annual Frank M. Engle Lecture in Economic Security, which was given in Tulsa, Oklahoma, that year by James M. Buchanan, a professor at Virginia Polytechnic Institute. The nationally recognized political economist advocated Constitutional reform to curb inflation.

In June Prudential Chairman Robert A. Beck, the trustee who led the College's $5.5 million capital gifts campaign organized only 18 months earlier, announced the successful completion of the fundraising drive. Beck made special mention of the Charter Founders program headed by fellow trustee William B. Wallace. The emphasis on this program elicited Golden Key Society pledges of $10,000 or more from some 450 individuals and institutions. Commitments were made with the understanding that 30 percent of the pledge would go for the 250-seat auditorium in the new building (which was to be called Founders Hall), with the remainder of each gift or grant to be spent for program development.[72]

Summer slipped by quickly and the College soon entered the last months of 1981, which featured several important academic events. In September Dr. Glenn Boseman arrived on campus as the third James S. Bingay visiting professor of creative leadership.[73] The College appointed Dr. Boseman for a one-year term but soon would make him a full professor, a position he would occupy for many years to come.

In October the Graduate Studies Center was dedicated. These ceremonies, which began on the 16th, accentuated the positive through one of the most memorable celebrations in the College's history. The Graduate Center dedication fulfilled a long-held dream of President Davis W. Gregg in that the academic/ residence/dining complex "created new vistas for resident study" at the College.

It has been said "that a building succeeds or fails on many different levels; as a practical object as well as a beautiful one, as a work of art, but also as a setting for life."[74] This third Mitchell/Giurgola *tour de force* on the Bryn Mawr campus could be compared to the Pennsylvania State Capital building in the sense that both buildings "combined structural soundness and aesthetic cohesion for later generations while also instilling the kind of pride and inspiration that becomes a landmark edifice."[75]

More than 300 people attended the dedication events, which spanned 2 days and included a ribbon-cutting and key-presentation ceremony in Founders Hall and a more formal observance for the Graduate Center. Board Chairman John T. Fey, President Davis W. Gregg, and Vice Chairman Robert A. Beck took turns presiding at the sequence of formalities near the Hall of Nations and the Hall of States. There were prayers, speeches, a time capsule ceremony and a horticultural walk. Paul M. Ingersoll, vice president of Christie's Fine Arts Galleries, lectured on art, and visitors enjoyed an exhibit of Hobson Pittman paintings loaned by Bryn Mawr College.

The art show enhanced the ambiance of the occasion, but it also began a popular art exhibition program that would continue for many years and win many friends for the College from the community. The trustees believed that beauty in the environment—art, horticulture, and architecture—is a positive, motivating force for educational achievement and that responsible stewardship includes sharing and outreach.

Finally, in November 1981, the fourth annual William T. Beadles Lecture was given by Dr. Eugene G. Kerr, president of Technology Resources of Belleview, Washington. Kerr spoke on "Technology and Education for Performance in the Eighties."[76]

*   *   *

In addition to Dr. Gregg's retirement, during the 1981–1982 period two corporate officers also retired and six trustees began their terms of office at the College. Senior Vice President Leroy G. Steinbeck retired after an on-and-off association with the College that started in 1950. Helen L. Schmidt stepped down as corporate secretary after 13 years in that position and a total of 33 years at the College, but she would remain employed in another capacity. Among the new board members were Vanguard investment chairman, John C. Bogle, and Detroit businessperson, Maxine B. Niemeyer, CLU. Niemeyer had earned MDRT membership six times, and at her election to the board, she enrolled in the College's Master of Science in Financial Services program.[77]

National news of 1982 emphasized monetary matters. AT&T divested itself of 22 Bell System operating companies. The country recorded the highest poverty rate since 1967. Interest rates would peak, and that summer would see the start of a bull stock market destined to last 5 years.[78]

The American College, always alert to the need for continued scrutiny of both course content and content description, had made a number of changes over the years, including the major revisions of 1970. Now the trustees, acting upon recommendations of the Special Planning Commission, approved further widespread changes that would strengthen Huebner School offerings and "assure their relevance in light of the many changes taking place in insurance and financial services."[79]

The ChFC educational, experience, and ethical requirements paralleled those of the CLU designation. The new arrangements specified course requirements for each program and provided for a 2-year transition period beginning July 1, 1982, during which CLUs could earn the ChFC credential by completing only three additional courses.[80] More than 2,000 CLUs responded with sufficient vigor to qualify for the new diplomas at the October conferment exercises.

That summer the Commonwealth of Pennsylvania approved the College's new Master of Science in Management degree (MSM), but the biggest news was on August 11 when the trustees named Edward G. Jordan, University of Pennsylvania executive vice president, to succeed Davis W. Gregg as president of the College beginning on November 1.[81]

NOTES

1. *Review of Activities,* 1976, pp. 1–2.
2. *World Almanac and Book of Facts* (Mahwah, NJ: World Almanac Books), 1994, p. 130.
3. Paul Dickson, *Timelines* (Reading, MA: Addison-Wesley Publishing Co., Inc.), 1990, p. 227.
4. *The American College Today,* March 1977, p. 2.
5. Mildred F. Stone manuscript, chapter x, pp. 1–2.
6. Ibid., p. 3.
7. *The American College Today,* July 1977, p. 2.
8. *Review of Activities,* p. 13.
9. *The American College Today,* July 1977, p. 3.
10. Ibid., p. 1.
11. Interview with the author, December 21, 1994.
12. *The American College Today,* November 1977, pp. 1–2.
13. Ibid., December 1977, pp. 1–3.
14. Interview with the author, November 12, 1994.
15. Marjorie A. Fletcher, "Official Number of American College Matriculants and Huebner School Graduates," 1994, p. 2.
16. Coopers & Lybrand, The American College, Report on Examinations of Financial Statements for the Year Ended June 30, 1977, p. 3.
17. Charles S. DiLullo, interview with the author, November 18, 1994.
18. *The American College Today* masthead statement, beginning July 1977.
19. *The American College Today,* April 1978, p. 1.
20. Ibid.
21. Ibid., p. 3.
22. *Review of Activities,* 1977–1978, p. 10.
23. Interview with the author, November 25, 1994.
24. *Annual Report,* The American College, 1978, p. 3.
25. *The American College Today,* July 1978, pp. 1–2.
26. Stone, unpublished manuscript, chapter ix, pp. 24–26.
27. Dickson, *Timelines,* p. 235.

28. *The American College Today,* December 1978, pp. 1–2.
29. Ibid., p. 3.
30. *Review of Activities,* 1977–1978, p. 9.
31. Dickson, *Timelines,* p. 239.
32. *The American College Today,* December 1978, pp. 2–3.
33. Ibid., April 1979, p. 4.
34. Ibid.
35. IBM letter to Charles S. DiLullo, January 11, 1979.
36. *The American College Today,* August 1979, p. 2.
37. Ibid., p. 4.
38. Stone, unpublished manuscript, chapter xvi, p. 12.
39. *The American College Today,* April 1979, p. 3.
40. Ibid., August 1979, pp. 3–8.
41. Ibid., pp. 6–8.
42. Ibid., p. 8.
43. The American College news release, September 11, 1979.
44. *The American College Today,* December 1979, p. 3.
45. *World Almanac,* 1994, p. 972.
46. Dickson, *Timelines,* p. 245.
47. *Business Week* (New York: McGraw-Hill, Inc.) December 3, 1979, p. 124.
48. *Best's Insurance Management Reports* (Morristown, NJ: A.M. Best Co.), November 12, 1979, p. 1.
49. *The American College Today,* April 1980, p. 3.
50. Ibid.
51. Ibid.
52. Ibid., p. 1.
53. Ibid., September 1980, p. 1.
54. The American College news release, July 22, 1980.
55. *Review of Activities,* 1980–1981, pp. 5–6.
56. *The American College Today,* September 1980, p. 7.
57. Ibid., December 1980, p. 5.
58. Ibid.
59. Ibid., pp. 7, 8.
60. Ibid., p. 1.
61. Ibid., pp. 1, 8.
62. Ibid., p. 1.
63. *Annual Report,* 1981, p. 1.
64. Dickson, *Timelines,* p. 253.
65. *Review of Activities,* 1980–1981, pp. 2–3.
66. *The American College Today,* April 1981, p. 1.
67. The American College news release, June 22, 1981, p. 1.
68. Davis W. Gregg, letter to trustees, July 1981.
69. *The American College Today,* January 1982, p. 1.
70. The American College, *Plaintiff v. Capitol Formation Counselors, Inc.,* Defendant Civil Action No. 82-0227.
71. Civil Action No. 82-0227, June 22, 1982.
72. *Review of Activities,* 1980–1981, p. 5.
73. *The American College Today,* January 1982, p. 5.
74. Witold Rybczynski, *Looking Around, a Journey through Architecture* (New York: Penguin Books), 1992, p. xvi.
75. Craig W. Hovle, et al, *Lawmaking and Legislators in Pennsylvania,* vol. one, University of Pennsylvania Press, 1992.

76. *The American College Today,* January 1982, p. 14.

77. Ibid., pp. 3–4.

78. Dickson, *Timelines,* pp. 258–260.

79. *The American College Today,* September 1982, p. 6.

80. Ibid., p. 7.

81. Ibid., p. 1.

The dedication of Myrick Pavilion in 1965 marks the first campus expansion. Left to right: Roger Hull, Charles J. Zimmerman, Julian S. Myrick, Joseph H. Reese, Sr., and Davis W. Gregg.

John O. Todd receives document for MDRT Foundation Hall time capsule from Alexander Tambouras of Athens, Greece, at the 1970 Board of Trustees dinner.

Ribbon cutting at the dedication of MDRT Foundation Hall in 1972. Left to right: James B. Longley, Davis W. Gregg, Charles J. Zimmerman, John T. Fey, Donald Shepherd, John O. Todd, and James B. Irvine, Jr.

Senior Vice President Vane B. Lucas (right)
presents the Solomon S. Huebner Gold Medal to
insurance educator William T. Beadles in 1976.

Joseph E. Boettner and Davis W. Gregg attend
first Boettner symposium on personal financial
security in December 1978.

Frank M. Engle with Yung-Ping Chen,
Frank M. Engle Professor of Economic
Security Research.

Frank M. Engle speaking to guests at the College's first
endowed Engle Lecture, which was held at the Union League
in Philadelphia in 1978.

The Educational Policy Board meets at the College in 1976.

Symposium for case study in management "Confrontation at Infinite Life" on May 13, 1977, an activity for the College's 50th anniversary.

In 1976 Davis W. Gregg, John T. Fey, and Charles J. Zimmerman with the new College Charter.

The first MSFS graduating class with President Davis W. Gregg following commencement in October 1977.

Groundbreaking for the Graduate Center. Left to right: Leo R. Futia, Charles J. Zimmerman, Davis W. Gregg, Joseph Ladd, James B. Irvine, Jr., and John T. Fey.

Ribbon cutting for the Graduate Center in October 1981 (renamed Davis W. Gregg Educational Conference Center in 1983). Left to right: William B. Wallace, Davis W. Gregg, Charles J. Zimmerman, and Robert W. Greig.

Davis W. Gregg announces the endowment for the Richard D. Irwin School of Management. Left to right: President Gregg, portrait of Richard D. Irwin, and Mr. Irwin (October 1982).

Clarence B. Walton, Charles Lamont Post Distinguished Professor of Ethics and the Professions, occupies his new office in the Graduate Center in 1981.

Helen L. Schmidt receives Huebner Gold Medal from Davis W. Gregg in recognition of her outstanding dedication to life insurance education.

Davis W. Gregg admires a silver tray engraved with 96 signatures of trustees at the recognition dinner in honor of his retirement. Left to right: Charles J. Zimmerman, Davis W. Gregg, Robert A. Beck, and John T. Fey.

Davis W. Gregg, retiring president of The American College, welcomes incoming president, Edward G. Jordan in 1982.

SECTION FIVE

Transition 1982–1987
Edward G. Jordan

10

A Different Emphasis

The president designate would bring both business and education experience to the position, but unlike his five predecessors, would assume the presidency without a life insurance background. Aside from a brief stint years earlier as the head of a California brokerage company with some pension plan and life insurance involvement, Edward G. Jordan's three previous posts had been in either transportation or university administration.[1]

A University of California graduate with an MBA from Stanford, Jordan served as chairman and CEO of Consolidated Rail Corporation (CONRAIL) from 1975 to 1980. Then he went to Cornell as dean of the Graduate School of Business for a few months before joining the University of Pennsylvania as executive vice president in 1981.

The College trustee presidential search committee organized in 1980 had moved slowly. It experienced difficulty in finding the right man for the job. The board had retained Spencer Stuart Associates of Chicago to facilitate the quest for Dr. Gregg's successor, but the right candidate proved elusive.

The Greggs knew the Jordans through membership in the Merion Golf Club where Davis W. Gregg often enjoyed a game. This acquaintance resulted in the search committee's Joseph C. Ladd approaching Jordan regarding the presidency of The American College. Interest was expressed and in due course the trustees offered Jordan the position, effective November 1, 1982.

When Board Chairman John T. Fey announced Jordan's appointment, he described the 52-year old executive as "a man of keen intellect and substantial management experience," who would "continue the dynamic, intellectually bold leadership qualities that enabled Dr. Gregg to elevate the College to one of America's leading nontraditional educational institutions in the financial sciences." Fey added, "Jordan is a man of proven leadership and substantial managerial experience. His background in business, government, and education equips him well to continue the College's pattern of growth and leadership in education and research for men and women in life insurance as well as other financial services professionals."[2]

Davis W. Gregg offered his personal recommendation by praising Jordan's "record of leadership, his understanding of the world of business, and his interest in and commitment to education." Gregg also stated, "The College is fortunate to have his strength of leadership in the presidency, especially in these times when the efficient utilization of human and other resources is so very critical to higher education in America."[3]

The president-to-be responded, "At a time when the dynamics of the field of financial services have caused the demarcation lines between the various components to become increasingly blurred, I find the challenge to contribute to the understanding and development of financial service irresistible." Jordan welcomed the trustees' invitation to be the College's chief executive, declaring he would marshal the strengths of the College "to have even more impact in the future, even when measured against the progress of the past."[4]

Summer 1982 flowed into autumn and introduced one of the most interesting months in the institution's 55-year history. In October Davis W. Gregg shared some ceremonial duties with Edward G. Jordan as the two men went through the last weeks of the former's presidency and the final days of the latter's apprenticeship. For example, Gregg went to New York City on October 5 for the 1982 conferment exercises, while Jordan addressed the MSFS graduates on the Bryn Mawr campus 3 days later.

At the conferment Davis W. Gregg led the Huebner School graduates in the traditional Professional Pledge. George G. Joseph, CLU, president of the Life Insurance Marketing and Research Association (LIMRA), delivered the conferment address. Huebner School designees included 2,194 men and women who received the CLU certification and 2,034 persons who earned the new Chartered Financial Consultant (ChFC) diploma.[5]

At the MSFS commencement Edward G. Jordan gave his first major address within the College family since his appointment as president 2 months before. Jordan hailed the MSFS degree earners, and he noted three factors that had brought him to the College: (1) its nontraditional nature, (2) its direction in the financial sciences, and (3) its understanding of and comfort with the new technology of communications.[6]

Both Gregg and Jordan were involved in the Richard D. Irwin convocation on October 13, when the College dedicated its recently established Graduate School of Management to the distinguished publisher and philanthropist. The new academic entity offered a Master of Science in Management degree (MSM), approved by the Commonwealth of Pennsylvania that summer (and first awarded in 1983). "Few colleges in America," said Irwin, "are as committed to finding new and effective ways to deliver professional business education on a nationwide basis as The American College."[7] Dr. Gregg paid tribute to Mr. and Mrs. Irwin for sharing their success with future generations.

A campus party for the Greggs rounded out the eventful month and concluded one of the most remarkable administrations in the history of The American College. When most college presidents complete their terms of office, they usually leave campus. Davis W. Gregg did not. Instead, he stayed on to become the Joseph E. Boettner Distinguished Professor of Financial Services Research, thereby achieving his dream of "returning to research, writing, and teaching."[8]

*   *   *

Although CLU designations actually awarded reached a cumulative total of 51,575 in the 55 years ending in 1982, matriculations continued to decrease and had declined by 40 percent since 1978. The College had been mindful of this trend and, as noted earlier, had introduced the ChFC designation as a partial response to the demand for wider educational opportunity within the financial services industry. The College realized, however, that a broader approach was needed to prepare fully for the challenges of the present and the opportunities of the future.

The 1982 *Periodic Review Report* prepared for the Middle States Association of Colleges and Schools concluded that "the College mission, goals, and objectives were unfocused and that there was some confusion as to the difference between ends and means."[9] Specific areas for scrutiny included improved methods of securing student information without delay and review of both board and faculty committee structure. The Jordan administration would give close attention to these and other such concerns as it moved ahead with plans for the installation of the new president in June 1983.

Meanwhile, the early months of 1983 featured a pair of campus events worthy of mention—a public service forum that March and the latest Frank M. Engle Lecture in May. The Joseph E. Boettner Chair in Financial Services sponsored the public service forum, "Social Security Reform: Legislative Debate and Your Voice." University of New Mexico professor Jerry L. Jordan, PhD, delivered the Engle lecture, "The Problem of Productivity in Restoring Prosperity," which was the sixth in the series of annual presentations named for the Tulsa, Oklahoma, insurance agent, business leader, and philanthropist.

An American College trustee of that era likened Edward G. Jordan's early summer installation to "a royal coronation."[10] The impressive event was planned with full pomp and circumstance in mind, reminiscent of the flavor of Edward Elgar's famous march with that title. After all, Jordan was the first new president of the College in almost 30 years.[11] *The American College Today* devoted an entire issue to describe the dramatic induction ceremonies, which were held within and without the handsome Graduate Center beginning at 4:00 p.m. on June 16, 1983.[12] At the appointed hour the academic procession in full regalia reached the Garden Court podium where Board Chairman John T. Fey welcomed the crowd and Senior Vice President Robert M. Crowe, CLU, ChFC, delivered the invocation. Eight representatives in the field of financial services brought brief greetings from their respective constituencies. Among them were Bruce C. Hendrickson, NALU past president; Richard S. Schweiker, American Council of Life Insurance president; and Dr. Dan M. McGill, Frederick H. Ecker professor of life insurance at the University of Pennsylvania. College librarian Judith L. Hill expressed welcome from the faculty.[13]

After remarks by Davis W. Gregg, Fey presented Jordan with a leather pouch, the College's governance symbol. This special leather pouch contained vellum copies of the original Charter of The American College dated 1927, the Charter reincorporating the College in Pennsylvania dated 1976, and the College's current bylaws. Jordan accepted the documents as he contrasted the traditional rites of investiture with the contemporary nature of the College. With "deep feelings of gratitude" he assumed the challenge and responsibilities of the office. Speaking for 20 minutes, Jordan declared, "I want The American College and the professions it serves to make a real contribution to the future quality of life in America." He added, "I don't think that is an unrealistic goal."[14]

After the ceremony, the Jordans, Greggs, John T. Fey, and Mr. and Mrs. Charles Zimmerman greeted guests in the Graduate Center's Hall of Nations before moving on to dinner in the dining hall. Charles J. Zimmerman acted as master of ceremonies at the recognition banquet to honor Davis and Mille Gregg. After greetings, anecdotes, and speeches, Vice Chairman Robert A. Beck gave Dr. Gregg an engraved silver tray with the signatures of all 96 persons who had served as trustees of the College.

June 1983 was a busy time for the governing board in other ways. When the trustees met that month, they accepted John T. Fey's retirement and honored him for 17 years' service and 11 years as chairman. Fey had held this post longer than any other chairman except Julian S. Myrick, who had been chairman for 22 years (1938–1960). Fey's Resolution of Appreciation contained such plaudits as "imaginative and visionary leadership," "keen judgment and visionary counsel," and "excellence of achievement."[15]

The board then named Robert A. Beck as Fey's successor. When Beck became the seventh chairman of The American College, he climaxed his rapid rise at the College, which began in 1979 with his election as a trustee. Heading the $5.5 million capital fund drive launched that year, he had also chaired the presidential search committee beginning in 1980 and moved up to vice chairman of the board in 1981.[16]

Beck had been equally successful in business, reaching the presidency of Prudential Life at age 48 and chairman and CEO 4 years later. He was a man accustomed to command. According to a member of the campus family, "He came on like gang-busters." President Jordan praised Beck's "assertive, confident attitude," which made him "a driving, stimulating man to work with," and added, "I think the College and all its constituencies will benefit tremendously from his leadership."[17]

Speaking of trustees, the board had welcomed five new members earlier that year, including Martin Meyerson, former president of the University of Pennsylvania, and Denis F. Mullane, CLU, CEO of Connecticut Mutual Life. In becoming a trustee Mullane followed the example of a former head of Connecticut Mutual Life who had joined the College board in 1951—none other than the redoubtable Charles J. Zimmerman. Mullane was destined to continue in

Zimmerman's footsteps when he, too, later attained the chairmanship of the academic trustees.[18]

Other June board meeting actions included changing the name of the Graduate Center to the Davis W. Gregg Educational Conference Center and voting Solomon S. Huebner Gold Medals for Robert M. Best and J. Carlton Smith, CLU. Veteran proponents of insurance education and professionalism, both men easily met the required criterion of distinguished service to education and professionalism. Best and Smith were to become the 19th and 20th persons to win the esteemed award since its establishment in 1975.[19]

As the Bryn Mawr, Pennsylvania, financial services College welcomed new people and honored others, the country at large observed the 10th anniversary of legalized abortion with a major protest march in Washington, DC. President Ronald Reagan first proposed a Strategic Defense Initiative (Star Wars), astronaut Sally K. Ride became the first American woman in space, and the synthetic drug PCP (angel dust) began to claim a large number of lives.[20]

Back at the College, President Edward G. Jordan knew that he must move from the ceremonial to the substantive without delay. The very morning of his inauguration he and the trustee Executive Committee met with a team from the New York consulting firm of McKinsey and Company. The trustees had retained McKinsey, once described as "one of the three great institutions left in the world"[21]—along with the U.S. Marines and the Catholic church—to advise the College how best to combat the declining enrollment and rising costs of recent years. McKinsey presented a 62-page report that analyzed these problems and proposed a multipoint plan to reverse them. The report urged the College "to pursue a customer-oriented strategy that recognizes a fundamental change in the marketplace."[22]

The report recommended that decreased matriculation and increased attrition in the Huebner School of CLU and ChFC, as well as less than expected enrollment in the School of Advanced Career Studies (SACS) and the masters degree programs, be countered in two ways. The College should rebuild its position in the life insurance industry and explore new financial markets.[23] Rising costs were to be countered by such things as utilizing the Gregg Conference Center to capacity, cutting overhead, reducing staff, and attracting major donors.

In the fall President Jordan traveled to San Francisco for the CLU and ChFC conferment on October 11 and was back on campus 10 days later to preside at the graduate commencement. Newly installed president of the American Society of CLU & ChFC, Irving N. Stein, spoke to the graduates, which included 118 Master of Science in Financial Services recipients and the first two Richard D. Irwin Graduate School of Management conferees to receive MSM degrees.[24] Davis W. Gregg presided at a Joseph E. Boettner invitational conference that examined the "Human and Financial Dimensions of Retirement Counseling."[25]

*   *   *

George Orwell's sobering novel *Nineteen Eighty-four*, published in 1949, warned of future totalitarianism by the date of its title and projected a world of economic stringency and political tyranny. Actual events of the intervening 35 years, however, led in the opposite direction. By 1984 the Soviet Union was stumbling and the United States was reaching out to China and successfully confronting dictators elsewhere around the globe. The Western world was said to "revel in individualism and free play."[26] The national mood was also upbeat, and justifiably so: Despite persistent federal budget deficits, prosperity was replacing recession. The economy would have its best year since 1951, expanding 6.8 percent, while consumer prices would rise only 4 percent.[27]

The scene at the American College proved equally sanguine. While competition in the form of alternate designations was pressing and internal financial burdens remained heavy, the College exuded a fresh air of confidence. Essentially proactive toward the industry in the early years of its history, the College was becoming more responsive to the needs of the financial services community in the 1980s. President Edward G. Jordan expressed it this way: "We look at today's competitive business climate as an opportunity to develop new strategies, an efficient organizational structure, innovative course offerings, and more responsive services."[28]

The personalities of the College's two new top officers set the tone. Robert A. Beck and Edward G. Jordan worked well together as they assumed their respective roles. Chairman Beck, known as "a catalyst for change," was "never reticent about presenting his views on controversial subjects."[29] President Jordan, also extremely forthright in manner, was described by a friend as a man who "could put forth a pyrotechnical display of new ideas." As the industry had left behind the stability of the 1960s, survived the rampant inflation of the 1970s, and found itself awash in the financial planning seas of the 1980s, Jordan tried to define a mission for the College as he maneuvered it through an ethos that had ranged from stodgy to tumultuous.

In his first *Annual Report* Jordan spelled out the broad new policy parameters: "In times past the College has properly emphasized expansion of new facilities and additional staffing to meet increased numbers of students. The task today is to guarantee that available resources in personnel, physical plant, and financial assets are used effectively as we continue to expand the program."[30] The College was to embark upon cost cutting and to emphasize academics.

Frank M. Engle excited The American College community in early 1984. January brought the announcement that the Tulsa, Oklahoma, philanthropist had further supported the College's educational mission by a new gift to establish an endowed professorship for research in economic security that would bear his name. In March the College presented the seventh annual Frank M. Engle Lecture as one of the public events offered on the campus that year. Congressional Budget Office Director Rudolph G. Penner, PhD, and former resident scholar at the American Enterprise Institute of Public Policy Research, spoke on "The Deficit Dilemma"—a subject relevant to Engle's interest in stimulating objective study of economic life in the United States.[31]

Government authority abruptly disturbed this academic atmosphere on April 3 through a letter from Frank J. Lynch, chairman of the Delaware County Council, with offices in the Media, Pennsylvania, Court House. The letter referred to the June 28, 1974, agreement between The American College and its three local taxing authorities (Delaware County, Radnor Township, and the Radnor School District) regarding voluntary payments by the College in lieu of real estate taxes, and it gave notice that these jurisdictions intended to terminate the agreement effective June 15, 1984.[32]

The County offered to meet College officials "to arrive at an amicable resolution of the tax-exempt status of the property in question."[33] Perhaps mindful of Alexander Hamilton's dictum, "The power to tax involves the power to destroy,"[34] President Jordan turned to College counsel William H. Lowery, Esq., of Dechert Price & Rhoads for guidance regarding an appeal. This was the beginning of a contest that would last more than 4 years and end in defeat for the College.

On July 20 when the taxing authority presented the assessment of the College property for the 1985 tax year, the worst fears of the College's trustees and its president loomed as a grim reality. Starting in 1960, the College had made a voluntary contribution for services provided by the township. In the beginning the College was the only college in Radnor Township to make a voluntary contribution. Through the years that contribution had been regularly increased until the last agreement was reached in 1974.

Obviously, the amount due was significant as the voluntary contribution would be replaced with a substantial tax burden. Moreover, because the College had made continual efforts to evidence good corporate citizenship beyond its voluntary contributions—with such ongoing neighborly overtures as making the service of the faculty and the use of College facilities available and opening the campus for community activities in the Radnor Township School District—the assessment had also damaged the College psychologically.

The College responded immediately. That very day Vice President and Treasurer Charles S. DiLullo filed an appeal with the Board of Assessment Appeals and requested the necessary forms.[35]

During the preliminary appeal, life proceeded as usual at the Bryn Mawr distance education institution. President Jordan's academic emphasis became apparent that summer. A new Office of Student Services began operations on July 23, 1984. Shirley Steinman, CLU, ChFC, the director of the program, and four student counselors served as an advisory liaison between the College and its student body. Soon Steinman and her staff were responding to some 250 telephone calls daily. They answered questions, gave information, and resolved issues for students whose problems, in the words of one counselor, "stemmed from the often hectic nature of an insurance career."[36] Students could call this office on a toll-free hotline.

In August a campus teleregistration was instituted. Teleregistration reached out to former students who had dropped out before completing their CLU courses. The five-person unit hoped to re-register 2,000 former students the first year. Despite the need to make an average of 100 calls just to reach 10 students, the convenience of the service brought immediate results. Teleregistration unit manager William A. Wolford and his staff re-enrolled more than 500 students in the first 2 months.[37]

On October 22 President Jordan went to Toronto for the Society's annual forum. The 1984 program for this event was of particular interest for two reasons: One, it was the first combined conferment/commencement exercise since the advent of the masters degree graduations, and two, it provided the occasion for Edward G. Jordan's announcement of the College's adoption of a formal Code of Ethics. Both subjects need amplification.

Conscious of the distinction between the CLU designation and the MSFS degree when the latter was first awarded in 1977, the College accentuated the difference by holding the respective graduation ceremonies on different dates, in separate places, and with individual names: the CLU *conferment* and the MSFS *commencement*. With the characteristics of each now clearly established, the College embarked on the first of a series of joint annual efforts with impressive results. The College awarded more than 6,000 diplomas in Toronto, including 2,106 CLU designations, 3,287 ChFC designations, 119 MSFS degrees, and 12 MSM degrees. The class of 1984 brought the total number of CLUs awarded in 57 years to more than 58,000.[38]

Regarding the College's adoption of a formal Code of Ethics, while love and marriage may go together like the proverbial horse and carriage, life insurance and ethics cannot be said to make the same claim. According to one industry official, these days ethics and life insurance are an oxymoron in some minds.

Although the American Society had adopted its own code of ethics in 1960, the College had not taken a similar step. The College felt the CLU Pledge, which had remained essentially unchanged since 1928, would suffice for maintaining high standards and good moral character. That pledge, as we noted earlier in this book, reads as follows:

> In all my professional relationships, I pledge myself to the following rule of ethical conduct: I shall, in light of all conditions surrounding all those I serve, which I shall make every conscientious effort to ascertain and understand, render that service which, in the same circumstances, I would apply to myself.[39]

By 1984, however, a new climate surrounded financial services, blurring institutional lines and prerogatives. President Jordan, in announcing the adoption of a formal Code of Ethics, explained, "In this climate the role of those who serve the financial needs of the public has changed. Competition has increased. New products and services abound. The College feels an imperative to be more forceful in the application of long-standing ethical principles. What was once a matter of persuasion is now an imperative."[40]

The College promulgated its Code of Ethics to assure postconferment fidelity to CLU and ChFC ethical standards by empowering the College's certification officer to investigate complaints and reports of violations. Code standards would apply to violations occurring after October 1, 1984, but also to CLU and ChFC students who matriculated on July 1, 1982, or later.[41]

In addition to the pledge, the 1984 code included eight rules, such as the following: "Conduct yourself at all times with honor and dignity." Over the years the pledge had been accompanied by certain suggested standards. In the 1960s they were called the "six admonitions." By the 1970s they had become the "seven precepts." In 1984 there were "eight canons."[42]

"The American College loses bid for tax-exempt status," a local newspaper headline proclaimed on November 15, 1984. The Delaware County Board of Assessment Appeals clarified the doctrine of pure public charity and then turned down the College's July appeal.[43] (This did not affect the College's federal tax charitable exemption.) The College reeled from the blow but promptly appealed to the Delaware County Court of Common Pleas. On December 6 this court allowed the appeal; the action would go before Judge Howard F. Reed, Jr.

These dramatic days of 1984 at The American College were played out against a national backdrop in which a gallon of gasoline cost $1.10 and an equal measure of milk $2.26. The average price of a new car came to $8,749, while the average cost of a new home stood at $86,730. Scientists discovered a totally effective chicken pox vaccine, Los Angeles hosted the 23d Olympic Games, and Ronald Reagan won reelection by an overwhelming electoral vote.[44]

*   *   *

As President Reagan began his second term, President Jordan began his third full calendar year as chief executive at The American College. Within the Bryn Mawr institution it would be a season of continuation, a time of further developments within two spheres of activity that had begun the previous year: the Jordan educational emphasis and the College's response to the tax-exemption threat.

The new administration's academic focus represented more than executive whim. The College sought better to serve the risk-protection industry, beset as rarely before by continuing threats to individual well-being and family security. (That February, for example, a new federal study established obesity as a major killer in the same category as smoking and high blood pressure.[45]) In 1985 therefore the College's concentration was curricular—partially in response to tax law changes that "affected almost every course in the CLU/ChFC program."[46]

In the past, faculty newsletters had conveyed course content updates to keep students informed about legislative, product, and service developments. A new publication, *The American College Outlook*, would now carry this information through its "Course Columns." The spring 1985 issue, for example, highlighted

10 specific courses, including HS 321 Income Taxation by James F. Ivers III, JD; HS 323 Financial Statement Analysis/Individual Insurance Benefits by Edward E. Graves, CLU, ChFC; and HS 329 Wealth Accumulation Planning by Robert J. Doyle, Jr., CLU, ChFC. The student-oriented *Outlook* replaced the broader *The American College Today,* which had carried articles of interest to the wider American College audience consisting of alumni, friends, neighbors, and benefactors.

Besides changes to existing courses, the College announced a major program restructuring that would affect the CLU and ChFC curricula. There would be three new personal insurance courses within the six required and four elective subjects leading to either designation. The CLU program would have two tracks: one for life insurance professionals and another for students involved in auto, homeowners, and health, in addition to life products. The College had worked out these new options and requirements in cooperation with the American Institute for Property and Liability Underwriters.[47]

The College also worked with the Control Data Corporation to create a computer-administered examination program called Examinations on Demand (EOD). The relationship had begun 3 years earlier when the College offered one course on an experimental basis. Immediately popular, the attractive EOD option revolutionized the testing process. By 1985 EOD involved more than 40 percent of students where it was available. The new system enabled candidates to set their own exam schedule, rather than wait until the January or June round of tests. Best of all, results of EOD examinations taken at Control Data "Education Centers" were immediately available instead of arriving in the mail 6 weeks later.[48]

President Jordan did not confine his administration's academic emphasis to the CLU/ChFC mainstream. The College at this time also actively promoted its School of Advanced Career Studies and its Graduate School for those with the basic designations and for other professionals. The Graduate School offered a graduate residency program for students working toward College masters degrees who had completed 15 credits. In 1985 it scheduled three of these on-campus, 2-week sessions in the Gregg Conference Center.

Intensive Learning Programs (ILPs)—regular courses presented in a concentrated study mode that covered 4 to 5 days, thereby eliminating the customary study method of one-a-week assignments—were also held at the Gregg Center. *The American College Outlook* announced ILP courses in such subjects as estate planning, pension planning, and business tax planning; courses were open to both examination candidates and "those who come for the knowledge only."[49]

Premier Schools—specialized programs created for individual life companies and agencies, banks, or accounting firms—occupied still another place in the College scholastic panoply. Company personnel and College meeting planners collaborated to design these events. The College also awarded continuing education units to the students and maintained permanent records of their achievements. Bankers Life of Iowa, Connecticut Mutual, Indianapolis

Life, and Occidental Life of North Carolina were among the early sponsors of Premier Schools.[50]

Finally, the College presented special seminars and workshops as additional outreach programs to the total financial services market of those days. These programs focused on topics of current interest such as the Tax Reform Act of 1984. The seminars and workshops spanned 2 days with overnight accommodations at the Gregg Center. Life agents, trust officers, accountants, and lawyers found these programs invaluable in updating their knowledge of specific current subjects.

Despite the vitality of these academic endeavors and the general strength of most of them, the College found the graduate degree programs less than an unqualified success. The Master of Science in Financial Services, begun in 1975, had done reasonably well with 802 MSFS degrees awarded through 1984. The Master of Science in Management, started some years later and serving a smaller pool of candidates, had awarded only 16 degrees by that time. Some uncertainty existed about the content of its courses. In 1985 therefore the College temporarily withdrew the MSM program and did not even list it in the 1985–1986 *Catalog*.

Following the preliminary real estate tax skirmishes of the previous year (which culminated in the Delaware County Court of Common Pleas permitting the College appeal), Hon. Howard F. Reed, Jr., on July 22, 1985, stayed the Board of Assessment order to pay these taxes. Judge Reed accepted the College's offer to continue voluntary payment of $30,000 per year under the 1974 agreement with the authorities, pending further order of the Court.[51]

The surcease proved temporary. The taxing authorities appealed Judge Reed's postponing order to Commonwealth Court. That body (in an opinion filed on October 22, 1985), stated that Reed lacked jurisdiction. The taxing authorities, however, agreed to let the College postpone payment of these taxes for a year based on the College's coming up with $34,206.58 interest on these levies.[52] End of round two.

There had been several administrative staff changes during these first 3 years of the Jordan presidency. Some people's employment was terminated, other people were moved around, and a number were brought to the College for the first time. Samuel H. Weese, PhD, CLU, CPCU, was one of the newcomers. In a move that a colleague described as "the best thing Edward Jordan ever did," Edward G. Jordan hired the former West Virginia insurance commissioner and Eastern Kentucky University professor to be The America College's vice president, assistant to the president, and secretary to the board of trustees.[53] A year later Weese became vice president of academic affairs upon the resignation of David D. Hemley, PhD.

*   *   *

Mission statements and long-range planning committees have become part of the mantra of contemporary corporate life. The American College had had its share of them from time to time in the past, and in January 1986, it announced its latest version of each. The list of newly defined institutional tasks had been long laboring, having begun 5 years earlier when the College prepared its 1982 self-study report for the accrediting authorities.

That document, as we explained earlier, was presented to the Commission on Higher Education Middle States Association of Colleges and Schools and concluded that "the College mission, goals, and objectives were unfocused and that there was some confusion as to the difference between ends and means." The report continued, "These goals were found to be inadequately communicated to the appropriate College constituencies."[54] President Jordan responded with a series of operational and strategic planning activities. He gave the trustees semi-annual briefings of the College business plan for each fiscal year. Furthermore, the College administration and faculty produced a restated institutional goal—"dedication to the advancement of learning and professionalism in financial services"—defining five specific areas of emphasis.[55]

Edward G. Jordan liked to work with outside consultants, as the 2 previous years had shown. To help achieve these latest objectives he again engaged an independent firm to provide guidance and administrative support, addressing such issues as the segments of the financial services industry the College should serve, the value of academic accreditation, the benefits of the large campus, the importance of nonprofit status, and the merits of closer cooperation between the College and the American Society of CLU & ChFC.[56]

According to Jordan, he had never been interested "in running the place"[57] but came to the College to solve financial problems and better define the financial services world. Nevertheless, committees, consultants, and credos had not fully sufficed to address the fiscal situation. Operating deficits escalated during the 3 consecutive years ending June 30: In 1984 they came to $130,901; the next year they were $277,811; by 1986 they zoomed to $1,707,526. Total College debt rose even more ominously to these levels: $9,021,955 (1984), $11,569,508 (1985), and $12,072,749 (1986).[58] The College needed more money. It decided to raise it through voluntary contributions.

Gifts and grants had long been important to the College, which had started its Development Fund in 1960. This fund was built up through 10-year pledges with annual contributions to the Golden Key Society from individuals, matching gifts, and from within the chapter structure. By 1975 the Endowment Development Fund had reached $5.2 million. The $20 million Golden Anniversary Fund had sought $7 million in major gifts and $13 million from Golden Key pledges (which were to be paid over a decade). This campaign was successful except for the $5 million needed for endowment, which was not fully subscribed and "deferred for more immediate needs."[59]

As previously noted, the College began a second capital gifts campaign in July 1979 for $5.9 million to help finance the new Graduate Center. Robert A. Beck led this campaign, which exceeded its goal within 24 months.[60] Although these efforts were substantial, because of the 10-year pledge payment period for

Golden Key Society commitments, the income was insufficient to cope with costly construction overruns and expensive debt service. This resulted in current financial exigencies that could no longer be denied.

Board Chairman Beck and President Jordan announced a new $30 million fundraising drive at an April 1986 campus celebration. Beck reiterated "The American College's capacity to deliver professional education better than we can get anywhere else in the world." Jordan emphasized the importance of the campaign by stating, "No institution of higher education can properly fulfill student needs while in debt."[61] Charles J. Zimmerman, honorary board chairman, also took part in the program, which included a retrospective look at the dreams of the College's founders.

The trustees organized the campaign into two phases. Kenneth C. Nichols, CLU, ChFC, president of Home Life Insurance Company, would chair Phase I with a $10 million goal from corporate pledges to retire the College's physical plant debt. William B. Wallace, Home Life general agent, would head Phase II, seeking $20 million for endowment from individuals in cash gifts or life insurance policies. This drive became known as the ACE (American College Endowment) campaign.

The fundraiser got off to a dramatic start: Both Board Chairman Robert A. Beck (Prudential Life CEO) and Vice Chairman John B. Carter (Equitable Life CEO) had secured $1 million grants from their respective companies. These pace-setting gifts, together with other contributions, enabled Beck to report almost $8 million already subscribed toward the Phase I $10 million goal.[62]

Wallace, as part of his Phase II accounting, reported a $.5 million gift from Frank M. Engle.[63] This particular announcement, coming only a month after the 1986 Engle Lecture by Anne O. Krueger, vice president of the World Bank, reemphasized the true dimensions of Engle's interest in and generosity to The American College. The Oklahoma benefactor, as we have noted, had previously endowed the lecture series and the Frank M. Engle Chair in Economic Security and Research.

In April 1986 the trial of the College's real estate tax exemption case began in the Court of Common Pleas of Delaware County. Since the October 24, 1985, Commonwealth Court's reversal of Judge Howard Reed's postponement of tax payment, both parties had been preparing for the showdown. The trial began on April 9 and continued off and on during the months of May and June. College counsel William H. Lowery told the trustees "not to expect a decision before fall at the earliest."[64] The case would eventually be determined by the College's qualification as an educational organization that serves as a purely public charity. Time would tell.

Two months later the trustees accepted the resignation of Robert A. Beck as chairman of the board and elected John B. Carter, CLU, to succeed him. Beck had served only 3 years in the position, but he had been a big factor in raising money for the College and sharpening its restated mission. Carter had risen through the ranks at the Equitable Life Assurance Society as his career took him from agent to CEO over a period of 30 years. Carter's advancement at The

American College proved equally noteworthy. Elected a trustee in 1982, he became vice chairman within 3 years and succeeded to the chairmanship in 1986. Beck and Carter had personally solicited a number of the major gifts in the current capital campaign.

In June 1986 the American Society of CLU & ChFC held its 40th Anniversary Institute in the Gregg Conference Center. Although the Society first offered its Institute to members in 1946 as part of an overall continuing education program, it had held these 5-day events for life insurance and other financial professionals in various parts of the country but had never presented the program on the Bryn Mawr campus. In those days the College could not provide the accommodations and instructional facilities for such a group.

By holding its 40th Anniversary Institute in the Gregg Center in June 1986, the Society could offer members an opportunity to visit the campus (many for the first time) and to stroll the same 35 acres frequented in the past by those who built the CLU movement such as the late Solomon S. Huebner, Paul S. Mills, CLU, Charles J. Zimmerman, as well as former College President Davis W. Gregg.[65]

This was the year when the *New England Journal of Medicine* announced that moderate exercise could significantly shrink the risk of death from all causes, when film actor Paul Newman won an Oscar for his role in *The Color of Money,* and the cost of a Levittown, Pennsylvania, house rose to $125,000 (from only $60,000 in 1980).[66]

Meanwhile, the College continued to expand its Examinations on Demand (EOD) effort by making its CLU and ChFC computerized exams available for nearly all Huebner courses. The College also granted graduates the right to use these designations quarterly instead of requiring them to wait for the annual fall conferment. In education, as in life, however, all steps are not forward. Some situations demand a step backward. President Jordan had placed a property-liability course in the 1983 MSFS curriculum, but it had proved to be less than successful. The College withdrew it in 1986 for further deliberation.

The American Society made more College news in October at its 1986 annual forum held in San Antonio. Society President Stanley Liss, CLU, presented Edward Jordan with a $1 million life insurance gift to the capital campaign in another dramatic illustration of the close relationship between the two organizations. The Million Dollar Round Table did its part, too, with a $250,000 cash pledge payable over 5 years. The first check was presented by Frank Friedler, Jr., past president of the MDRT. These contributions brought the total amount of campaign cash and pledges to more than $14 million.[67]

Previous gifts from Joseph E. and Ruth E. Boettner had endowed the Boettner Chair in Financial Services Research (which Davis W. Gregg occupied when he retired from the College presidency in 1982). Earlier activities led to the establishment of the Boettner Research Institute, which held its inaugural convocation on November 5, 1986, with the theme "Improving Life Quality in the Retirement Years." Following an address by M. Powell Lawton, Gerontological Society of America president, and a panel discussion—

"Psychological, Spiritual, Physical and Financial Well Being"—President Jordan noted the close ties between the College and the Institute.[68]

Over the years the College had continually revised its courses to reflect legislative changes, but the College set a record for fast response toward the end of 1986. President Reagan signed the Tax Reform Act in late October, and the College prepared *The Financial Services Professional Guide to the Tax Reform Act of 1986* and published it in less than 6 weeks time! The volume, prepared by a faculty team led by professor Stephan R. Leimberg, JD, CLU, was priced at $12.95 and quickly sold 24,000 copies.

*   *   *

The College's 60th anniversary year of 1987 began without drama. At a time when President Ronald Reagan submitted the nation's first trillion-dollar budget to Congress, the College's plan of operations climbed to more than $17 million. Increased student fee income and reduced debt service expense had eased the institution's current financial condition. The capital campaign had also helped.[69]

Fundraising "all stars" John B. Carter, Robert A. Beck, Kenneth C. Nichols, and William B. Wallace continued to move the drive forward. By February, 75 corporations were listed on the contribution honor roll, and more than 200 donors had made minimum gifts of $50,000 in face-value life insurance to the endowment fund. The College had organized several regional celebrations across the country in such locations as Chicago, Los Angeles, Seattle, Atlanta, and Boston to augment the solicitation efforts of the trustee leadership quartet and their hard-working committees. President Jordan and other administrative officers attended these meetings and talked with alumni and other constituents.[70]

The College and the American Society continued their efforts to bring about greater interorganizational cooperation. The Society's executive vice president, John R. Driskill, likened the relationship between the two organizations to that of the American Bar Association and an individual law school (except that the Society relates to only one school in the life insurance field).[71] The two entities created a joint task force to consider future cooperative efforts in the spring of 1987. College Chairman John B. Carter and Society President Stanley Liss announced the formation of an eight-member group with representatives from the boards of both bodies. Denis F. Mullane would head the College team, which included Dr. Dan M. McGill and William B. Wallace; President Jordan was an ex-officio member. Liss, former NALU trustee and MDRT president, explained that although the College and the Society competed with each other in continuing education, "they have always been not only cooperative, but close."[72]

College officials had made preliminary plans for the College's 60th anniversary as early as the fall of 1986 when they considered the possibility of an appropriate program to be held in the Philadelphia area.[73] Some months later President Jordan told the trustees that the administration had reevaluated the matter and concluded, "As the premier distance education institution . . . it would be more fitting to celebrate nationally with all our constituency in Washington,

DC."[74] A modest campus commemoration featured an April 9 reception at the Gregg Center when Jordan and 38-year employee Helen L. Schmidt shared the honors in a cake-cutting ceremony to which all employees had been invited. [75]

Paul N. McCracken, PhD, economic adviser to President Ronald Reagan, gave the 1987 Frank M. Engle Lecture at a special College convocation on May 6, which marked three simultaneous anniversaries: the 10th anniversary of the Engle Lecture series, the 60th of the College itself, and the 90th year of Engle's life. A panel that included Michael P. Darby, assistant secretary of the Treasury; A. Gilbert Heebner, Eastern College distinguished professor; and Lindley H. Clark, Jr, editor of the *Wall Street Journal,* elaborated on McCracken's subject, "Can Economic Policy Manage the Economy?" [76]

When the trustees met in June they approved a newly structured graduate program in the School of Financial Sciences designed to improve upon and partially replace the existing MSFS offerings, which some felt had not differed markedly enough from the basic CLU and ChFC programs.[77] As Academic Affairs Vice President Samuel H. Weese expressed it, "We found a need for greater professional education in two distinct areas—professional services management and financial planning applications."[78] The board decision came after extensive student surveys, formation of a blue-ribbon advisory panel, faculty committee work, and focus group activity that finally produced a new curriculum with more faculty-student interaction.

No official word had come from the authorities regarding the real estate tax imbroglio since the trial of the previous spring and summer. The Common Pleas Court of Delaware County finally broke the silence on July 22 when Judge Howard F. Reed, Jr., decreed "that the action of the Board of Assessment Appeals . . . holding that American College is not entitled to real estate tax exemption be and the same is hereby affirmed. It is hereby further ordered that the property of American College . . . be and the same is assessed at one million, one hundred fifty thousand dollars, but without prejudice to appeal such assessment."[79]

Six days later the College filed a motion for post-trial relief in the Court of Common Pleas and followed it up with an appeal to Commonwealth Court. After 2 months, no action had been taken on this application, increasing the likelihood that an argument would not be scheduled until December or early January.[80]

The anniversary year reached a climax in the first week of October during the 4 days of activities at the Sheraton Hotel in Washington, DC. There, Edward G. Jordan made the surprise announcement that he would "step down from the presidency of The American College."[81] He named December 31 as the effective date. (He had officially resigned at the June 26 trustees meeting although there had been no public announcement until more than 3 months later.[82])

Five years seemed a short tenure, particularly when compared to the 28 years that Davis W. Gregg had held the office. The Jordan years were fast paced and reflected the two major trends in the life insurance industry of those days: declining agent recruitment and growing segmentation. One group of companies diversified its activities into broad financial services; another segment—known as multiline companies—concentrated on personal lines casualty coverage and some life insurance.[83]

Edward Jordan could count a number of definite accomplishments during his presidency. He had achieved a meaningful academic reorganization: In 1987 both matriculations and course registrations had reversed a declining trend and actually increased. Jordan had also refinanced the cumulative debt at more favorable rates. Former Board Chairman Robert A. Beck is reputed to have claimed that "Jordan saved the College." Be that as it may, The American College still faced a formidable financial challenge. Despite fundraising success, total debt stood at $9,220,285 on June 30, 1987, which was almost $200,000 more than 3 years before.[84]

Jordan stated that he "had the satisfaction of working with an outstanding group of people" at the College, but his abrupt and aloof manner had often strained those relationships. As one industry executive opined, "He did not suffer fools gladly." Trustee comments describing Jordan ranged from "brilliant" to "combative," and one faculty member claimed that Jordan never made eye contact with those he addressed. A later board chairman reflected, "His 5 years were not a happy time."[85]

A cluster of other 60th anniversary events closely followed Jordan's resignation announcement. The very next day, for example, the College presented its fourth annual Masters Seminar for forum attendees who held MSFS or MSM degrees. Board Chairman John B. Carter concluded the Society's annual forum on October 7 with a "stimulating conferment address,"[86] when he awarded 1,965 CLU and approximately 1,800 ChFC designations. Nearly 200 persons earned both designations that day, and an additional 131 individuals graduated from the MSFS and MSM programs. By this time, some 65,000 men and women had earned the CLU designation since 1928.[87]

The College concluded the celebrations with a by-invitation-only educational program at the National Press Club on October 8. Dr. Charls E. Walker spoke on "The Economic Environment in the Final Decade of the Century and Beyond." A panel then discussed "The Future Role of Financial Services—for the Major Financial Institutions, the Individual Practitioners, and the Consumer." Panelists included U.S. Senator Christopher J. Dodd, Dr. Robert Litan of the Brookings Institution, and the president of John Hancock, T. James Morton.[88]

As autumn deepened, the stock market crashed on October 19, but The American College continued on its steady course with both off-campus outreach programs and on-site events. The College completed its 1987 *Periodic Review Report* for presentation to the Commission on Higher Education of the Middle States Association of Colleges and Schools as a requirement for continued accreditation. The Vane B. Lucas Library held an open house for faculty, staff, and constituents to mark its 50th year of operation. Librarian Judith L. Hill noted that the library, which had begun as a small collection of books housed in the College's 3924 Walnut Street location at the University of Pennsylvania, "now occupies the first floor of MDRT Foundation Hall and comprises a collection of

8,000 books and 500 periodicals."[89] Outgoing president Jordan had been a proponent of the library during his 5 years in office.

NOTES

1. *Who's Who in America* (Chicago: Marquis-Who's Who, Inc.), 1996, vol. 1, p. 2136.
2. *The American College Today*, September 1982, p. 1.
3. Ibid.
4. Ibid., p. 3.
5. Ibid., December 1982, p. 5.
6. Ibid., p. 3.
7. Richard D. Irwin convocation program, October 13, 1982.
8. *The American College Today,* December 1982, p. 3.
9. *Periodic Review Report,* 1982, p. 2.1.
10. John C. Bogle, interview with the author, January 23, 1995.
11. Marjorie A. Fletcher memorandum, February 1996.
12. *The American College Today,* vol. 14, no. 2, summer 1983.
13. Ibid., pp. 5–10.
14. Ibid., front cover.
15. Ibid., winter 1984, p. 5.
16. Ibid., p. 2.
17. Ibid.
18. Ibid., p. 3.
19. Ibid., p. 4.
20. Paul Dickson, *Timelines* (Reading, MA: Addison-Wesley Publishing Co., Inc.), 1990, pp. 264–266.
21. *Hoover's Guide to Private Companies 1994–1995,* p. 95.
22. *Creating a Strategy,* McKinsey & Co., Inc., September 12, 1983, p. 4.
23. Ibid., p. 17.
24. *The American College Today,* winter 1984, p. 10.
25. Ibid., p. 9.
26. Dickson, *Timelines,* p. 271.
27. Ibid., p. 272.
28. Stewardship Report, *Annual Report,* The American College, 1984.
29. *The American College Today,* winter 1984, p. 2.
30. Stewardship Report, p. 1.
31. Rudolph G. Penner, "The Deficit Dilemma," Frank M. Engle Lecture, 1984, front page, no. 3.
32. Letter addressed to Davis W. Gregg, April 3, 1984.
33. Ibid.
34. *McCullough v. Maryland,* 4 Wheaton 431, 1803.
35. Delaware County, Pennsylania, Board of Assessment Appeals, July 20, 1984, folio no. 2858, wd. 3.
36. *Outlook,* November 1984, p. 4.
37. Ibid., pp. 1, 2.
38. Ibid., p. 2.
39. *The American College Catalog,* 1984–1985, p. 22.
40. The American College Code of Ethics, 1984, p. 1.
41. Ibid., p. 2.
42. Ibid.

43. *Philadelphia Inquirer,* November 15, 1984, p. 13-M.
44. Dickson, *Timelines,* pp. 271–275.
45. Ibid., p. 277.
46. *The American College Outlook,* spring 1985, p. 6.
47. *Society Page,* American Society of CLU & ChFC, June 1985, pp. 1, 2.
48. *Outlook,* spring 1985, pp. 1–2.
49. Ibid., p. 4.
50. Ibid.
51. William H. Lowery, "Confidential Communication to the Board of Trustees of The American College," June 21, 1985, p. 2.
52. Lowery, "Advice to the Board of Trustees," January 16, 1986.
53. *The American College Catalog,* 1985–1986, p. 65.
54. *Periodic Review Report,* 1987, p. 2.1.
55. Ibid.
56. Ibid., p. 2.2.
57. Edward G. Jordan, interview with the author, August 8, 1995.
58. Reports on Examination of Financial Statements, Coopers & Lybrand, June 30, 1984, 1985, 1986.
59. *Self-Study,* 1982, The American College, pp. 11.1–11.2.
60. Ibid.
61. *Outlook,* summer 1986, p. 3.
62. Ibid.
63. Ibid.
64. Lowery, "Confidential Communication," June 17, 1986.
65. *Society Page,* April 1986, pp. 1, 10.
66. Dickson, *Timelines,* pp. 284, 286.
67. *Focus, The American College Newsletter,* fall 1986, pp. 4, 5.
68. Inaugural convocation program, Boettner Research Institute, November 5, 1986.
69. Report on Examination of Financial Statements, June 30, 1987, p. 3.
70. *Outlook,* spring 1987, p. 2.
71. Interview with the author, November 9, 1994.
72. Interview with the author, June 15, 1995.
73. Marjorie A. Fletcher, memorandum to David W. Bruhin, November 17, 1986.
74. Letter to the trustees, April 17, 1987.
75. *Outlook,* summer 1987, p. 5.
76. Paul N. McCracken, "Can Economic Policy Manage the Economy?" Frank M. Engle Lecture, May 6, 1987.
77. *Outlook,* summer 1987, pp. 1–2.
78. Ibid.
79. Court of Common Pleas of Montgomery County, Pennsylvania. Civil Action-Law No. 84-16202, p. 1.
80. Lowery, "Report on Status of American College's Real Estate Tax Appeal," September 25, 1987.
81. Edward G. Jordan, "The American College Now—In its 60th Year," p. 11.
82. *Outlook,* fall/winter 1987, p. 2.
83. *Self-Study,* 1987, p. 6.1.
84. Report on Examination of Financial Statements, June 30, 1987, p. 6.
85. Personal interviews with the author.
86. *Outlook,* fall/winter 1987, p. 1.
87. Ibid.

88. Ibid.
89. Ibid., p. 6.

President Edward G. Jordan, Clarence C. Walton, and Richard D. Irwin celebrate the newly endowed Richard D. Irwin School of Management.

The inauguration of Edward G. Jordan as the sixth president of The American College took place on June 16, 1983. He had been appointed on November 1, 1982.

A masters degree recipient receives congratulations from President Edward G. Jordan at the Graduate School commencement in 1983.

Examinations on Demand—testing by computer—became available for CLU and ChFC courses between 1982 and 1987, and the first software to use with courses was developed.

President Edward G. Jordan addresses the Graduate School commencement in 1982.

Under President Jordan, Premier Schools were developed using College faculty for the intensive education programs. Here, Clarence C. Walton teaches a Bankers Life Premier School seminar.

President Edward G. Jordan presents the Huebner Gold Medal to Gen Hirose, president, Nippon Mutual Life Insurance Company of Japan.

SECTION SIX

Fruition 1988–1997
Samuel H. Weese

11

Striking a Balance

Time is the Subtle Thief of Youth.

John Milton

"It is now well established that presidential leadership is the main imperative for the revitalization of higher education," writes academic governance authority James L. Fisher. "However, the presidential search process has become popularized to the point of being more important than the outcome."[1] This ironic circumstance is the result of trustees' loss of control and excessive faculty and even student involvement in what is essentially a board responsibility. On the national scene many educators, including Harvard's David Reisman, lament this symptom of the current leadership dilemma in higher education.[2]

The American College successfully avoided this issue when it effected the transition of executive authority from Edward G. Jordan to Samuel H. Weese in early 1988. Board Chairman John B. Carter had kept control of the succession situation and announced the unanimous decision of the trustee Executive Committee with these words: "Dr. Samuel H. Weese, PhD, CLU, CPCU, vice president for academic affairs, has been appointed to serve as acting president of the College, effective January 1." The chairman also indicated that Dr. Weese would "continue in his present capacity while assuming the additional responsibilities of acting president."[3] Thus began a decade destined to bring more changes to The American College than the pioneer distance education entity had experienced during its previous 25 years.[4]

Behind Carter's succinct statement stretched 6 months of tightly focused but largely inconclusive presidential search activity. Before the end of the June 26, 1987, board meeting at which the trustees received Jordan's resignation, Carter had named himself chairman of the search committee whose other members he would appoint in the near future. The president of Prudential Insurance Company of America, Joseph J. Melone, CLU, ChFC, became involved, as would Stanley Liss, CLU, New York Life; Jack L. Nix, CLU, Insurance Services, Inc.; and William B. Wallace, Home Life Insurance Company.

Within a few weeks Carter received a letter from the chairman of the Wharton School Department of Insurance, Dan M. McGill, who urged the committee "to give serious consideration to the suitability of Samuel H. Weese for the position."[5] Dr. McGill recommended Weese both for his "sterling personal and professional qualities and in the belief that the next president of the

167

College should have academic qualifications."[6] Former president Davis W. Gregg echoed this sentiment.

The committee retained the worldwide executive search consulting firm of Spencer Stuart and worked initially with the New York office. Spencer Stuart cast a wide net. The company began a process that eventually involved conversations with hundreds of sources, including senior officers of almost every insurance company of consequence in the United States and every academic institution remotely involved with insurance.[7] The College sought a candidate with both academic and insurance managerial experience, but the quest proved more difficult than first imagined.

After some months, the consultants narrowed the field to a few potentially strong applicants. One of these, a former university president and life insurance company CEO, came to Bryn Mawr and met with members of the campus family. His credentials were impressive, but before the board took action, this candidate withdrew his name for personal reasons.

The unexpected development forced the succession issue. Time was running out. With Jordan's departure only weeks away, Board Chairman Carter took immediate action. He asked the academic vice president, Samuel H. Weese, to serve as acting president for an indefinite period until the trustees could select a permanent president.

Dr. Weese accepted the interim appointment on two conditions: that he be given full chief executive authority from day one and that he be considered for the position on a permanent basis. Weese also requested that other applicants be measured against his experience and performance.[8] The trustees accepted these conditions, and the man from West Virginia thus earned his second promotion in 2 years as he moved steadily upward from vice president, assistant to the president in 1985, to academic vice president in 1986, and now succeeded Edward G. Jordan in the top spot, albeit on an acting basis. Throughout these title changes Samuel H. Weese retained another position that could not help but be advantageous to his prospects—that of secretary of the Board of Trustees. President Jordan had made this position available for Weese in 1985 to help bring him to the College.

Born in 1935 in Morgantown, West Virginia, Samuel H. Weese spent his first 29 years in the Mountain State except for a 3-year period as a U.S. Air Force navigator. The son of a high school teacher and college professor, young Weese was drawn to the academic world. His early goal was to become a college teacher like his father. After earning a bachelor's degree at West Virginia University, he continued there for an MBA and then joined the faculty at Davis and Elkins College in Elkins, West Virginia, where he served as an instructor in business and economics for 2 years.

At business school, impressed by the impact of insurance on people's lives, Weese was strongly influenced by his insurance professor, Fred E. Wright, who was one of the most popular professors in the West Virginia University Business School. It was Wright who told Weese about the Huebner Foundation and its attractive fellowship program for those interested in teaching careers in insurance, and Wright who recommended Weese to Dr. Dan M. McGill, then the director of the Huebner Foundation. Dr. McGill selected Weese as a Solomon Huebner fellow. He earned his MA degree in 1966 from the University of Pennsylvania and his PhD in 1969.[9]

Weese's first teaching position after leaving the University of Pennsylvania was in the College of Business Administration at the University of Florida. During his second year in Gainesville, his former college professor, Fred Wright, brought Weese to the attention of Wright's college friend, Arch A. Moore, Jr., who had recently been elected governor of West Virginia. The governor-elect needed an insurance commissioner, and he liked Wright's recommendation. Moore named Weese insurance commissioner, and the young educator served in that capacity for 6 years.[10] Wright, Moore, and Weese—along with five members of the governor's cabinet who took office in 1969—had been members of the Beta Theta Pi fraternity while in college.

Samuel H. Weese enjoyed public policy issues and followed his role as commissioner with 3 years' experience as general manager of the National Flood Insurers Association, which was created as a government-industry partnership for providing flood insurance to residents in flood plain areas. Higher education, however, continued to call, and Weese returned to academia with teaching posts first at the University of Hartford and then at Eastern Kentucky University, where he held a chair of insurance from 1981 to 1985 to round out 2 decades of professional experience in the educational and insurance worlds.[11] It was while he was at Eastern Kentucky University that he earned his CLU designation in 1983 and his CPCU designation in 1985.

Samuel Weese easily met the presidential search committee's specification for a person who "could contend with curriculum development, faculty appointments and the like" on the one hand, as well as "control costs, hire and fire people, and maintain external corporate relationships" on the other.[12] By 1987, 2 administrative years at The American College had further refined Weese's overall talents and added the bonus of in-house familiarity.

The acting president stood in stark contrast to his predecessor. Their disparate backgrounds were one difference. Personality and temperament were another. Jordan seemed brusque and aloof to most of the campus family, reputedly never even speaking to some people. Weese's steadying influence had earned him respect and support from both faculty and staff during the previous 5 turbulent years.[13]

Samuel H. Weese worked under significant pressure as acting president. After all, he was holding two full-time jobs since his appointment included continuing as academic vice president. Furthermore, he had to work with incumbents, at least one of whom was a competitor for the top job. Finally, he had to convince the board that he had the qualifications to run the College. Dr. Weese faced this third challenge decisively by taking full responsibility for his actions. Firsthand knowledge of College personnel and operations proved helpful in this regard. He had no difficulty in accepting accountability for his leadership.[14] The energetic top executive at The American College oversaw a variety of events and programs, several of which had been in the planning stage for some time.

It was important that the College continue to function in an uninterrupted manner because the life insurance industry was in the midst of unprecedented change, and The American College had to keep pace. Helpful to the acting president was the opportunity to bring with him to the new position his administrative assistant, Vicki Doyle, who joined the College in 1980 and had been Sam Weese's assistant in his two previous positions. She has functioned in this capacity to the present.

In February, for instance, there was news from the Immigration and Naturalization Service of the U.S. Department of Justice. The government had approved the College's application for permission to accept and enroll foreign nonimmigrant students into its Master of Science in Financial Services degree program.[15] This authorization would allow foreign students to remain in the United States for 2 years, provided they maintained full-time status at the College for that period. While the MSFS degree was a distance education offering, the curriculum also required 2 weeks of resident study on the Bryn Mawr campus. Then, too, course examinations were offered only on computer at some 50 testing sites in the continental United States.

"This academic credential provides confirmation of the status of our graduate school," Dr. Weese noted. It illustrates, he said, "another advantage of Middle States accreditation."[16]

The College and the Society collaborated in another special effort at that time. They issued a joint statement calling for an industry summit to emphasize educational standards as a higher priority than a single designation throughout the financial planning profession. Dr. Weese, for his part, declared, "The source of confusion for the consumer is not the proliferation of designations and credentials, but the broad range of educational levels they represent."[17] Society President John B. Peyton, CLU, ChFC, agreed and added, "Discussions which focus on designations rather than educational levels can lead to nonproductive debates."[18]

March marked another American College outreach to a wider constituency. In addition to serving foreign nonimmigrant students and TV financial viewers, the College signed an agreement with the Life Underwriters Association of Canada to make the Chartered Financial Consultant designation available to Canadian CLUs. Through a contractual arrangement, Canadian CLUs could thus earn their ChFC designations by completing three additional courses. LUAC was to be responsible for the curriculum and examination development under the overview and approval of the College.

In a joint signing ceremony with LUAC's John E. Wahl, CLU, College Board Chairman John B. Carter affirmed the College's dedication to participate in international professional education for those in life insurance and other financial services. "This agreement . . . is an example of the significant role The

American College can play in bringing about coordination and cooperation," Carter said.[19]

Canada had offered its own independent CLU designation for more than 60 years, and in 1988 was joined by Israel when 37 insurance representatives of that country received their CLUs in Jerusalem after completing a professional program modeled after that of The American College. Israeli professor Yehuda Kahane designed the Israeli program with in-depth knowledge of the College's CLU curriculum and with the cooperation and support of The American College. A contractual agreement was arranged with the College for the Israeli program to use the Chartered Life Underwriter designation.[20]

In April Federal Reserve Board Governor H. Robert Heller visited Bryn Mawr as the Frank M. Engle lecturer for 1988. Dr. Heller delivered the 11th Engle lecture with a cogent address titled "Imbalances and Asymmetries in the World Economy." He discussed the perennial tensions between free trade and tariffs and favored lower government expenditures over higher taxes as a sounder U.S. fiscal policy.[21]

The College undertook another joint venture that spring, this time with the Commerce Clearing House of San Rafael, California. The two organizations cosponsored a financial planning conference that focused on "a review of financial and estate plans in light of the volatile economic environment of those days."[22] The conference was held in two locations: at the Fairmont Hotel in San Francisco, May 5–6, and at the Crystal Gateway Marriott in Washington, DC, May 23–24. The College's Stephan R. Leimberg, professor of taxation and estate planning, and Sidney Kess, JD, a nationally recognized authority on law, accounting, and financial and estate planning, served as cochairmen.[23]

A few weeks later, during the early part of what proved to be the final month of Samuel H. Weese's probationary period, five Japanese insurance industry senior managers came to the College for a meeting with faculty members and local insurance and brokerage officials. The Japanese executives' visit (part of a 10-day tour of the United States and Canada) brought back memories of Solomon S. Huebner's visits to that Far Eastern nation decades earlier—visits that helped to build close ties between The American College and the Japanese life insurance industry.[24]

Not long thereafter, two faculty members went to Washington, DC, as cowinners of the International Association of Financial Planning's "Case Study Competition." Burton T. Beam, Jr., CLU, CPCU, associate professor of insurance, and William J. Ruckstuhl, CLU, ChFC, assistant professor of economics, shared the $2,000 first prize.[25]

The supervision of these myriad events, to say nothing of the ongoing administration of academic affairs, gave Weese ample opportunity to demonstrate his leadership qualities to Board Chairman John B. Carter and the other members of the presidential search committee. The committee now included both trustees and three faculty members: Glenn Boseman, Edward E. Graves, and Stephan R. Leimberg.

The acting chief executive made formal application for the job on a permanent basis, and at least one other member of senior management also applied for the position. The search committee compared these in-house contestants with a number of outside candidates. Some of these candidates seemed strong initially, but upon closer scrutiny they did not measure up or did not show sufficient interest in the position.

By June 8 it had become apparent that the strongest potential president was none other than Samuel H. Weese. Spencer Stuart consultant David R. McCarthy of Philadelphia, who was now in charge of the search, told the trustees that day, "We have always had to deal with the question as to why the College would look beyond Sam Weese for the position." McCarthy went on to say, "People were puzzled about the fact that Weese is not in the position. You have an extremely strong candidate in Sam Weese."[26]

That did it. Faced with such overwhelming reinforcement of its own somewhat belated realization, the board acted without further delay. Chairman Carter announced the "unanimous confirmation" of Samuel H. Weese as the seventh president of "the nation's oldest and largest college devoted exclusively to financial services education."[27]

Carter extolled Weese's "proven leadership and significant organizational experience. His background in government, associational leadership, and higher education makes him particularly well qualified to serve the College's needs at this time,"[28] said Carter. The 53-year-old Weese acknowledged that the College and its constituencies were at "a critical juncture in history," which would require "this institution to allocate its resources carefully to meet new educational needs."[29]

On the world scene in mid-1988 Soviet troops withdrew from Afghanistan, the *USS Vincennes* shot down an Iranian jetliner over the Persian Gulf, and British Prime Minister Margaret Thatcher celebrated 9 years in office. The American agenda of those days included Alfred Whry's Pulitzer Prize for his popular *Driving Miss Daisy,* the installation of lights in Chicago's Wrigley Field, and a Census Bureau report that revealed that the proportion of one-parent families had grown from 12.9 percent of all families with children in 1970 to 27.3 percent in 1988.[30]

The life insurance community had its own problems. It was not at that time America's best-loved business. A leading American Life Insurance Association executive lamented that some critics unfairly "compared it to chemicals and nuclear power."[31] The relationship between the College and those who sold life protection plans reflected what a trustee of that era called "a philosophical problem rising from industry drive in tension with academic freedom."[32]

The new president faced at least two external challenges, as well as an internal situation that demanded his immediate attention. Dr. Weese believed that further improvement in the relationship between the College and American Society of CLU & ChFC was needed. While much has been said about the apparent cooperative relationship between the two organizations, those close to the scene knew this was not the case. He also had to repair industry ties that had become strained in 1982 when the College broadened its curriculum and introduced the ChFC designation. Finally, Weese knew he must reverse a negative financial picture.[33]

In endorsing the Weese candidacy, a task force led by professors Boseman, Graves, and Leimberg praised Weese's style and substance to their colleagues in those late winter-early spring days of 1988 when faculty morale was low. The tensions of the Jordan years had taken their toll. Jordan's frequent absences and the College's stubborn financial problems had created a mood of uncertainty and discontent. The faculty wanted a president who would be a hands-on executive.

In this wish they would not be disappointed. Soon after the June 24 announcement of his appointment as president, Samuel Weese met with the campus family and declared that he would be "a manager who knows the operation and focuses upon finding the most cost-effective means of achieving operational objectives."[34]

Dr. Weese's presidency was not the only position announced at the College that month. At their June meeting the trustees elected four men to the board for the first time: William W. Fenniman, Manufacturers Financial Group manager; John Gummere, Phoenix Mutual Life board chairman; Harry J. Hohn, JD, New York Life's board vice chairman; and Sidney Kess, CPA, Peat Parwick Main & Co. partner. The trustees also named a former board member (1978–1987), George J. Hauptfuhrer, Jr., to take Weese's place as corporate secretary. Hauptfuhrer, who had previously served as secretary, was the chairman of the Philadelphia law firm of Dechert Price & Rhoads, which had enjoyed a long legal relationship with the College.[35]

In addition, the board met the new vice president of academic affairs, Gary K. Stone, who would take office on August 1. Dr. Stone had many qualifications for the position. First, he had been a Huebner fellow at the Wharton School, University of Pennsylvania, where he earned his PhD in 1966. While a student at the Wharton School he corrected essay examinations for The American College and became a CLU in 1968. Second, he had enjoyed a solid career of more than 20 years at Michigan State University, where he became a full professor in the insurance field and later directed the MBA program. In fact, his Michigan State experience had been so satisfying that he took a leave of absence from MSU to "try out" The American College post with the opportunity to return to Michigan State if his Bryn Mawr, Pennsylvania, assignment did not prove satisfactory. Third, he had served as an insurance consultant to several organizations, including the Federal Trade Commission. Finally, he had known Samuel H. Weese for a long time, since they were Huebner fellows together at the University of Pennsylvania. The men would work well together, and the trial period would quickly pass and become the foundation for a long tenure.

Before Robert W. Cooper, who was dean from 1979 until he resigned in 1987, the Huebner School deanship had experienced considerable turnover. William H. Rabel held the position from 1976–1978, followed by Denis T. Raihall, who held it in 1978–1979. Prior to Weese's presidency, there was an even higher turnover rate in the position of vice president for academic affairs, with Raihall in the position in 1977–1980, Charles E. Hughes in 1980–1984, Robert M. Crowe in 1984–1985, and David D. Hemley in 1985–1986.

The new president therefore merged the positions of Huebner School dean and Graduate School dean into the position of vice president of academic affairs and at the same time downgraded the title of dean of examinations to director of examinations. New positions were created as directors for the Huebner and Graduate Schools. This reorganization was designed to consolidate the Academic Division's authority into the vice president's position that Gary Stone had accepted. It was a reflection of the confidence that President Weese, who wanted consistent long-term leadership for the Academic Division, had in his new appointee. No single appointment had a more stabilizing effect for the College as it entered the decade of the 1990s.

In August The American College moved closer to confirming Benjamin Franklin's maxim about the certainty of death and taxes as the Pennsylvania Commonwealth Court, by Order and Memorandum Opinion dated the 3d of that month, "affirmed the Order of the Court of Common Pleas of Delaware County."[36] Within days Dechert Price & Rhoads recommended that the College appeal to the state Supreme Court.[37] The College elected to take this step; thus began another interval of waiting for a judicial decision in the tax contest that had begun in 1984.

Soon after Dr. Stone assumed his duties, Dr. Weese announced another new faculty appointment. He introduced former Connecticut Mutual Life general agent John W. Cronin, CLU, ChFC, as the first holder of the George G. Joseph Chair in Management Education. Leaders of the General Agents and Managers Conference (GAMC) had proposed the George G. Joseph Chair as early as 1982. Led by future trustee Vincent C. Bowhers, CLU, ChFC, a veteran group of agency managers launched a campaign to fund an endowment to support a management chair. The sum they raised fell below the target. As a result, the amount was inadequate for a traditional faculty chair. A viable alternative was to take a nontraditional approach by naming a retired practitioner to the position, someone who could bring practical experience to the management faculty while working part-time for the College.

In selecting Georgia Institute of Technology graduate John W. Cronin for the position the joint College/Agency Management Committee headed by trustee Edward K. Leaton, CLU, ChFC, deliberately chose a veteran who was preparing to retire as an active general agent. The highly successful Cronin, MDRT life member and a retired rear admiral in the U.S. Naval Reserve, had been a respected local agency manager for years. However, he lacked a graduate degree and had no experience in higher education. Cronin described himself as "the bridge between academia and the real world."[38] For the next 7 years he served the College extremely well as a part-time employee.

The new president took part in an October "American Culture and Business Ethics Conference" jointly sponsored by the College and Arthur Andersen & Co., the nation's largest public accounting firm.[39] This ethics program had been assembled by Clarence C. Walton, who as mentioned earlier, was the first Charles Lamont Post Chairholder of Ethics and the Professions at the College and the former president of Catholic University of America.

Later that month, Dr. Weese went to Nashville, Tennessee, to present a Huebner Gold Medal to Benjamin N. Woodson at the 1988 conferment exercises in conjunction with the American Society's annual forum. The biggest event of the fall, however, was held on November 18—Dr. Weese's formal inauguration as the seventh president of The American College. The inauguration ceremony, which had been planned by a committee of Davis W. Gregg, George J. Hauptfuhrer, Jr., and Clarence C. Walton, included an academic procession of more than 20 college and university delegates, the singing of "America the Beautiful," and a closing recessional prayer.

Eight organizations sent congratulations to Dr. Weese through personal representatives. Glenn Boseman, James S. Bingay professor of leadership, expressed greetings from the College faculty; William B. Wallace spoke for the Board of Trustees and William E. Kingsley for the American Council of Life Insurance; Maxine B. Niemeyer did the honors for the American Society of CLU & ChFC. Alan Press, NALU president, also took part, and other participants included Norman A. Baglini, president of the American Institute for Property and Liability Underwriters, and Dan M. McGill, chairman of the Insurance Department at the Wharton School of the University of Pennsylvania. "I think the College trustees showed good judgment in selecting Sam Weese as the president," said Dr. McGill. "I predict [he] will lead the College to new heights of achievement."[40]

Following remarks by former president Davis W. Gregg, Board Chairman John B. Carter introduced the new president and presented him with the traditional leather pouch containing the Charter of The American College and appurtenant documents.[41] Weese's inaugural address reviewed the College's history, noting 68,000 CLU designations granted since 1928 with approximately 42,000 active in the life insurance business 60 years later.

Dr. Weese predicted that the 1990s would be the decade of education in America, touching every segment of the country's instructional system, including adult professional education. "We must be ready to play a leading role in this educational revolution." he said. "It is the opportunity of a lifetime. We don't plan to miss it."[42]

*   *   *

George W. Bush took office in January 1989 as president of the United States, Samuel H. Weese began his first full year as president of The American College, and Marvin D. Bower, CLU, assumed his position as newly elected board chairman. The new chairman merits a closer look.

Marvin Bower, a graduate of Illinois Wesleyan University, rose through the State Farm organization until he became executive vice president of its young life insurance company. During his years at State Farm, Bower led the company, a predominately personal lines insurer of autos and homes, into the life insurance business. When he retired as head of its life company, State Farm had become one of the largest life insurers in this country.[43]

Bower had American College experience as well. Beginning in 1973 he served 9 years as a trustee and gained certification board experience. He was also active in development work for the College, particularly with the National Committee of the Golden Anniversary Fund. In 1985 Bower rejoined the College trustees and was elected chairman of the board in 1989 upon the resignation of John B. Carter.

Vice Chairman William B. Wallace was slated to succeed Carter, but Wallace became president of Home Life Insurance Company that year and could not devote the necessary time to the responsibilities of the board's top position. The trustees therefore elected Bower chairman based on his experience in the industry and his knowledge of The American College.

Unlike some tongue-tied business leaders, Samuel H. Weese knew the value of communication with both the outside public and the campus family. In response to questions from the editor of an industry magazine, for example, Dr. Weese explained that the College would be revising its MSFS degree program to keep up with developments in the industry that "will not ever be as they were in the 1970s or 1960s."[44] In discussing his goals for the College, Weese added, "We have to work more closely with the American Society. Too often in the past the two organizations have gone their own ways."[45]

On January 18, 1989, Weese sent a Boettner Research Institute "personal update" to all College and Society personnel to announce the appointment of Neal E. Cutler as professor of gerontology and social policy and as a director of the Boettner Research Institute. Cutler, a Northwestern University PhD, had been a Fulbright fellow and had held a University of Southern California professorship of political science and gerontology.[46]

Although Dr. Cutler's official title differed somewhat from that held by Davis W. Gregg, the new professor actually replaced Gregg in the Boettner teaching chair. Davis W. Gregg would now become the founding director of the Boettner Research Institute. Helen L. Schmidt, recently honored for 40 years' work at the College, also moved to part-time status as a research associate.[47]

In a world increasingly accustomed to acronyms and an industry positively addicted to their use, the College and the American Society introduced still another one in early 1989—PACE, which stands for Professional Achievement in Continuing Education. The PACE program, which had been in the planning stage for more than a year and mentioned in general terms by President Weese early in his administration, was now reported in detail and hailed as an excellent example of cooperative effort by the two organizations.

PACE was designed to become a mandatory program as new matriculants joined the College, in keeping with the continuing education requirements of other professions. Dr. Weese noted, "To remain fully equipped to meet the public's needs CLUs and ChFCs have to continually update their knowledge."[48]

PACE would work on a system of 2-year reporting periods during which 60 hours of academic credit had to be earned. Noncompliance would bring suspension of the right to use the CLU and ChFC designations and ineligibility for American Society membership.[49] The new program would become effective on July 1, 1989. It would be offered on a voluntary basis to persons holding these designations at that time and to current students who had already matriculated before that date. It was made clear, however, that "once an individual volunteers to commit to PACE, the commitment is irrevocable."[50] By their example, President Samuel H. Weese, Academic Vice President Gary K. Stone, and Board Chairman Marvin D. Bower got the new PACE program off to a strong start by signing their "Consent Forms" to participate in the effort.[51]

Soon after the PACE announcement in the United States, College Vice President and Treasurer Charles S. DiLullo, CLU, ChFC, went to Israel for the second annual CLU conferment at the Jacob Sharin College of Insurance at Tel Aviv University. He described the PACE program to the graduates and presented a "Proclamation of Lasting Friendship" to the sponsors of the Israeli CLU program.

Charles DiLullo was an ideal representative for the College, having joined the institution in 1970 as controller and adding the role of vice president for financial administration in 1973 and the title of treasurer in 1975. In recent years he has added faculty responsibilities to his wide-ranging duties. As a senior member of management, DiLullo has served under three of the College's seven presidents.

When people think about life insurance careers, the first job that often comes to mind is that of sales representative. Yet the success of salespersons depends heavily upon the qualifications of management, particularly the general agent in the field who has the responsibility to recruit and train new agents, as well as oversee their development in the years that follow. As former John Hancock Mutual Life general agent Vincent C. Bowhers explains, "The vast majority of personal producers respond very favorably to a close working relationship with their agency managers."[52]

The American College had long recognized the need for management education. As early as 1930 it had offered certificate courses and diplomas in agency and company management. These were followed by the Management Learning Series courses. The major opportunity to advance management education came about when Richard D. Irwin gave the College a $2.5 million gift that was used to endow the graduate management program in 1982, which made possible a Master of Science in Management. The College created the Richard D. Irwin Graduate School of Management in his honor.

Richard D. Irwin was president of the famous publishing firm that bears his name. He and Davis W. Gregg had been friends and business associates for years. Many of the College textbooks were published by Irwin while Gregg was editor of the Irwin Insurance Series. An oil painting of the well-known publisher hangs on the third floor of the Gregg Conference Center as a lasting tribute.

During the Jordan years 1985–1988, the College had plans to introduce an Executive Management education program that would include formal classes on campus for the students selected by companies for the program. The concept never became operational, however, and was abolished when Sam Weese became president. He directed the management faculty to return to the previous management curriculum and to immediately begin an update of these earlier developed courses.

By early 1989, with these courses restructured, President Weese announced the reactivation of the MSM degree program. It would combine customary distance education methods with periods of Bryn Mawr campus study. "We have the faculty and support resources to help meet these educational needs, and the College is dedicated to this challenge," the president said.[53]

Dr. Weese presided over an educational first for the College that spring by hosting a 3-day symposium May 3–5 titled "Brussels to Beijing: Prospects and Challenges for Life Insurance and Financial Services."[54] The symposium for senior management officials focused on the opportunities and challenges facing U.S.-headquartered financial services companies operating in the Far East and Europe. Richard Collins, president of American Life Insurance Company, and Prudential's International Insurance Department CEO Nicholas Graves cochaired the symposium. "The American College has an obligation to take a leadership role in considering emerging issues that will impact our industry in the 1990s," said Dr. Weese.[55]

Three weeks after the symposium, W. Lee Hoskins, president of the Federal Reserve Bank of Cleveland, delivered the 1989 Frank M. Engle Lecture at the Bryn Mawr campus. Hoskins titled his lecture "Reforming the Banking Industry: Assessing Structure, Regulation, and Risk."

With the coming of summer Board Chairman Marvin D. Bower announced a number of new trustee appointments made at the annual meeting when three men, among them John B. Carter, retired from the board and seven new trustees joined the governing group. The freshmen included company leaders, Million Dollar Round Table members, a former university president, and a University of Pennsylvania professor.[56] Four were CLUs and three were PhDs. One of the new trustees, Jerry S. Rosenbloom, now Insurance Department chairman at the Wharton School, was a former American College professor. Among the others were Warren W. Deakins, CLU, ChFC, Fidelity Mutual Life CEO; and Edwin T. Johnson, CLU, president of Johnson Companies, Newtown Square, Pennsylvania.

One of the ongoing trustees, Equitable agent Millard J. Grauer, who had visited Israel the previous year, served as chairman of the Executive Steering Committee of an International Forum in Bryn Mawr that June. In an endeavor that would have pleased Solomon S. Huebner and that also echoed the earlier efforts of Davis W. Gregg, the College hosted 25 educators and insurance leaders from such countries as Belgium and India, Japan and the United Kingdom to discuss the International Forum's feasibility and to delineate its mission. A press release explained, "Membership in the International Forum will consist of not-for-profit institutions with interest in the professional development of life insurance and related financial services."[57]

Although the concept of such an international forum appeared at that time to have merit, the practical aspects of limited budgets and wide-ranging educational levels in different countries inhibited the organization's progress. As a result, it was defunct within 3 years.

Behind the scenes, Dr. Weese had begun to confront the internal financial difficulties facing the College. While the balance sheet for the year ending June 30, 1988, showed an excess of income over expenditures of $1,750,764, this seemingly favorable result included contributions of $3,269,376.[58] Operating revenues were insufficient to cover costs, which were too high.[59] The College's pattern of running operating deficits could not continue.

Faculty and staff positions had grown from 145 in 1975 to 183 a decade later—an increase of 26 percent. This fact forced the president to be more pragmatic about jobs and to reduce the payroll. By June 30, 1989, he had cut expenditures for salaries and employee benefits by more than $720,000 as the number of College employees dropped to 172. Meanwhile, gross operating revenues rose by more than $1 million that year to reach $18,898,307, compared to only $13,002,990 in the 12-month period ending June 30, 1983.[60]

Dr. Weese initiated a major restructuring of the College's organization with changes beginning at the highest levels. He accepted the resignations of C. Carter Marsden, vice president of marketing, and Richard Lincoln, vice president of evaluation and planning. President Weese also accepted the decision of Gordon K. Rose, CLU, ChFC, director of the Development Office, to join the ranks of the retired after serving the College faithfully for 20 years in a variety of capacities.

As previously mentioned briefly, Dr. Weese had also accepted the resignation of Robert W. Cooper, dean of the Huebner School. If the College had named a most valuable player during the decade of the 1980s it surely would have been Cooper. Unanimously recognized as the hardest-working academic at the College, Dr. Cooper was known for his hands-on style of management. He carefully reviewed and critiqued nearly every course manuscript that was printed. His knowledge of the technical content of each course was legendary among faculty and staff; his standards for high-quality educational output were recognized by all. Dr. Cooper had been planning for some time to return to a traditional academic faculty position, and when the opportunity arose at Drake University, he decided to accept it.

Two prominent graduate faculty members also resigned in the late 1980s to pursue new opportunities. Herbert Chasman, the former dean of the Graduate School, decided to join a Philadelphia law firm after nearly 10 years as a well-known professor of estate planning at the College. Shortly thereafter, Robert LeClair, PhD, a highly regarded College finance professor, decided to join the faculty at nearby Villanova University. LeClair had played a key role in the 2-

week graduate residency programs of the 1970s and 1980s that were extremely popular with the students who attended them.

As individuals left the College, new people joined. One of them, Stephen D. Tarr, CLU, ChFC, took charge of the Development Office, replacing Gordon K. Rose. Vane B. Lucas had hired Rose in 1969 as director of candidate development to increase the matriculation of designation candidates. He was ultimately asked to serve in the Development Office as manager of annual giving. By 1988, Golden Key activity had slumped to only 242 new pledges in contrast to well over 1,000 new pledges 10 years earlier.

Weese brought Tarr in as vice president of development to improve the situation. Stephen Tarr had gained experience at College Life Insurance Company Indianapolis, Lincoln National Life, and as agency head for Farm Family Life in Albany, New York.[61] In bringing Tarr to the College the president said, "He is a welcome addition to the College management team."[62]

National news of those days included a revelation that the IRS lost 2 million tax returns and related documents a year and that *Modern Maturity* (with a circulation of over 23 million copies) had become the best-read magazine in the country.[63]

The College sponsored several campus conferences in late summer that year. Although humorist Fred Allen describes a conference as a gathering of important people who singly can do nothing but together can decide that nothing can be done, the College had proved the value of conferences on many past occasions. On August 28 a 3-day Agency Management meeting began, which stressed leadership skills and was presented by such faculty members as John W. Cronin and Glenn Boseman.[64] A month later the College's Boettner Institute hosted a 3-day Retirement Planning session led by Neal E. Cutler.[65]

During the last months of 1989, the College recognized a number of individuals for their exceptional service. Samuel H. Weese honored Davis W. Gregg with a campus reception to mark 40 years of leadership. Solomon S. Huebner Gold Medals went to former trustee Leo R. Futia and to life trustee Sidney P. Marland, Jr. Futia was also the former chairman and CEO of Guardian Life Insurance Company; Marland had been a distinguished career educator.

Board Chairman Marvin D. Bower addressed more than 900 new CLUs and ChFCs at the 62d conferment exercises in San Diego on October 7, 1989. Urging the new designees to support the PACE program, Bower said, "All of us are finding the need to continue our professional education."[66]

That fall the College also announced the inauguration of the recently endowed Henry A. Deppe Lecture Series devoted to pensions and retirement security issues. The Deppe Lectures would be supported by friends and associates of the former Guardian Pension consultant who had built his own organization, National Pension Services, in White Plains, New York. Deppe presented the first lecture that November and titled it "Life Insurance in Qualified Retirement Plans—Forty Effective Reasons."[67]

*   *   *

January 1, 1990, began not only a new year but a new decade as well. It would be census time again, and this time the tabulation would reach 249 million people, compared to 226 million in 1980. Life expectancy at birth continued its rise to 75.4 years, up from 73.7 years a decade before. At The American College, however, a number of measurements moved in the opposite direction compared to the previous year. There was a decline in student matriculations from 12,389 to only 6,771. (Much of the decline was attributed to a rush by many new enrollees to matriculate before July 1, 1989, in order to escape the new continuing education mandate for all matriculants. Thus, the drastic decrease in the number of matriculants in 1990 was somewhat of an aberration since the number of new Huebner School students rose to nearly 8,000 in 1991.) Of greater concern was the decline of new CLUs from 2,264 to 1,574 and new ChFCs from 2,284 to 1,293 that same year.

The new president faced these decreases head-on as he continued to address the three priorities he had set upon taking office: attending to the College's financial situation, strengthening its relationship with the Society, and improving industry ties. The Golden Key Society's 30th anniversary gave him an opportunity to emphasize all three simultaneously. Although improving the College's income-expense ratio began with cutting costs, increases in gift income would further help the financial picture. The Development Department had organized a Golden Key Society focus group that had come to the campus a few months earlier to study the Golden Key Society program. Trustee William W. Fenniman had conducted this meeting, which had brought together a mix of people who had been involved with the Golden Key Society for a long time and some who had not been involved before at all.[68]

Soon thereafter Development and Society Relations Vice President Stephen D. Tarr announced a 1,000-key goal to be met by June 30, 1990. Since some of the earlier Golden Key Society 10-year pledges had not been renewed and others had lapsed before completion, fresh commitments were crucial. Tarr involved both the College National Annual Giving Council and the Society's 228 Golden Key Society chapter chairpersons in this new effort. Six such chapters hosted special one-day programs in their respective cities for local leaders to meet representatives from the College and the Society. Alumni and friends would now have the opportunity to upgrade old pledges, make new ones, or if neither option met a donor's needs, to make a contribution on a year-to-year basis.[69]

In February the *National Underwriter* reported that the College's customized education for individual companies was "a big hit with agents and insurers."[70] Because the NALU's initial opposition to the ChFC designation had been a problem in the early 1980s, this endorsement was particularly welcome. At one time the NALU president, H. Kirke Lewis, CLU, ChFC, had declared that the ChFC program "would have an enormous and confusing impact on the public perception of life underwriters."[71] Later, however, the NALU renewed its commitment to The American College and pledged wholehearted support.[72]

Close cooperation with another industry association was evident in March 1990 when president Samuel H. Weese announced a new policy with the Life Underwriter Training Council, whereby an LUTCF (as a holder of its designation was called) would automatically receive credit for one course toward the CLU or ChFC designation. "This means," Weese explained, "those who meet the criteria can earn a CLU or ChFC designation by successfully completing nine Huebner School courses rather than the 10 courses usually required."[73]

James Tobin, PhD, Sterling professor of economics emeritus at Yale University, gave the 13th Frank M. Engle Lecture on April 19, 1990. Dr. Tobin, a former adviser to President John F. Kennedy and Federal Reserve System consultant, titled his address "Social Security, Federal Debt, and Economic Growth."[74] The formal invitation to the lecture indicated that attendance would earn CLUs and ChFCs 2 hours of continuing education credit under the PACE program.

A month later several distinguished visitors came to the Bryn Mawr campus for a 2-day conference cosponsored by the College and the Life Insurance Marketing and Research Association to discuss "Post-1992 Opportunities for U.S. Financial Services in an Integrated Europe." Dr. Weese noted that the conference would "recognize the interdependence of banking and insurance in the European marketplace."[75]

Within a matter of weeks the College participated in a different program with another organization. This time two American College professors went to Newark, New Jersey, to take part in the Society's Agent and Broker Liability Conference on June 8. Robin Derry, PhD, Charles Lamont Post professor of ethics, spoke on "Professionalism, Liability, and Ethical Behavior." Her cohort, Jeffrey B. Kelvin, JD, associate professor of taxation, presented "An Overview of Federal Securities Law."[76]

While these outreach programs to and with other organizations were taking place, President Weese found time to plan another event in connection with the June trustees meeting. He proposed that the College honor two retiring life trustees—James B. Irvine, Jr., and Sidney P. Marland, Jr.—at a special dinner on June 21.[77] The former MDRT president and the one-time U.S. Commissioner of Education both held the Solomon S. Huebner Gold Medal. The College had named a total of 21 life trustees since creating the title in 1938, but these two men were the first to reach mandatory retirement age while holding that rank.[78]

After more than 18 months in office, Samuel H. Weese had managed to cut payroll costs and increase operating revenue, and he was pleased to see the beginning of a new fundraising effort. The fundraising campaign, however, had not been in effect long enough to make a difference (contributions actually declined from $2,665,632 for the year ending June 30, 1989, to $2,275,581 by June 30, 1990). Furthermore, reduced enrollment had lowered student-fee income, which partially offset the decrease in personnel expenses. These various factors reduced total income from $19,293,568 to $18,033,925 within the same 12-month period. Even worse, $1,673,194 in deferred real estate taxes had become due and had to be paid.[79] Much remained to be done to assure the financial stability of the College.

Most academic endeavors experience a renascence in late summer and early autumn. The American College was no exception, forming a partnership at that time in 1990 with the Financial Satellite Network to effect nationwide television distribution of continuing education material. Within a year, however, the network was in financial trouble and soon disappeared—an idea ahead of its time.[80]

The Boettner Research Institute made College news in October by sponsoring a lecture by Miltida White Riley, Rutgers University professor of sociology emerita, on "Aging in the 21st Century." Soon thereafter Helen L. Schmidt, who had recently been working as a part-time Boettner associate, received the Solomon S. Huebner Gold Medal for 41 uninterrupted years of service to the College. Dr. Davis W. Gregg made the presentation in a special ceremony on the Bryn Mawr campus.[81]

President Weese presented a second 1990 Huebner Gold Medal to Home Life CEO William B. Wallace at the New Orleans conferment exercises on October 20. At that time Wallace served as vice chairman of the College trustees.[82]

The graduates that day brought the total CLU designees in 63 years to more than 70,000 and the number of ChFCs since 1982 to over 22,000. Nevertheless, LIMRA reported a 17 percent decline in the number of policies sold in the period 1983–1989, as well as a decrease in earnings throughout much of the industry. Despite what conferment speaker Denis F. Mullane called "disconcerting trends," he resolutely forecast that the new decade would provide "a marvelous opportunity to create a new, more beneficial industry structure."[83]

Mullane's statement proved to be more than wishful thinking, and the College would have the satisfaction of knowing that its program of continued high-quality education brought tangible benefits to its graduates. A Life Insurance Marketing and Research Association survey that fall confirmed higher income for CLUs than for nondesignees and even greater advantage for holders of the ChFC. This LIMRA survey also disclosed that designation-educated agents were far more likely to achieve Million Dollar Round Table status than nondesignee salespeople: 59.7 percent of ChFCs and 42.5 percent of CLUs, compared to only 26.2 percent of those without either title.[84]

The merging of the two Germanys and Iraq's invasion of Kuwait dominated world events that year, while the United States healthcare spending topped $650 million and the District of Columbia area counted 703 homicides. The American College conducted its own survey of the nation's most successful financial consultants and found that a majority of them believed that the field was growing or at least remaining stable. Although a substantial minority were less optimistic, Weese remarked, "There is unanimity on at least two key issues: the critical importance of professional education and credentials in building public confidence, and the continuing urgency of informing the public of the precise nature of the valuable services we provide."[85]

NOTES

1. James L. Fisher, *The Board and the President* (New York: Macmillan), 1991, p. 42.
2. Ibid.
3. The American College news release, February 1, 1988.
4. John D. Gatewood, interview with the author, May 2, 1995.
5. Letter to John B. Carter, July 30, 1987.
6. Ibid.
7. *Search Status Report,* Spencer Stuart Consultants, June 1988.
8. Memorandum to the author, April 26, 1996.
9. *The American College Outlook,* spring 1988, p. 1.
10. Interview with the author, April 27, 1996.
11. *Who's Who in America* (Chicago: Marquis-Who's Who, Inc.), 1996, vol. 2, p. 4386.
12. *Search Status Report,* p. 1.
13. Dan M. McGill, letter to John B. Carter, July 30, 1987.
14. Interview with the author, April 25, 1996.
15. The American College news release, February 1988.
16. Ibid.
17. Ibid., March 25, 1988.
18. Ibid.
19. *Outlook,* summer 1988, p. 5.
20. Doremus Public Relations news release, April 11, 1988.
21. H. Robert Heller, Frank M. Engle Lecture, "Imbalances and Asymmetries in the World Economy," April 21, 1988.
22. *Outlook,* spring 1988, p. 3.
23. Ibid.
24. Doremus Public Relations news release, June 8, 1988.
25. *Outlook,* summer 1988, p. 1.
26. *Search Status Report,* p. 4.
27. The American College news release, June 28, 1988.
28. *Outlook,* summer 1988, p. 1.
29. Ibid.
30. Paul Dickson, *Timelines* (Reading, MA: Addison-Wesley Publishing Co., Inc.), 1990, pp. 297–299.
31. William E. Kingsley, American Life Insurance Association, interview with the author, April 7, 1995.
32. John C. Bogle, interview with the author, January 23, 1995.
33. Interview with the author, April 25, 1996.
34. President's report to the trustees, June 24, 1988.
35. The American College news release, August 1988.
36. *Brief in Opposition to Petition for Allowance of Appeal from the Order of the Commonwealth Court,* Henry B. Fitzpatrick, Jr., Esq., November 23, 1988, p. 9.
37. William H. Lowery, Esq., memorandum to Samuel H. Weese, August 30, 1988.
38. Interview with the author, November 11, 1994.
39. The American College news release, October 10, 1988.
40. *Outlook,* spring 1989, pp. 1–3.
41. Ibid.

42. Ibid., pp. 1–4.
43. The American College news release, January 6, 1989.
44. *Life Association News,* January 1989.
45. Ibid., pp. 39, 42.
46. *Outlook,* spring 1989, p. 3.
47. Samuel H. Weese memo, January 18, 1989.
48. *Outlook,* spring 1989, p. 1.
49. Ibid.
50. The American College news release, February 16, 1989.
51. *Outlook,* summer 1989, cover and p. 2.
52. *Readings and Applications in Ethics for Field Managers* (Bryn Mawr, PA: The American College), 1993.
53. *Outlook,* spring 1989, p. 1.
54. Proceedings of the Symposium, The American College, May 3, 1989.
55. The American College news release, April 17, 1989.
56. Ibid., August 9, 1989.
57. Ibid., July 28, 1989.
58. Coopers & Lybrand, Certified Public Accountants.
59. Charles S. DiLullo, interview with the author, April 1996.
60. Carl Marinelli, memorandum to Samuel H. Weese, October 10, 1995.
61. Stephen D. Tarr, interview with the author, April 6, 1995.
62. The American College news release, October 15, 1989.
63. Dickson, *Timelines,* pp. 306, 307.
64. *Outlook,* spring 1989, p. 4.
65. Ibid., summer 1989, p. 3.
66. Ibid., fall/winter 1989, p. 1.
67. *The American College Catalog,* 1989–1990, p. 43.
68. *Outlook,* spring 1990, p. 2.
69. Samuel H. Weese, interview with the author, May 16, 1996.
70. *National Underwriter,* February 12, 1990, p. 1.
71. Letter to Davis W. Gregg, April 30, 1981.
72. *National Underwriter,* July 11, 1981.
73. The American College news release, March 12, 1990.
74. Frank M. Engle Lecture, April 19, 1990, invitation.
75. Doremus Public Relations news release, April 16, 1990.
76. The American College news release, May 9, 1990.
77. Letter to Board Chairman Marvin D. Bower, March 29, 1990.
78. Ibid.
79. Report on Examination of Financial Statements, Coopers & Lybrand, June 30, 1990.
80. Gavin Anderson Doremus & Company news release, September 12, 1990.
81. *Outook,* spring 1991, p. 7.
82. Ibid., p. 8.
83. Ibid., p. 3.
84. Doremus Public Relations news release, September 12, 1996.
85. The American College news release, December 28, 1990.

12

The Margin of Excellence

Time Bears Away all Things, Even our Minds.

Virgil

Fresh concepts and new procedures that had been developed during the previous decade or so created a commercial climate in the early 1990s that dramatically changed the circumstances of American business. Copiers replaced carbon paper and the mimeograph machine, computers superseded card files, and numerous jobs disappeared, including those of most gas station attendants, paperboys, and milkmen.

The stock market boomed as the number of mutual investment funds jumped from 564 in 1980 to 3,347 in 1991; consumer spending rose as supermarket products grew from 9,000 in 1976 to more than 30,000 by 1991.[1] The life insurance industry, however, did not keep pace. Although by this time Americans had invested over $1.6 trillion (or about 5 percent of their disposable income) in 2,115 life insurance companies in the United States, the risk-protection business had experienced flat sales for 20 years.[2]

In response to the rampant inflation and unfixed interest rates of the 1970s, the industry during the 1980s had moved toward financial planning and equity-based life insurance products. The 1990s brought more annuities and universal, then variable, life products, which in effect cannibalized traditional business—companies scored record sales, but many of those sales were replacements of products sold earlier. During this period, survival had become the key issue for insurers.[3] Several companies merged; a few failed. Many reduced dividends and hired fewer sales representatives. Some sought experienced agents from competitors rather than train their own.

These factors affected The American College through lower student matriculations, reduced course registrations, and ultimately fewer designations awarded. As previously noted, the College's 1989 PACE program of mandatory continuing education for CLU and ChFC designees may have been aggravating this situation. In his 1991 annual report President Samuel H. Weese noted a drop from 11,800 to 8,200 new student matriculations between 1989–1990 and more than 4,000 fewer Huebner School course registrations for the same period.[4]

The resilient president did more than merely chronicle the challenge, however. He moved purposely to confront it within the framework of a long-range plan developed by consultant John Glennie, the College management, faculty, and the trustee Steering Committee and approved by the board the previous June. At that time the College endorsed a strategy "to develop more fully the opportunities that currently exist as well as those that would appear in the future."[5]

In this decision, which echoed the 18th century wisdom of Edmund Burke's warning "never to plan the future by the past,"[6] the College would steer a middle course between cutting back the institution's size and scope to gain quick financial strength and moving into areas in which it had no experience. "We have made a commitment to proceed toward becoming a fully developed educational institution," Dr. Weese explained. "Our plan is to continue to provide quality education, primarily on a distance basis, for the life insurance professional."[7]

A succession of annual business plans designed to make the College a financially stronger educational enterprise, and in this way to improve its ability to meet its mission, facilitated the tactical implementation of the strategic plan.[8] The long-range plan was not simply a reflection of executive ego or institutional prestige but was based upon product value and program merit.

The College designations had long represented both attributes, a fact that gave credibility to early 1991 efforts to promote a new combined study program awarding successful candidates both the CLU and the ChFC designations upon graduation. A survey at that time revealed that CLU agents earned an average gross medium income 54 percent higher than agents without either credential.[9]

In the broadest sense all The American College courses and programs represented continuing education.[10] The original CLU designation and the later ChFC could be so described, as well as the subsequent masters degree offerings. PACE reconfirmed this commitment in 1989 as the College intensified its efforts toward insurance agents and brokers who needed to fulfill state continuing education requirements to maintain their licenses.

Now with a clearer definition of institutional mission in hand, the College began a course of action to achieve those objectives. President Weese went to New York City on March 12, 1991, for a press briefing to introduce a new series of self-study guides designed specifically for continuing education (CE) programs. He was joined by vice presidents of major insurance companies that had already endorsed the program.

Noting that "for 63 years The American College has set the educational standard for the life insurance industry," Samuel H. Weese announced that the new CE courses would be accepted for PACE credit. Furthermore, Weese reported that a number of state insurance departments had already approved the new courses and assigned credit value to them.[11]

Institutional plans are effective only if they are able to move out of the planning stages and become a reality. It is at this juncture that the right kind of corporate leadership proves pivotal. Weese provided that leadership. Although a contemporary management consultant, Richard Hagberg, believes that many CEOs are "lousy leaders" and compares them to "Rambos in pinstripes"[12] because they fail to build relationships with boards and employees, that certainly does not describe the executive style of Samuel H. Weese.

The American College president, from the start of his administration, had established close ties with his department heads. He worked well with Vice President Gary K. Stone, Vice President and Treasurer Charles S. DiLullo, Marketing and Communications Vice President William J. Lombardo, and Vice President of Development Stephen D. Tarr, speaking with these men on a daily basis.

Much as he depended on these core relationships, the president also continued his efforts to strengthen the entire faculty and total management team. In spring 1991 he announced two new appointments. In April Richard H. Viola, PhD, was named director of the Richard D. Irwin Graduate School of Management where he had been a professor for several years.[13] Before coming to the College, Dr. Viola had spent 17 years in the School of Business and Management at Temple University, and he had studied under the renowned Peter Drucker.

A few months later M. Donald Wright, JD, CPA, was named to head the Graduate School of Financial Sciences on the Bryn Mawr campus. Wright, an adjunct professor of financial planning at the College since 1988, had been a partner with Arthur Andersen & Company for more than 20 years. At the internationally known public accounting firm Wright had gained experience in financial planning seminar leadership and the development of internal training courses in financial and estate planning. "We're delighted that Don has agreed to build the MSFS curriculum," Weese said. "His years of leadership in financial services will keep our program in the forefront of financial education."[14]

The Frank M. Engle Lecture in Economic Security helped maintain academic momentum for the 14th consecutive year when the campus hosted the annual event that April 30. Newly appointed Frank M. Engle Professor of Economics Michael D. White, PhD, CLU, ChFC, introduced the 1991 speaker, Robert E. Litan, JD, PhD, senior fellow in economic studies at the Brookings Institution in Washington, DC. The noted banking expert addressed some 200 insurance and banking professionals on the subject "Trouble in the U.S. Financial Service Industry: Why Should We Care and What Should We Do about It?"[15] Dr. Litan told the audience that "banks should only be permitted to sell insurance through separate affiliates funded with uninsured instruments and then only if the bank operations of the conglomerate are heavily insulated from the nonbanking activities."[16]

Dr. Richard Viola presented a 1991 campus Leadership Forum in early May. The College limited the program to 25 general agents and managers with less than 5 years' experience in their current positions. Industry leaders joined College faculty to examine such subjects as "Evaluating Your Leadership Style" and "Effective Leadership in an Era of Unprecedented Change."[17] These forums were highly successful and have been continued to the present.

The administration kept the Gregg Conference Center humming with activity that season with the second annual Advanced Business Planning

Conference during the first week of June. The 2 1/2-day program concluded with a hands-on workshop to address issues affecting a closely held business. Theodore T. Kurlowicz, JD, CLU, ChFC, and Jeffrey B. Kelvin, JD, CLU, ChFC, associate professors of taxation, headed a faculty group that took part. Participants in the Leadership Forum and the Advanced Business Planning Conference earned PACE credits for their attendance.[18]

The Professional Achievement in Continuing Education program began to prove its worth as an increasing number of states agreed to accept the College's PACE courses for credit in their respective mandatory CE programs for life insurance agents seeking to retain their licenses. In May that year John R. Driskill, the Society's executive vice president, announced that Kentucky had taken that important step. Washington would soon follow, with Iowa, Maine, and New Hampshire joining the growing group of states whose departments of insurance endorsed the PACE program.[19]

Since part of the College's emphasis on continuing education involved encouraging CLUs and others to attain the Chartered Financial Consultant designation, President Weese was very pleased about that summer's poll results showing strong alumni support for the ChFC program. Solomon S. Huebner School Director James F. Ivers, III, reported that 85 percent of recent designees "enjoyed the prestige and professionalism imparted by the credential."[20]

These 1991 campus and insurance industry events took place against a backdrop of the liberation of Kuwait on the world scene as United States and allied forces defeated Iraq in a sensational 100-hour war. Domestic news combined culture and commerce. John Updike's novel *Rabbit at Rest* won a Pulitzer prize, as did Neil Simon's play *Lost in Yonkers*. The Dow Jones stock average topped 3,000 for the first time, but unemployment rose to a 5-year high of 6.7 percent. AT&T acquired NCR to create a $7.9 billion company in one of the largest corporate mergers of those days.[21]

In Bryn Mawr The American College trustee family experienced several changes in 1991: The board mourned the sudden death of its recently retired leader, replaced the chairman who had completed his term, and elected six new members. Let's take a closer look at these changes and the contributions the individuals made to the College.

Former chairman John B. Carter died unexpectedly on May 21 of complications following heart surgery. He had been an extraordinary supporter of The American College as he climbed the ladder of success at the Equitable Life Assurance Society to become its president and CEO. According to College President Samuel H. Weese, "Few people realize how much influence John Carter has had over the infrastructure of the industry. He chaired search committees that selected leaders of HIAA, LUTC, and The American College. No one has made a greater contribution of time to these industry organizations in the past several years."[22] The trustees passed a memorial resolution that said, "Throughout his momentous career, John Carter was recognized for his genuine affection for people. He was a charismatic leader and a caring humanitarian."[23]

At the annual board meeting that summer Marvin D. Bower completed his 2-year term as chairman. An enthusiastic fellow trustee noted that while the State Farm chief executive was not a highly visible person throughout the industry, his somewhat retiring nature enabled him to provide subtle and effective leadership at the College, which awarded him the Solomon S. Huebner Gold Medal that year. Bower's advice to the president was to "keep it simple, do it well."[24]

When William B. Wallace succeeded Bower, he became the 10th board chairman in the 64-year history of The American College. Wallace, a former varsity football star at Columbia University (where he graduated in 1952), served briefly in the U.S. Navy and then spent his entire business career with the Home Life Insurance Company, later overseeing its merger with Phoenix Mutual Life in 1993. He completed his illustrious career as president and COO of the new company, Phoenix-Home Mutual Life.

Wallace began his association with The American College by flunking his first CLU examination, but the experience "taught me respect for the program,"[25] he later said. Davis W. Gregg invited him to become a College trustee in 1978 after hearing his articulate executive address at the General Agents and Managers Association (GAMA) conference.[26] Wallace progressed from one influential role to another as an able and enthusiastic board member. He served on the Educational Policy Committee, and he proved to be a particularly successful College fundraiser. Wallace would continue to be both a forceful speaker and a thoughtful listener.

This change of command was accompanied by the election of new trustees. The freshmen board members brought the College a combination of company executive experience and industry association leadership. Four of the six were alumni. One of the others was an insurance company president, while the sixth had been a state insurance commissioner and former president of the National Association of Insurance Commissioners. The new trustees were Vincent C. Bowhers, CLU, ChFC, general agent at John Hancock; Glenn A. Britt, CLU, executive vice president of State Farm Life; Louis G. Lower, II, Allstate Life president; John B. Peyton, CLU, ChFC, former Society president; Paul J. Shevlin, CLU, ChFC, MSFS, National Life Insurance Company of Vermont general agent in nearby Newtown Square; and Richard E. Stewart, chairman of Stewart Economics, Inc., and a former state insurance regulator. Glenn Britt's election is noteworthy in that, with Marvin Bower's retirement, Britt continued the connection between the College and State Farm Life Insurance Company. Britt's service on the board would lead to his succeeding Bower as chairman.

After a relatively tranquil summer, the campus featured a number of interesting autumn programs, beginning with the third annual Henry A. Deppe Lecture on September 12. The lecturer was Andrew J. Fair, Esq., whose subject was "Life Insurance in Qualified Plans."[27]

The most significant event of the fall, however, was the October 25 dedication of the John F. Savage Educational Forum, which formalized the completion of a $325,000 construction project of the fourth floor of the Gregg Conference Center. The space was transformed into a professional classroom facility, a reception area, and a multitude of small breakout rooms. The funds were raised in tribute to John Savage by 20 friends and associates of the legendary life insurance salesman, whose lecturers on successful selling were unmatched in the industry.

Librarian Judith L. Hill added icing to the academic cake at year-end by announcing that the Vane B. Lucas Memorial Library had installed a new on-line cataloging system called Sophie Z in memory of Charles J. Zimmerman's late sister, Sophie, in whose name the honorary board chairman had contributed $10,000 for the new system. (Later, Denis F. Mullane added $4,000 to complete the funding of the system.)

*   *   *

American business sent the nation mixed signals early in 1992. R.H. Macy went bankrupt on January 27, followed by TransWorld Airlines a few days later. Yet the Dow Jones industrial average reflected optimism about the future and reached an all-time high of 3,283 on February 24.[28] At The American College President Weese maintained the management style he had adopted at the beginning of his presidency 3 1/2 years before. That style is consistent with the words of Lord Sieff, former chairman of Marks & Spencer, who once remarked, "Leaders must be seen to be up front, up to date, up to their job, and up early in the morning."[29]

In early 1992 Dr. Weese reported that 51 computerized examination centers were added to the 54 available the year before. Although the College would still offer paper-and-pencil exams at some 60 centers overseas, the emphasis would now be on computer-based testing.

As we explained earlier, Examinations on Demand at the College began in 1983. They were first listed in the 1984 *Catalog* and contributed to the College's growth in the late 1980s and early 1990s. According to President Weese, "At a time when professional education is critical to the success of life insurance agents, we continue to find ways to better serve our 45,000 students. Now with these added centers, nearly every section of the country has an exam center within easy driving distance."[30] Not only did all CLU and ChFC courses have computerized EOD exams but the testing centers also had the capacity to offer EOD exams in the College's masters degree programs.

On campus the highly visible academic CEO determined to be heard as well as seen. Therefore Dr. Weese augmented his regular birthday luncheons and quarterly All Employee Meetings with monthly "President's Updates" beginning on February 25, 1992, "to keep everyone better informed as to what is happening at the College."[31] Although he knew the importance of positive employee momentum and the value of what another corporate head called "an atmosphere of mental excitement,"[32] the president struck a somber note in his first epistle. He reported an unacceptable $900,000 deficit for the first 6 months of the current fiscal year, and he announced plans to eliminate the deficit by the end of the year and to move the College's operations into a positive position.

President Weese's management plan was to reduce expenses for the first 6 months of 1992. There would be less use of outside consultants and vendors, more emphasis on implementing the strategic business plan, and greater focus on institutional accountability. In referring to the excellent ideas reaching him through the campus suggestion boxes, the president expressed confidence that this program would also be beneficial to the College.[33]

Ever seeking greater outreach to broader insurance markets, the College began a series of regional meetings to encourage the inclusion of minorities in the College's CLU/ChFC program. Working in conjunction with William Klauber, Life Underwriter Training Council president, the College held focus groups around the country (the first had been held in New York City in December 1991). President Weese then went to the West Coast in April 1992 for five meetings in Los Angeles and San Francisco with focus groups of Asian-Americans, Hispanics, and African-Americans.[34] There he gained valuable insights into the cultural differences of these groups in the context of providing professional education to meet their needs.[35]

By now the Frank M. Engle Lecture was a highly respected academic event that was known by thousands. Each year the lecture was published and distributed to a wide-ranging audience of academic and business economists. The 1992 lecture, held on campus in May, was given by the widely read *Business Week* columnist Paul Craig Roberts, III, whose topic was "Takings: The Economy and Legal and Property Rights." Dr. Roberts, holder of the William E. Simon Chair in Political Economy at the Center for Strategic and International Studies in Washington, DC, brought a conservative philosophy to his well-delivered presentation.

Although it had been almost exclusively male for a long time, the life insurance profession had gradually welcomed women, and The American College had done its part. In the early days there was author Mildred F. Stone, followed by Solomon S. Huebner gold medalist Helen L. Schmidt and Maxine B. Niemeyer, a college trustee for 14 years beginning in 1981. The College added more women to the faculty—for example, Constance J. Fontaine, JD, LLM, CLU, ChFC, associate professor of taxation, and Robin Derry, PhD, holder of the Charles Lamont Post Chair of Ethics and the Professions. During the 1980s the number of female students grew consistently, and the class of 1991 had 575 women. More than 20 percent of the matriculants in the Huebner School were female.

The College maintained this forward momentum by sponsoring a June 1992 "Women Managing in the Financial Services Professions" seminar. Professor of Management Richard H. Viola coordinated the event, which featured Linda S. Mayhew, CLU, ChFC, First Colony Life Insurance Company vice president; Christina Seix, Macay-Shields Financial Corporation CEO; and former trustee Maxine B. Niemeyer, president of Business and Estate Financial Coordinators, Inc.[36] President Weese summed up the event by saying: "It is imperative for industry leaders to realize the virtually untapped potential of females in the higher levels of corporate and field management."[37]

The crowded June that year reflected the increased activity level at the College compared to the less hurried tempo of earlier times. The College published a *Personal Financial Fact Finding* handbook coordinated by Graduate School of Financial Sciences Director M. Donald Wright. It also cosponsored a computerized bulletin board system with the Life Underwriter Training Council to provide information about the two organizations to agents throughout the country via personal computers.[38] The fiscal year that closed that June was a benchmark both financially and academically.

Dr. Weese made the most of the achievement when he reported 1991–1992 a positive 12-month period. Operating revenues reached a new high of $18.4 million with net revenues of $600,000. All academic statistics surged upward, too. New student matriculations reached 9,600, Huebner School course registrations rose 12 percent to 46,800, and graduate student numbers reflected similar growth.[39] To assure a continued sound fiscal base, the trustees voted an 8.7 percent tuition increase in the Huebner School registration fee, effective July 1. One justification for the increase was the inclusion of audio cassette review tapes as part of the study materials.

It is important to remember that the total revenues the College received each year had long included contributions from life insurance companies and alumni. This continued to be the case in the late 1980s and early 1990s. For example, the Golden Key Society honored Mutual Life of New York at its autumn 1991 annual luncheon for being the first insurance company to total 1,000 individual givers—MONY agents and employees who made personal gifts to the College— since the Golden Key Program was started.[40] Acacia Mutual Life of Washington, DC, gave $25,000 to upgrade the Hurson Exercise Room in the Gregg Conference Center (Daniel L. Hurson was a former chairman and CEO of Acacia Mutual). Company grants and agent gifts made possible the John F. Savage Educational Forum; New York Life and Top of the Table contributions paid for the New Hampshire Room in the residency wing of the Gregg Center to honor legendary agent Ben Feldman, CLU. Another $200,000 raised by the Advanced Association of Life Underwriters made possible the AALU-John Todd Research Foundation endowment to fund faculty and outside research projects. Best of all, 1992 marked the successful completion of payments totaling $9.3 million from the 1985 Corporate Capital Campaign designed to reduce the College's $14 million mortgage debt. The year also brought an increase of 13 percent in the number of individual donors over the 1991 level.[41]

On October 8 the College's former president, Davis W. Gregg, delivered a lecture on "The Human Wealth-Span: A Life-Span View of Financial Well-Being." Although the occasion seemed similar to other economic information programs at the College, it differed completely in background and therefore warrants a reprise of the events preceding it.

The College provided the venue for the lecture, but the Boettner Institute of Financial Gerontology at the University of Pennsylvania—named for benefactors Joseph and Ruth Boettner who had pledged a $1 million gift—actually sponsored it to publicize the Boettner Institute and add to the literature on this subject. It was the fourth in a series of such lectures that began in 1987, the year the Boettner Institute was accepted as a division of the College. Davis W. Gregg was director of its activities. Philosophical differences soon emerged, however, between Edward Jordan, then president of the College, and both Gregg and Boettner.

When Samuel H. Weese became president, he tried to recapture Boettner's enthusiasm but this proved difficult; when Neal E. Cutler replaced Gregg as director of the Boettner Institute in 1989, the situation became even more strained. Dr. Cutler wanted more policy independence. He saw value in affiliation with The American College, but he fought against College control. President Weese, on the contrary, saw the gerontology program as an arm of the College.[42]

Dispute arose over Dr. Gregg's desire to solicit contributions for the Boettner Institute using the same address as the College. College trustees believed that those solicited would be unaware that the Boettner Institute was not part of the College. Before year's end, it was decided by mutual agreement that the Boettner Institute would reorganize as an independent corporation and move its headquarters off campus.

Accordingly, on March 20, 1991, with the help of counsel Dechert Price & Rhoads, two things happened. The Commonwealth of Pennsylvania granted a charter to the Boettner Institute, and that same day the U.S. Internal Revenue Service confirmed its status as a tax-exempt 501(c)(3) charitable, educational, and scientific organization.[43] Helen L. Schmidt and Davis W. Gregg, however, continued to function in an office at the Gregg Conference Center on the College campus. The Boettner Institute's operations led by Dr. Cutler moved to the University of Pennsylvania's School of Arts and Sciences and signed a 5-year agreement of affiliation on April 1, 1992.

Soon after the Boettner Lecture that October, President Weese went to Orlando, Florida, for the American Society CLU & ChFC national conference and the annual College conferment. At the conference banquet Dr. Weese posthumously awarded the Solomon S. Huebner Gold Medal to the late John B. Carter and presented the medallion to his widow, Hope Carter, with these words: "The life insurance industry has been indelibly influenced by his caring, dedication and generosity." The president went on to say, "John Carter gave his heart and soul to this institution, leading the College at a crucial time when we were facing substantial problems and doubts about our future success."[44]

At the conferment exercises the following day the College awarded 2,181 CLU designations and 1,221 ChFCs for a total of 3,402 new Huebner School graduates. The median age of the Chartered Life Underwriters was 37; for Chartered Financial Consultants it was 38. More than 50 percent already held a bachelor's degree.[45] When Ernest E. Cragg, CLU, president emeritus of the Life Insurance Marketing and Research Association (LIMRA), delivered the conferment address, he told the graduates, "Your mission is to continuously place behind the family of the individual standing alone the incomparable strength of persons standing together. To ascertain and to understand this is, and must be, a part of your creed at all times."[46]

State Farm, Prudential, Equitable, Northwestern Mutual, and New York Life (in that order) led the list of life insurance companies with the largest number of new CLUs. The Equitable graduates included the mother/daughter combination of Patricia and Mary Jo Duncan who announced that they were also studying for their ChFCs.[47]

The shorter days of autumn presaged the finish of another year at The American College. President Weese and his colleagues had much to do before December 31, which, for the first time, would mark the simultaneous end of the College's calendar and fiscal years. The trustees had earlier approved the change from a July 1–June 30 operating schedule to match the prevailing pattern of the life insurance industry and most of the business world.

In late October there were two events worth mentioning. The Richard D. Irwin Graduate School of Management sponsored another in a series of 3-day Leadership Forums under the direction of Dr. Richard H. Viola. A few days later the College hosted its first graduate school homecoming, which featured both educational sessions and reunion activities for the classes of 1977 and 1982. As Dr. Weese explained, "We wanted to give graduates something of professional value along with the opportunity to renew old acquaintances and build new friendships."[48]

The College scheduled the fourth annual Henry A. Deppe Lecture on November 5 in New York City, where two of the three earlier talks had been given. Previous lecturer Andrew J. Fair, Esq., assumed the podium once again and spoke about "Distribution Planning and Uses of Life Insurance." A number of New York area chapters of the American Society of CLU & ChFC, along with the New York Estate Planning Council, cosponsored this event with the College. Much of the administrative support in New York came from Meryl Greyer, PhD, CLU, the executive director of the New York Chapter of CLU and ChFC. Guardian Life continued its financial support of the lecture, which attracted some 200 persons.

On the national scene Bill Clinton won the presidential election; in Bryn Mawr The American College closed the season with its ninth annual tax conference on December 8.

*   *   *

The barometer of the life insurance industry continued to register unsettled—even negative—conditions through the early 1990s. For example, the number of people entering the life insurance business was declining. Companies were hiring fewer trainees at a time when it had become socially fashionable to condemn insurers.[49] Even the best in the business reported problems. Million Dollar Round Table members experienced shrinking margins as expenses rose faster than income across the United States and Canada.[50]

Yet the College showed distinct improvements in its operations at that time. President Weese described 1992 as a banner year—and deservedly so.[51] The trustees' long-range plan and the annual business plan were paying off. At their January 21–22, 1993, meeting the trustees were pleased to learn that there were 10,000 more new matriculants in 1992 than in the previous year, and the total course registration figure was more than 56,000—the highest student activity level in over 10 years. These results reflected the change in the College's marketing strategy, which, among other things, encouraged general agents and managers to urge prospective students to continue their studies.[52]

Knowing that the past would not automatically guarantee the future, Dr. Weese nevertheless looked ahead with confidence to the challenges 1993 would bring. The year got underway with an early Gregg Conference Center reception to honor three artists whose pictures would be on exhibit through February. This watercolor show continued a College custom that began in 1977 of holding art exhibitions from time to time as a community service, as an employee benefit, and in the belief that "beauty in the environment is a motivating force for achievement in education."[53] Under the direction of one-time librarian, later archivist, Marjorie A. Fletcher, these popular programs enhanced the College's reputation as neighbors became better acquainted with the institution and artists gained greater respect for the gallery.

February that year was important for two more reasons. First, five employee action committees completed the reports arising from the Life Office Management Association (LOMA) personnel survey of the previous summer in which 87 percent of those on the College payroll participated. These committees had focused on the following areas: corporate values, management style and communication, training and education, position descriptions, and evaluation and reward.[54] Second, the College introduced an Insurance Warfare program in collaboration with the management consulting firm Baker, Rakich, Shipley & Politzer, Inc. The 3-day leadership program was designed to help industry leaders be more effective in their current positions and better prepared for added responsibilities in the future. The program presented by Baker, Rakich, Shipley & Politzer executives and College faculty members offered "a holistic understanding of life insurance in today's competitive environment."[55]

In addition to such one-time, specific-event joint endeavors, the College maintained ongoing relationships with such organizations as the American Society of CLU & ChFC, the American Institute for Chartered Property Casualty Underwriters, and the Society of Chartered Property and Casualty Underwriters. The College and these organizations sponsored an Ethics Awareness Month that March to increase awareness of the ethical issues facing the insurance and financial services industry. They conducted the program at local CLU/ChFC and CPCU chapter meetings across the country.[56]

While these nationwide sessions were taking place, the College president welcomed a six-person Middle States Association team, which visits the campus every 10 years as part of the accreditation evaluation process.[57] The College first achieved accreditation (according to a dictionary definition, accreditation means "certification of a school or college as meeting all formal requirements as of academic excellence, facilities") in 1978 and secured reaffirmation of this status at 5-year intervals thereafter. Each of these periodic reviews was preceded by a comprehensive *Self-Study.*

Preparation of the 1993 version began 2 years earlier and ran to more than 120 printed pages. As noted by Academic Vice President Gary K. Stone, the *Self-Study* involved most faculty members, many administrators, and other employees under the guidance of a steering committee. Ten subcommittees did much of the work. They reviewed the entire institutional operation but paid special attention to the graduate program, the ChFC designation, the examination delivery system, and the cost of student attrition.[58] The *Self-Study* reflected Dr. Stone's educational philosophy, which since his arrival 5 years earlier in 1988 was to simplify the curriculum, concentrate on courses in the academic areas of faculty expertise, include more practical applications in educational materials, and incorporate more of the basics of life and health insurance in introductory courses.[59]

The College's 5-year progress, particularly the improved financial picture, impressed the Middle States Association team, which sent President Weese a report following the visit. Word concerning formal accreditation renewal, however, would not come until the Middle States Association board of directors took action later that year.

While the College faculty and administration carried the major responsibility for the reaccreditation, the trustees oversaw the effort and concentrated on several issues distinctly their own. Two such matters came to the fore: debt elimination and tax reduction.

The Executive Committee met in New York City to plan liquidation of the long-term debt resulting from the construction of the Gregg Conference Center and the cumulative tax liability caused by the unsuccessful property tax litigation of the 1980s. The Executive Committee also discussed the possible sale of the 9+ acres of land known as the Carter property to help reduce annual real estate taxes.[60]

This property had been acquired in 1977 to complete Davis Gregg's master property acquisition plan. The size of the campus, however, had proven to be more than adequate without the additional acres, and because of real estate taxes, the extra land appeared to be a liability rather than an asset. Negotiations for its sale began in 1993.

Although T.S. Eliot described April as "the cruelest month," that adjective seemed inappropriate at The American College in 1993 when it held the 16th annual Frank M. Engle Lecture and published an important new book for life insurance general agents and managers throughout the industry. Walter E. Williams, PhD, distinguished professor of economics at George Mason University, delivered the lecture, "The Legitimate Role of Government in a Free Economy." Publication of *Managing Sales Professionals* maintained the College's tradition of offering high-quality educational materials. The 441-page volume was written by 25 successful managerial leaders with support from the

College faculty; Professor Glenn Boseman was the editor. Samuel H. Weese called the book "an extremely valuable resource for general agents and managers of all levels of experience."[61]

A present day educator writes, "In faculty eyes a president is 'new' if in office for less than 3 years and 'old' if in office for more than 5 years."[62] In June 1993 it had been 5 years since Dr. Weese's inauguration as president, but whether "new" or "old," the vigorous executive continued to address the constant challenge of changing business and social environments with a variety of innovative concepts and fresh techniques. The president took a "first-ever," 2-week family vacation but otherwise spent the summer hard at work. He announced certain new programs and revealed the results of ongoing projects. He also began a different working relationship with Denis F. Mullane, Connecticut Mutual Life chairman, who moved up from vice chairman to chairman of the Board of Trustees on June 18.

In assuming the board chairmanship Mullane became the fourth man to hold that post in the first 5 years of the Weese presidency. Samuel H. Weese had, in this short time span, worked under John B. Carter (1986–1989), Marvin D. Bower (1989–1991), William B. Wallace (1991–1993), and now Denis F. Mullane, since the revised bylaws of 1991 limited occupancy of the top position to 2 years.

Mullane had played varsity football at West Point, graduated from the Military Academy in 1952, served for 4 years as a lieutenant in the U.S. Army Corps of Engineers, and then resigned his commission to work at Connecticut Mutual Life Insurance Company. He began as a career agent, enjoyed each job that came his way, and rose to become CEO and chairman of the board of directors.

Along the way, Mullane became involved with The American College, joined the board of trustees, assumed increasing responsibility, and found himself the head of the College Board of Trustees and Connecticut Mutual concurrently. In achieving the top post at both organizations Mullane followed the example of his predecessor, Charles J. Zimmerman.

The new chairman, long accustomed to working with and leading groups, expressed enthusiasm about the board. "Ninety percent of the trustees," he proclaimed, "have real zeal for The American College."[63] As vice chairman for 2 years, Mullane had already established a harmonious working relationship with President Weese.

At that time, as part of an effort better to serve student needs, the College established a computerized registration and information system. Known as CRIS, the automated phone service could process 24 simultaneous student queries easily and quickly. Kathryn L. Rushford, a Prudential Insurance Company agent in Bethlehem, Pennsylvania, who was the first student to use CRIS, reported that registration for a new course took "only seconds," and that within one week she had received her textbook and study materials.[64]

In another effort to serve its students better, the College redesigned its mentorship program for Huebner School students in a plan to gradually replace the College's traditional sponsorship program that began in 1958. The new plan placed greater emphasis on a continuing student-mentor relationship to increase the likelihood of each candidate's earning his or her designation. Mentors would remain in contact with their charges throughout their CLU/ChFC studies.

Dr. Weese hoped that this effort would reduce the traditionally heavy dropout rate of 70 percent, which meant that, over the years, only three of every 10 matriculants succeeded in earning their first designation.[65] A recent study had revealed that "an improvement of one percent in the attrition level, all other factors being held constant, would yield approximately $207,000 per year or more than $1 million over the next 5 years."[66] Even more important, it would mean that there would be a substantial increase in the number of students earning a designation from the College and being better prepared to service their clients.

Quantity alone, however, was never the sole consideration; quality was equally important. To increase the effectiveness of the College's mission to maintain quality professional education and high ethical standards, the trustees voted that June to begin "publishing the name, city, and state of those persons whose designations have been suspended because of a violation of the College's Code of Ethics."[67]

The College's latest efforts to improve student service were particularly relevant in light of a recent report from a task force led by Charles S. DiLullo and composed of faculty members Charles E. Hughes and Michael J. Roszkowski and Registrar Shirley P. Steinman. That group studied more than 2 decades of CLU matriculations and course registrations and concluded that the College must remain flexible to hit the moving target of continued change in the life insurance industry.[68]

Shirley Steinman deserves some elaboration. She has been a loyal employee of the College since 1970 and in many respects is a self-made person, having earned her CLU, ChFC, and masters degrees from the College while handling each position she has been asked to fill with dedication and commitment. During her career with the College, she has been in the Finance Division, the Marketing Division, and then in the Academic Division. She became the registrar in 1990 upon the retirement of William McCouch. In recent years she has taken the full administrative responsibility of running the annual designation conferments and graduate commencements. Steinman is truly one of the unsung heroes of the College.

The Commission on Higher Education of the Middle States Association of Colleges and Schools reaffirmed the College's academic accreditation based on what Samuel H. Weese called the College's "solid track record of achievement and stability from which to move forward."[69] In a mid-summer report to the faculty the pleased president pointed out that accreditation was far from automatic and that there were distance education colleges similar to The American College that had previously tried unsuccessfully to meet such standards.[70]

National news that year was the usual blend of the somber and the bright. A World Trade Center bomb blast killed six people and injured 1,000. The

Mississippi River flooded eight million acres of land, killed 50 people, and left 70,000 homeless. David McCullough won a Pulitzer Prize in history for his biography of Harry S. Truman, and the Motion Picture Academy of Arts and Sciences awarded an Oscar for the best film to Steven Spielberg's *Schindler's List.*[71]

October had traditionally been a busy month for the College. The yearly conferment exercises and their relationship to the American Society's annual forum were a case in point, but three other events made October 1993 particularly noteworthy. The College had planned two of them, but the third was unforeseen.

First, David A. Lester, CLU, ChFC, a 20-year Prudential agency manager in Pittsburgh, Pennsylvania, was hired as director of multicultural activities and the first African-American to hold a management position at the College. In this newly created position he hoped to stimulate growth of CLU and ChFC education among minorities.[72] Lester's appointment continued the 1992 emphasis on minority focus groups around the country initially undertaken with the Life Underwriter Training Council. Advisory committees for African-, Asian-, and Hispanic-Americans would soon be formed, along with a speakers bureau and a series of newsletters. Of the 10,000 new students enrolled the previous year, approximately 10 percent belonged to one of these racial groups.[73]

Second, the College honored two individuals who had contributed much to the institution. A State Farm Companies Foundation grant made possible the establishment of a new archives area in the Gregg Conference Center lobby in honor of Marvin D. Bower. Bower returned to the campus to cut the ribbon at the dedication ceremony.

At the same time the College paid tribute to another leader who provided unparalleled educational support to both State Farm and The American College. That person was Professor William T. Beadles, for whom a lecture series had been named in the early 1970s. Through a State Farm grant the College built a suite of two offices on the ground floor of MDRT Foundation Hall and named them the Beadles Suites in his honor. Beadles was a long-time educational consultant to The American College.

The third event that October was a tragic one. Davis W. Gregg died on October 27, ending a 4-decade involvement with the College he had so capably served as president for 28 of those years. Dr. Gregg had been in ill health for some time so his demise did not come as a complete surprise. Nevertheless, the College family was deeply saddened by his death. Suffice it to say that no other person had made a greater contribution to The American College in its 66-year history.[74]

That year the annual October American Society conference and American College conferment exercises were held in Kansas City, Missouri. Participating were Board Chairman Denis F. Mullane, President Samuel H. Weese, and trustee Roland C. Baker, CLU, who was the first African-American to give the conferment address. The 66th exercises awarded 1,804 CLU designations and 1,239 ChFCs. Chairman Mullane congratulated Kevin J. Messer, CLU, of

Cincinnati, Ohio, as the 25,000th person to earn the Chartered Financial Consultant designation.

Another Solomon S. Huebner Gold Medal was awarded that season; the 1993 recipient was Edmund L. Zalinski. Dr. Zalinski, former president of the Life Insurance Company of North America and an American College trustee from 1954 to 1971, had served on almost every College board committee and had been chairman of several. He was perhaps best recognized in the industry as a founder of the Life Insurance Training Council in 1941 and its first executive director.

The American College could not have become the national leader in life insurance distance education without substantial voluntary financial support from corporate grants and gifts from individuals. Successful capital campaigns and consistent Golden Key Society activity had made the difference.

Development Committee Chairman Brian S. Brown, CLU, ChFC, and Vice President Stephen D. Tarr presented the College constituency with an outstanding record of 1993 stewardship, which counted more than 4,600 donors—an increase of 18 percent over the previous year.[75] The College's annual financial report showed $1,595,200 in contributions that year.[76]

As the year drew to a close, Samuel H. Weese was able to report, "Nineteen ninety-three was a good year for the College in every respect."

NOTES

1. Robert J. Samuelson, *The Good Life and Its Discontents (The American Dream in the Age of Entitlement 1945–1995)* (New York: Random House), 1995, p. 57.
2. Morey Stettner, *Buyer Beware, An Industry Insider Shows You How to Win the Insurance Game* (Chicago: Probus Publishing Co.), 1994, p. 57.
3. Stan Tulin, Coopers & Lybrand address to Covenant Life Insurance Company Board of Directors, October 14, 1993.
4. *Annual Report,* The American College, June 30, 1991, p. 2.
5. *Self-Study,* The American College, 1993, pp. 1, 4.
6. Edmund Burke, letter to the members of the British National Assembly, 1791.
7. *Annual Report,* 1991, p. 2.
8. Ibid.
9. The American College news release, January 14, 1991.
10. *The American College Catalog,* 1990–1992, p. 35.
11. Gavin Anderson Doremus & Co. news release, March 12, 1991.
12. *Fortune,* June 24, 1996, p. 147.
13. The American College news release, April 12, 1991.
14. Ibid., July 25, 1991.
15. Ibid., April 2, 1991.
16. Ibid., May 1, 1991.
17. *The American College Outlook,* summer 1991, p. 8.
18. The American College news release, May 17, 1991.
19. Ibid., May 3, June 3, and July 3, 1991.
20. Ibid., August 5, 1991.
21. *World Almanac and Book of Facts* (Mahwah, NJ: World Almanac Books), 1996, p. 123.

22. Samuel H. Weese as quoted by Alan Press in "Why I Will Miss John Carter," May 1991.
23. *Outlook*, summer 1991, Board Resolution, p. 11.
24. Samuel H. Weese, interview with the author, May 16, 1996.
25. William B. Wallace, Oral History interview, January 24, 1991, p. 3.
26. Interview with the author, December 12, 1994.
27. The American College news release, September 20, 1991.
28. *World Almanac,* 1995, p. 509.
29. *The Best of Business Quotations* (Mt. Kisco, NY: Exley Publications), 1993, p. 56.
30. The American College news release, January 13, 1992.
31. Memo to American College employees, February 25, 1992, p. 1.
32. Joseph P. Viviano, president, Hershey Foods Corporation, talk at the Union League, Philadelphia, April 11, 1996.
33. "President's Update," February 25, 1992.
34. Ibid., April 30, 1992.
35. The American College news release, April 6, 1992.
36. "Women Managing in the Financial Services Professions," seminar program agenda, June 1992.
37. The American College news release, July 23, 1992.
38. Ibid., June 19, 1992.
39. *Annual Report,* June 30, 1992, pp. 1–3.
40. *Outlook,* spring 1992, p. 10.
41. *Annual Report,* December 31, 1992, p. 6.
42. Clarence C. Walton, interviews with the author, January 12, 1995, and June 7, 1996.
43. Boettner Institute of Financial Gerontology, *Annual Report,* 1992–1993, p. 1.
44. *Outlook,* winter 1992, p. 4.
45. Ibid.
46. Ibid.
47. The American College news release, December 9, 1992.
48. Ibid., November 17, 1992.
49. Stettner, *Buyer Beware,* p. 2.
50. *Million Dollar Round Table News,* January 20, 1993.
51. *Annual Report,* December 31, 1992, p. 2.
52. Ibid.
53. Marjorie A. Fletcher, memorandum to the author, June 14, 1996.
54. *Self-Study,* The American College, 1993, pp. 8.3–8.4.
55. The American College news release, March 5, 1993.
56. Ibid., January 11, 1993.
57. "President's Update," April 22, 1993.
58. *Self-Study,* 1993, preface, pp. vi, vii.
59. Ibid., p. 2.6.
60. "President's Update," April 22, 1993.
61. The American College news release, April 27, 1993.
62. *How Academic Leadership Works* (San Francisco: Jossey-Bass), 1992, p. 73.
63. Interview with the author, December 1, 1994.
64. *Outlook,* fall 1993, p. 3.
65. "President's Update," August 31, 1993.
66. *Self-Study,* 1993, p. 6.9.
67. *Outlook,* fall 1993, p. 9.
68. *Student Activity Study,* 1967–1992.
69. *Annual Report,* 1993, p. 3.
70. "President's Update," August 31, 1993.
71. *World Almanac,* 1996, p. 509.

72. *Annual Report,* 1993, p. 6.
73. *Outlook,* fall 1993, p. 5.
74. Ibid.
75. *Annual Report of Gifts,* The American College, 1993, p. 5.
76. *Annual Report,* 1993.

13

Full Flower

Time will rust the sharpest sword.

Sir Walter Raleigh

January 1994 brought harsh weather to the Bryn Mawr campus and a devastating earthquake to Los Angeles, which cost some 60 lives and $20 billion in damage.[1] The life insurance industry also continued to experience tumultuous times, but the storm clouds of the 1980s seemed to be dissipating somewhat as mergers and downsizings strengthened companies' ability to function in a highly competitive marketplace.

This emerging new environment ushered in new opportunities. Waning corporate paternalism and the disappearance of 30,000 pension plans since 1990 made the now middle-aged baby boom generation more apprehensive about the financial stability of their approaching retirement. There was a growing awareness among the population that the greater financial risk is living too long as opposed to dying too soon. The American College would respond to these developments astutely, drawing on the influence gained from its more than 65 years of leadership as the premier educator in the life insurance industry.

Early that year the College honored former trustee Dan M. McGill, professor emeritus at the Wharton School of Business at the University of Pennsylvania, in a manner that both personally recognized the noted life insurance authority and provided a valuable teaching tool for all professionals involved in the dynamics reshaping the industry. In January 1994 the College published what President Weese called "its own life insurance textbook," *McGill's Life Insurance*. The book was based on Dr. McGill's earlier classic volume and edited by Associate Professor Edward E. Graves. McGill had graciously assigned his original copyright to the College. The new book would be used in two American College courses and offered off campus to professors teaching life insurance in traditional colleges and universities. It would give the College broader visibility and greater influence across the country. Academic Vice President Gary K. Stone described the book as "the essential reference book for every life insurance professional."[2]

The publication of the McGill life insurance text was part of a larger strategy that was instituted at the beginning of the decade. This strategy was to have College faculty write the textbooks for the Huebner School courses and thereby systematically replace all books written for the traditional College market by outside authors. (By 1996 the College had 11 hardback texts in use, all with distinctive gold trim on a dark blue background. Various college and university professors were beginning to use some of these textbooks, known as the Huebner Series, in their classes.)

There were several advantages to the College in producing its own textbooks. One, it meant that the faculty was not using books that had been written for an audience that was somewhat different from the College's. Two, the College faculty would not be under the control of outside authors or publishers regarding decisions about when to update a text. Three, the College could maintain a substantially higher percentage of the revenue from the sales of its books than it could if an outside publisher held the copyright.

The trustees paid tribute to Dr. McGill at their January 27 meeting by dedicating the Kentucky Room in the residence wing of the Davis W. Gregg Conference Center in honor of the distinguished insurance educator, a testimonial made possible by a grant from the Equitable Life Assurance Society of the United States. The commemorative citation noted McGill's "major contribution to society as Chairman of the Pension Research Council (1952–1990) and his five-volume study that led to the vesting of pensions, to the reform bill ERISA, and to his role in the establishment of the Pension Benefit Guaranty Corporation."[3]

Several events enlivened the campus during the next few months. First, the palette of programs that season included a number of one-week class sessions known as graduate residencies. (To obtain their MSFS or MSM degree students are required to attend residencies scheduled at the beginning and at the conclusion of their Financial Services or Management program.)

In addition, since 1990, March had been known as Ethics Awareness Month. Each year the College, with the American Society of CLU & ChFC, the American Institute for Chartered Property Casualty Underwriters, and the Society of CPCU cosponsored a nationwide effort "to increase awareness and facilitate the discussion of ethical issues in the insurance and financial services industry."[4] In 1994 almost 5,000 professionals from these fields participated in 160 ethics education meetings that were endorsed by more than 150 insurance companies and professional societies/associations.[5]

Samuel H. Weese loved being at the heart of campus activity. He enjoyed presiding or otherwise participating in institutional events. From time to time, however, the vigorous executive took advantage of opportunities to leave Bryn Mawr to wave the institutional flag and spread the College's academic gospel far afield. April 1994 provided such an occasion—an invitation to represent the College at the 20th anniversary celebration of Japan's Life Underwriting Academy.

Accompanied by Academic Vice President Gary K. Stone, Dr. Weese made the trip to Tokyo, where he spoke at the anniversary gala and met with Japanese industry executives. He and Dr. Stone also traveled to Hong Kong and Singapore, where they discussed the possibility of offering the College's CLU program there. The president enjoyed these opportunities "to generate additional interest of students, potential students, and companies in our program throughout the Pacific Rim countries."[6]

It had become a tradition for a group of new graduates of the Japanese CLU program to visit The American College each summer as part of a week-long tour of the United States, and 1994 was no exception. Twenty new designees, nearly all of whom were women, enjoyed a day at the College. This 1994 sojourn marked the eighth consecutive year that a Japanese delegation had visited the College campus.[7] It also continued the relationship between the College and Japanese life insurers that had begun during Dr. Solomon S. Huebner's first visit to that country in 1927.

In June 1994 the trustees took action to begin a $1 million corporate gift campaign. When combined with the $1.3 million received for the sale of the Carter property and the $2.7 million accumulated from operating revenues and annual giving, the additional $1 million would enable the College to pay off the remaining $5 million of long-term debt by the spring of 1997.[8]

Viable institutions depend on new employees to replace those who leave because of death, discharge, resignation, or retirement. Although the American College has been fortunate to have had a relatively stable work force over the years, the period 1991–1996 introduced a host of new faces to the College.

The group included David A. Littell and David M. Cordell, who joined the faculty in 1992 as professors of taxation and finance, respectively. Ken Cooper came in 1994 as visiting professor and holder of the Charles Lamont Post Chair of Ethics and the Professions, G. Steven McMillan and Carol N. Marais joined the management faculty in 1995, and Roger C. Bird was hired as the Frank M. Engle Chairholder in Economic Security Research. In 1996 Ronald F. Duska joined the College as professor of ethics and the Charles Lamont Post Chairholder of Ethics and the Professions.

New employees also filled several important professional support positions during these same years. In early 1991 Ann M. Casey joined the College as general manager of the Gregg Conference Center; her considerable experience as a conference center manager made her a valuable asset to the College. The following year Joan L. Zaremba, a New York University MBA with extensive direct marketing experience, was named director of marketing. In 1993 Bruce B. Makous joined the Development Office as a director and immediately became the administrator of the Golden Key program. In 1995 Prudential's Anthony C. Smith, CLU, ChFC, joined the Marketing Department as a director of marketing. Robert A. Reiser also arrived on campus that year as public relations director after a lengthy career with CNA, and John G. Wells became a director in the Finance Department after 8 years with Hay Associates. Another new employee that year was Diane J. Kyker, who was named director of planning and evaluation and assistant to the president. Dr. Kyker had previously been an associate director of the Office of Senior Institutions in the New Jersey Department of Higher Education.

In 1996 there were two more important new hires. The first was Jennifer J. Alby, a young attorney who joined the Development Office to become responsible for an increased emphasis on deferred giving. Her experience in advanced underwriting had been for both Security Mutual and Lutheran Brotherhood. The second new employee was Sandra K. Stuckert, who became vice president of management information systems and the head of this increasingly important division of the College. Joining the College with more than 20 years of experience in corporate technology and systems, she replaced Michael Scott, who had come to the College in 1991 to build its computerized student information system. Sandra Stuckert's role and responsibilities were considered to be at the core of the College's future success.

Facility dedications and book publications, guest speakers and international visitors, special programs and fundraising campaigns were important ingredients in the life and image of The American College. Nevertheless, although each contributed to the stature and influence of the pioneer distance education institution, none could match the significance to the College of student enrollment. President Weese defined the issue in mid-summer when he told the entire administration, faculty, and staff, "The financial success of the College is tied to how well the Huebner courses are doing. Student matriculations and course registrations carry high volume expectations, and these activities generate the majority of our annual revenue when the study materials are included."[9]

No longer could the College rely on automatic growth in Huebner School activity as it had prior to the 1980s. In the early years of that decade, student matriculations and registrations became increasingly volatile, and the number of new CLU designees ranged from a high of 2,690 in 1988 to a low of 1,871 in 1989. The 1990s began with the lowest number of new CLU designations in 25 years. New matriculants also remained flat in the early 1990s but showed growth with periodic volatility through 1996. Huebner School registrations grew from 1990 to 1993—increasing from 40,400 to 48,000—but then flattened out during the period 1994–1996.[10]

Although graduate school registrations rose substantially from 914 to 1,780 during the first 4 years of the 1990s and admissions to masters degree courses more than doubled from 106 to 266 for the same period, both leveled off in the middle 1990s. While revenue from the graduate program is less than revenue from the Huebner School, the graduate programs are considered to be very important to the mission the College.

William J. Lombardo, the dynamic vice president of marketing, was not about to accept flat registrations. He implemented marketing activities to increase student enrollments, organizing a 3-day November phonathon to contact all students who has passed a course in the past 18 months but had not recently registered for another course. The calls augmented an earlier CLU/ChFC mailing that offered incentives for registrations before December 31, 1994.[11]

Bill Lombardo had joined the College as the first full-time manager of the Gregg Conference Center. A Cleveland native with an MBA from Syracuse University, Lombardo came to the College highly recommended, with experience as a development officer at Fairleigh Dickinson University and a marketer of professional education for Golle & Holmes in New York. His management style was to motivate individuals as team players. His optimism and enthusiasm were contagious.

Flat enrollment figures and the College's response to the situation reflected more than the usual concern about operational income and expenses that is germane to every institutional enterprise. The 1980s had been years of continual operating deficits, and President Weese and the Board of Trustees had no intention of returning to those years. Recruiting more students obviously strengthened the College, but it also enhanced the professionalism and improved the personal fortunes of the men and women in a smaller field force, who found themselves working longer hours just to do as well as they had the previous year. As President Weese wrote that fall, "There is no greater security for the future than increased knowledge, because those who have the ability to answer the client's questions or have solutions that satisfy the client's problems are better prepared to succeed, regardless of the competition and industry structure."[12]

One faculty member who had seen more classes of new matriculants than most was C. Bruce Worsham, having joined the College faculty in the examination unit directly from his tenure as a Huebner fellow in 1969. During his years at the College he, like several others, continued his professional education by earning a JD degree at night from Widener University. As we mentioned earlier, Worsham became director of the Huebner School and associate vice president in 1992, and he quickly proved that his long experience on the faculty made him invaluable in overseeing the Huebner School curriculum.

The American Society held its 1994 national conference on October 9–12 in Seattle, Washington. The annual affair included the election of a new American Society of CLU & ChFC president, presentation of the Huebner Gold Medal to the third woman in the 20-year history of the award, and the 67th conferment exercises of The American College. Each of these events needs to be explored more fully.

Millard J. Grauer, who had held a succession of leadership positions in the life insurance industry, became president of the Society. The Equitable Life agent had been MDRT president and a trustee of The American College. In addition, he had been active in Society affairs and had served on its Executive Committee.[13] Upon taking office the new Society president immediately stressed the importance of industry ethics and the CLU Pledge as he urged all Society members "to take a stand against the few bad apples in the business."[14]

The Board of Trustees had created the Solomon S. Huebner Gold Medal in 1975 to honor persons whose support of The American College and its programs and whose dedication to professionalism had been of particular meaning to the College's mission and progress. After 2 decades it had presented the award to 36 people. Although there had been more than one honoree in the earlier years, after 1990, President Samuel H. Weese made it known that he preferred only a single recipient each year. In 1994 the College conferred this distinction upon Maxine B. Niemeyer.

Niemeyer's career consisted of one achievement after another. President of her own company (Business and Estate Financial Coordinators, Inc., in Grosse Pointe Woods, Michigan) and a Phoenix Home Life brokerage consultant, Maxine Niemeyer had been a long-time MDRT qualifier as well as president of the American Society (1988–1989). She had also become virtually part and parcel of The American College, earning both Huebner School designations and Graduate School masters degrees, serving on the governing board, and achieving life trusteeship in 1990—one of only 16 people to receive this honor in the College's 67-year history.[15]

The 1994 annual conferment exercises in Seattle added 2,378 CLUs and 1,398 ChFCs—a total of 3,776 new designation holders—to the College's alumni ranks. Because of the lower matriculation and registration figures of those days, the College exulted in this large class, which represented a 32 percent increase in CLU numbers and a 13 percent jump in the number of ChFCs over the class of 1993. Grand totals since 1928 had reached 76,926 CLUs and 26,438 ChFCs. William B. Wallace, former board chairman and Phoenix Home Life CEO, gave the conferment address.[16]

The Seattle activities also included a meeting of the College's Asian-American Society Advisory Committee. The College's Minority Committees had met earlier that summer on the Bryn Mawr campus with College President Samuel Weese, Society Executive Vice President John R. Driskill, and other College officials, including Multicultural Activities Director David A. Lester. In each of the next 2 years these Advisory Committees would meet during the annual conference and conferment. In Seattle, the College hosted a multicultural reception for the new designees who were of the minorities making up the Advisory Committees.[17]

Less than 3 weeks after the Seattle conferment, 42 men and women received the Master of Science in Financial Services degree and 14 people earned the Master of Science in Management degree. Local historian D. David Eisenhower, the grandson of President Dwight D. Eisenhower, told the graduates at the commencement in Bryn Mawr, "Adaptation to change is a law of life." Eisenhower also noted that "mid-life education [is] no longer a matter of choice, but an actual necessity."[18]

The commencement/forum weekend program also included dedication of the Barry Kaye Media Center in MDRT Foundation Hall, naming the audio/video technology facility in honor of the charismatic CLU whose generosity, vision, and appreciation for the College had made the center a reality.[19] Kaye had made the College owner and beneficiary of the largest life insurance policy—its face value was $1,025,000—ever gifted to the institution. "This gift," said President Weese, "will allow us to streamline the process by which we produce the Huebner School cassette reviews and the College-produced promotional videos that help us spread the word about CLU and ChFC."[20]

As these 1994 College and Society events took place, the national economic scene had the lowest inflation rate in 7 years and the gross national product was $6,727 billion. A baseball strike that began in August cancelled the World

Series, and the Republicans swept the off-year November elections to capture both the United States House and Senate for the first time since the days before Franklin D. Roosevelt's New Deal. *Forrest Gump* won an Oscar as the best motion picture, and a Pulitzer Prize went to David Remnick for his *Lenin's Tomb: The Last Days of the Soviet Empire.*[21]

That November an assistant vice president of organizational assessment at LOMA presented the results of the 1995 Life Office Management Association survey of American College employees to the College's Senior Management and Management Coordinating Committees. Overall, 91 percent of those taking the survey said they were "satisfied with the College as a place to work."[22] Although employee dissatisfaction was noted in the areas of job pressure and managers' promptness in handling work group problems, the results of the survey were substantially more favorable than a similar survey taken in 1992, when College employees were still somewhat shaken by several terminations and early retirements that had taken place. The lower morale at that time was in direct contrast to the more upbeat responses in the 1995 survey.

Two members of the College faculty terminated their full-time faculty positions at the end of 1995. The first was Dr. Michael D. White, holder of the Frank M. Engle Chair in Economic Security Research; the second was Dr. Richard H. Viola, professor of management and director of the Richard D. Irwin Graduate School of Management. While White had been with the College for 4 years and it had been his first full-time academic experience, Viola had joined the College faculty in 1989 after an 18-year career at Temple University.[23]

Despite extraordinary marketing efforts, new student matriculations were down by 7 percent in 1994 and course registrations were down by 10 percent from the previous year.[24] Effective cost controls, however, still made it possible for the College to end the year with $1 million of net operating revenues. Moreover, Stephen Tarr's Development Office reported another strong year, as annual giving dollars grew by 17 percent over 1993 to top $1 million. The number of donors increased approximately 20 percent to more than 5,700. These positive results—a larger net worth and a steady reduction of debt—continued to strengthen the College's financial position. With that fiscal stability, combined with its quality educational programs, publications, and other activities, The American College could claim to be well positioned to take advantage of future opportunities.[25]

*   *   *

"Let's keep the momentum going," President Weese exhorted the campus family early in 1995 in an ambitious statement of expectations early in the new year.[26] Things got underway on January 5 with a public announcement of conferences and seminars already scheduled for the new calendar period in the Davis W. Gregg Educational Conference Center.[27]

The College played out the first 4 impressive months of 1995 during a time of various calamities on the national and world scenes. An earthquake that hit

Japan on January 17 killed 5,000 people. In March the Bosnian truce collapsed and fighting in that troubled place resumed. A terrorist bomb killed 169 innocent victims on April 19 in Oklahoma City.[28]

The trustees met on January 19–20. Diane J. Kyker, assistant to the president, presented the 1995 business plan, which projected increases in both CLU and ChFC matriculations and registrations, along with continued growth in the MSFS and MSM degree programs. The administration also submitted a draft of a strategic plan that the board agreed to consider for adoption at its summer meeting. Instead of the traditional 5-year plan, this was a more flexible document that recognized the uncertainties inherent in a newly structured, integrated financial services industry.

A number of trustees completed their terms of service, including two people who had been employees of the College in the early days of their distinguished careers. Dr. Joseph J. Melone, a former Huebner fellow, had taught at the Wharton School and later been director of research at The American College before joining the Prudential Insurance Company, where he rose to the position of president. He later moved to the Equitable where he became its CEO and played a leading role in the conversion of this well-known mutual insurer into a stock company. Dr. Jerry S. Rosenbloom, also a former Huebner fellow, left The American College to join the faculty at Temple. Later, he became a member of the faculty at the Wharton School, where he rose to chairman of its Insurance and Risk Management Department. Both men had served the College well as trustees.

The two new board members were James M. Benson, CLU, president of Equitable Life, and L.J. Rowell, Jr., CLU, Provident Mutual Life chairman and CEO. Benson was a young executive on the rise, while Rowell's long successful career was nearing its completion.

A few days before the trustee meetings, John W. Cronin, former Connecticut Mutual general manager in Philadelphia and holder of the George G. Joseph Chair in Management Education at the College, flew to Dallas, Texas, with Development Vice President Stephen D. Tarr. There, they met with an ad hoc committee of Connecticut Mutual agents and managers from across the country who wanted to honor Charles J. Zimmerman, the former chairman of the board and CEO of Connecticut Mutual, by raising funds to supplement his estate gift to the College. Their goal was to endow a faculty chair in Zimmerman's name.

Charles J. Zimmerman had left his estate to Dartmouth College and The American College. The portion bequeathed to the College exceeded $750,000, but the minimum amount needed for an endowed chair was $1 million. It was decided to organize a $250,000 gift campaign to seek support from Connecticut Mutual's Foundation and the 300 people in the home office and throughout the agency structure who knew and admired the long-time industry leader and supporter of The American College. The new chairholder would be responsible for contributing to the College's life insurance courses and programs, conducting applied research, and publishing professional materials related to this field. The corporate offices committed $150,000 to a campaign that was scheduled to run through the calendar year and be successfully completed by December 31, 1995.

A February 2 seminar on Insurance and Financial Planning for the Older Client was the first in a series of what the College termed "a full lineup of exciting programs" for the new year. Theodore T. Kurlowicz, JD, professor of taxation, and adjunct faculty member Kenn B. Tacchino, JD, prepared the program designed to help enrollees look beyond the expected issues of retirement planning to examine the special needs of the retired older client.[29]

The College then teamed with Fairleigh Dickinson University to sponsor two other one-day seminars in New Jersey on the subject of "Retirement Planning in the Current Tax Environment." The first session convened in Hackensack on February 28, followed by a second class in Madison on March 23. Both featured American College faculty members John J. McFadden, JD, and David A. Littell, JD. Attendees could expect to earn state continuing education credits and PACE credits for these programs. This was the first of the College's partnerships with traditional colleges and universities around the country, in which the College supplied the continuing education course materials and the schools provided the attendees.

Cognizant that the average age of the College's main buildings was approximately 25 years and that minimum amounts of capital had been invested in them over the years, the trustees sensed the need for an audit of campus facilities to determine the real state of property conditions. In 1994 therefore the board had commissioned Burt Hill Kosar Rittlemann Associates to conduct such a study with the assistance of the College Facilities Audit Committee composed of President Samuel H. Weese, Vice President Charles S. DiLullo, and Robert D. Varner, the director of physical plant and grounds.

The architects presented their completed report in March 1995. It called for capital expenditures of approximately $7.2 million over a 6-year period. The proposed work included repairs needed to meet original building functions, replacement of major components and systems owing to changes in functional requirements, and cost-justified improvements to increase marketability and productivity and to avoid utility costs.[30]

The College approved the project and authorized 1995 expenditures of $1.1 million in first-year capital upgrades and improvements. Major investments were made in Huebner Hall and MDRT Foundation Hall with additional work in the Gregg Conference Center. President Weese explained, "These property enhancements will be completed with funds made possible from operations, annual giving, and restricted contributions."[31]

As the president had noted in his 1994 annual report, the College would remain alert to new opportunities for expanded capacity and broader outreach to its professional constituency. Such an opportunity arose when the College was approached by the leaders of the National Association of Health Underwriters (NAHU) to provide the education for its two designations. After considerable discussion that addressed the concerns of the National Association of Life Underwriters (NALU) and the Association of Health Insurance Agents (AHIA), the College, with the involvement of trustee Chairman Denis F. Mullane, was able to purchase the designations from NAHU. The understanding was that the RHU—Registered Health Underwriter—designation would serve the health insurance interests of the entire industry, while the REBC—Registered Employee Benefits Consultant—would be the designation for employee benefits specialists. The RHU was the better known of the two new designations; about 6,000 persons had earned the designation since 1979. Only about 250 individuals had earned the REBC designation, which had begun in 1990.[32]

Continuing Education Director Burton T. Beam, Jr., CLU, ChFC, would supervise these acquired programs. Although both programs required revisions and upgrades to reach the educational quality of the CLU and ChFC designations, each offered genuine potential for growth.[33]

Beam was another of several former Huebner fellows at the University of Pennsylvania to join the College faculty, having come to the College in 1977 as an assistant professor, initially to write examinations. Prior to joining the College he had taught at the University of Florida and the University of Connecticut. As the years passed, his expanding knowledge in the many technical areas of the Huebner curriculum further increased his value to the College. During Dean Cooper's tenure, Beam oversaw faculty course development and added administrative responsibilities for State Continuing Education filing to his faculty role in 1988.

In the early 1990s economists, politicians, and many thoughtful citizens engaged in (often dramatic) debate over the North American Free Trade Agreement. The American College examined this controversy on May 1, 1995, when the Director of the Center for Latin American Economics of the Federal Reserve Bank of Dallas, William C. Gruben, PhD, delivered the 18th Frank M. Engle Lecture, "The Implications of NAFTA."[34] Dr. Gruben, who described NAFTA as a process and not a static product, pointed out that the meaning of this trade agreement will continually change as the laws and regulations of the countries involved change.[35]

The spring calendar that year included a number of other campus events besides the annual Engle Lecture. Two are distinctive enough for specific mention. First, the College held an open house and reception on May 10, 1995, in the Gregg Conference Center so that local area guests could inspect the College archive room, enjoy a juried art exhibit, and take a walking tour through the arboretum. Second, 9 days later, the College's African-American Advisory Committee held an educational program primarily for African-American agents, which was presented by several very successful African-American life insurance practitioners. The occasion was called the Lang Dixon Professional Education Day in memory of one of the 15 charter members of the African-American Advisory Committee that had been formed at the College in 1992. Lang Dixon, CLU, was a highly respected Philadelphia life insurance agent who succumbed to cancer in 1994.[36]

The June commencement exercises for graduate degrees differed from the usual ceremony in that Denis F. Mullane took part twice. He first appeared as chairman of the board to present a number of special guests. He later stepped forward to receive his MSFS degree from President Samuel H. Weese.[37] The significance of Mullane's accomplishment was obvious: A true professional never stops growing.

At its June 1995 trustees meeting the College governing body elected Brian S. Brown to a position of life trustee.[38] Brian Brown, known informally as "B.B.," had held executive positions with Guardian Life, Canada Life, and Prudential. A former president of the American Society of CLU & ChFC, Brown had been an American College board member for only 5 years, but during that time had provided substantive leadership as cochairman of National Annual Giving and then head of the Development Committee of the Board of Trustees. Brown was the 17th person to become a life trustee in the history of the Bryn Mawr institution.[39]

That summer in the wide world beyond the campus boundaries, New York's Chase Manhattan and Chemical Banks merged to form a $297 billion financial institution.[40] At about the same time, The American College filed a five-course curriculum, which was designed to meet the requirements to sit for the CFP designation, with the Certified Financial Planners Board of Standards. Considering the previous competition between the ChFC and CFP designations, a review of earlier events will put the new relationship into proper perspective.

Once upon a time (up to and including the 1960s) life insurance flourished with little competition in the risk-protection business. In the 1970s, however, as the public developed an interest in a broader financial approach, financial planning emerged as a new career field. Sensing this opportunity, Loren Dunton founded the College of Financial Planning in 1972 to fill this niche; The American College maintained its concentration on the CLU designation and the traditional life insurance agent. The new institution offered a Certified Financial Planner designation. In the late 1980s during a legal dispute with Adelphi College in New York over ownership of the designation, the College of Financial Planning transferred all ownership rights in the designation to an independent organization, the Certified Financial Planners Board of Standards.

Because the life insurance industry had brought the College into being (in 1927) and had supported it all these years, The American College had been reluctant to branch out into financial planning. However, the time came when the College realized the need to expand its educational mission to reach a wider audience of financial services professionals. For a decade the trustees, who had resisted the move to a broader curriculum, were criticized by many for being blind to wider opportunities. In 1981 therefore the College introduced the Chartered Financial Consultant designation and thereby soon experienced a "damned if you do, damned if you don't" reaction. Some life insurance agents were already calling themselves financial planners, while life insurance purists complained that by beginning the ChFC program, the College had betrayed its core constituency.[41]

From its inception the ChFC was a 10-course designation for those who had not earned the CLU. The CFP, in contrast, was a six-part program and hence considered less time-consuming to achieve. Since 95 percent of all those earning the ChFC designation at that time already held the CLU designation, the Certified Financial Planners program competed with only 5 percent of potential ChFC students not already in The American College fold.[42]

Nevertheless, in 1994 the College realigned its 10-course ChFC curriculum so that the first five courses matched the curriculum required for taking the CFP certification examination, and it registered these five courses with the CFP Board of Standards. Although the College would not actually award the CFP certification, it could furnish students who completed the necessary five courses with a transcript verifying that they met the education requisites to sit for the CFP examination. It was the College's expectation that these CFP students would continue their education, taking (and passing) five additional courses to earn the more comprehensive ChFC designation. The curriculum realignment is a further example of the College's ongoing commitment to serve practitioners in an ever-changing and growing industry.

Both the College and the CFP Board of Standards issued affirmative statements about the venture. S. Timothy Kochis, CFP board president said, "The continuing increase in institutions registered to provide the Certified Financial Planner curriculum indicates a growing interest in financial planning as a career."[43] President Samuel H. Weese responded, "Our registration by the Board of Standards should allow the College to take advantage of the continued integration of the financial planning industry."[44]

The American Society of CLU & ChFC held its annual national conference in Atlanta, Georgia, in mid-October, followed immediately by the College's annual conferment. On October 15, 1995, the College presented its highest award—the Huebner Gold Medal—to New York Life's Stanley Liss, who had served so well as the first consultant to the Joint Planning and Policy Committee created in 1989 to enhance the relationship between The American College and the American Society of CLU & ChFC. Three days later, the College awarded 1,805 CLU designations and 1,354 ChFCs as part of the 68th conferment exercises.

Since starting his career as a New York Life agent in 1948 and earning his CLU in 1955, Stanley Liss consistently supported professional education within his company, at The American College, at the American Society, in the Million Dollar Round Table, and in other professional associations in which he invariably won leadership positions. In being honored with the Gold Medal, Liss received special recognition for "orchestrating a structure that fostered enhanced cooperation and coordination between the College and the Society."[45]

The profile of designees in the class of 1995 revealed that more than 85 percent of them were active in the insurance industry, with the remainder in investment counseling, accounting, law, banking, and related financial services. Women now represented 19 percent of the group and were recognized as a growing segment of the life insurance field force. State Farm, Northwestern Mutual, Prudential, New York Life, Equitable Life, Met Life, Massachusetts

Mutual, and John Hancock were the life insurance companies with the largest number of CLUs and ChFCs.[46]

Service could be called the very essence of The American College. Indeed, the College existed to help individual agents and managers and, through them, the life insurance industry, as well as other financial services professionals. The College had achieved remarkable success, but it could not rest on its laurels, given the unfavorable publicity that beset Prudential and Metropolitan—and the industry as a whole—in the mid-1990s. Newspaper headlines of those days ran from "New York Life Agrees to Settle Lawsuits over its Vanishing Premium Policies"[47] to "Eleven-State Probe of Insurance Sales to Open."[48] "Scary" is the word used by one life insurance veteran to describe industry conditions in 1995 as public criticism mounted against misleading sales practices by some companies and certain agents.[49]

Ever alert to professional agents' needs arising from changing conditions, the American Society offered agents the "Insurance Questionnaire" and "Replacement Questionnaire" as guides to better serve their clients.[50] The College introduced its own Customer Awareness Month, during which all employees were asked to recommit themselves to their customers, The American College students.[51]

Furthermore, the College joined forces with Insurance Marketing and Management Services, a Santa Monica, California-based organization serving property-liability insurance agents, whereby IMMS would offer these independent agents professional education in life insurance and financial services by publicizing The American College's products, programs, and services.[52] This was also the 3d year of the College's Professional Growth Award program, which now included 21 companies, 1,100 agencies, and 35,000 agents. The annual award is given to qualifying agencies that meet threshold levels of CLU and ChFC activity.[53] Under this program the College awards points to agents and agency staff who register for a course, pass an exam, and earn a designation or degree from the College. Recognition is then given to those agencies that meet or exceed the Professional Growth Award Program's level of education throughout the year.

In addition to these responses to industry pressures and students' needs, President Weese proudly announced at year's end that the administration had invested $1.1 million in capital improvements as part of the multi-year plan based on the 1994 facilities audit. The College's fiscal plans, which included a continued increase in its surplus balances, were on target.[54]

*   *   *

Negative publicity dogged the life insurance industry as it began the second half of the 1990s. For example, a *Wall Street Journal* article referred to the industry's "severely tarnished image."[55] A respected financial magazine noted "a frenzy of unease among consumers,"[56] and an internationally known newspaper wrote of "an outdated industry."[57] While much of this negative publicity was an exaggeration, the industry was concerned about the deterioration of public confidence.

Life insurance had faced adverse publicity 90 years before when corporate fraud and marketing misrepresentations led to the 1905 Armstrong Report, which inspired reform legislation and set the foundation for modern life insurance regulation.[58] Now, after more than 80 years of what a contemporary authority described as "exemplary service to its policyowners and beneficiaries," the issue of marketing misrepresentations surfaced again, owing largely to the use of computer-generated illustrations.[59]

State regulators and the federal courts were beginning to play a more influential role in how insurance was sold and who was eligible to sell it. California, to illustrate, began forcing insurers to provide a "standardized yield comparison index" for cash-value policies, which drew attention to the performance activity of low-load policies that are sold directly to consumers without sales commissions.[60] The United States Supreme Court handed down an important doctrine when it ruled that national banks could sell annuities.[61]

Some companies embraced the low-load, direct-sale concept on a national basis. The *Atlantic Monthly* ran a series of advertisements offering "Affordable Life Insurance" with coupons requesting application forms. The format remained constant; only the company name and specific monthly premium rates changed from issue to issue.

The American College believed that the best response to eroding public confidence and a tarnished industry image was education, concurring with the noted professor and business adviser Peter F. Drucker (who had delivered the first William T. Beadles Lecture at The American College in 1971) that the significance of professional education in today's fast-changing and complex world cannot be overestimated. Drucker described the new economic order of the mid-1990s as one in which "knowledge, not labor or raw material or capital, is the key resource."[62]

The College was well equipped to do its part and then some. Its mission statement was dedicated to this very purpose. The College's academic panoply of designations and degrees—together with the College-Society joint PACE programs, mentoring arrangements, and Professional Growth Award opportunities—offered a veritable cornucopia of educational options for every ambitious and qualified life insurance and financial services professional.

The College began its first major construction project on campus since the completion of the Gregg Conference Center in 1981. Mitchell Hall, as it would be called, would combine the former Dechert Hall with the adjacent General Services Building through a new central MONY Plaza entrance to yield a large, modern, multipurpose complex. This project, however, was a much less expensive undertaking, with an expected completion cost of $1.6 million. Also in contrast to the Gregg Center project, the funds to complete the newest construction were already on hand. Roy Mitchell, a Mutual Life of New York agent in Pittsburgh, Pennsylvania, had left the vast majority of his wealth to The American College. When the trust fund was liquidated in 1996, the College received over $800,000 for the new projects, along with an additional $200,000 from the fund's earnings over the past 10 years, which was also allocated to the new building. This was supplemented by a gift of $125,000 from Ellen and Eugene Seamen of Corpus Christi, Texas, plus $250,000 from Mutual of New York corporate offices and its field force. The proceeds of a $50,000 life insurance policy donated to the College by the late John McCole of Wilkes-Barre, Pennsylvania, were also allocated to the project. The College could make up the difference between expected costs and revenues raised without going into debt of any kind.

"The American College has given so much to me," Eugene Seaman said. "I am honored to help build a home for those insurance men and women who will follow me and reap the harvest of professional education."[63]

The 1996 winter trustees meeting is noteworthy on numerous counts: The board elected seven new members, affirmed its cooperative relationship with the American Society of CLU & ChFC, endorsed an ambitious 1996 business plan, adopted a new mission statement, and passed the gavel to the new board chairman. The sessions confirmed the educational board members' fundamental role "to serve as sentries to ensure that the president and faculty devise and implement strategies in fulfillment of the institution's mission."[64]

Robert M. Devlin, CLU, president of American General Corporation; Samuel J. Foti, CLU, president and COO of Mutual Life Insurance Company of New York; and Anita Jin-Ming Hsiao, CLU, ChFC, general manager, The Prudential, Monterey Park, California, were among the new trustees in 1996. The College and the Society signed a 10-year lease for the Society to occupy Huebner Hall, and the Society pledged its support in celebration of the College's 70th anniversary in May 1997. The College's new four-paragraph mission statement that the board approved had less functional detail and greater emphasis on continuing education than the previous credo. Finally, the trustees congratulated and thanked Denis F. Mullane for his successful term as chairman and presented him with a handsome, framed citation and the beautiful Philadelphia Bowl before electing Glenn A. Britt, State Farm Insurance Companies executive vice president, as his successor. President Samuel Weese declared, "The American College is extremely fortunate to have the accomplished leadership of Glenn Britt at this time, as the College and the financial services industry continue to face the challenges of change."[65]

Concomitant with this natural emphasis on present and future board chairmanship, the College paid tribute to a former holder of that position—the legendary Charles J. Zimmerman. Even after his death, Zimmerman continued to serve the College he had deeply loved through a generous legacy under his will. Ever forward looking, Charles Zimmerman wanted to help make sure there would always be an American College. In 1995, the trustees had recognized his more than 60-year relationship with the College by creating the Charles J. Zimmerman Chair in Life Insurance Education to be endowed through various funding sources, beginning with Charles J. Zimmerman's legacy.[66] There could be no more appropriate way to honor that remarkable individual, who said,

"Remember that no person has ever been honored for what he received. Honor is the reward for what he gave."

Ethics continued to occupy financial services professionals on the national scene—and for good reason. A Gallup Poll at that time rated lawyers, insurance agents, and used car salesmen near the bottom of the list of various occupations in terms of people's trust and respect. "This is alarming," a financial magazine editor wrote, noting that many people who control wealth "view estate planning professionals with a jaundiced eye."[67]

On campus the mood was more optimistic. The College made the first public announcement of plans to commemorate its 70th anniversary. In addition, it organized selected archival objects into a Special Traveling Presentation, which began a projected 9-month, nationwide tour at the General Agents and Managers Association (GAMA) 1996 Life Agency Management Program (LAMP) conference.[68] "Ben Franklin"—a well-known Philadelphia professional who dresses in the Colonial attire and looks very much like the original Benjamin Franklin—even joined the exhibit at most locations.

May had often been a busy time for the trail-blazing distance education College in Bryn Mawr, and the 1996 campus schedule maintained the custom. This time, the College designated the entire 31 days as RHU/REBC Month as part of a cooperative effort with the National Association of Health Underwriters to raise the visibility of these two designations.

The 19th Frank M. Engle Lecture on May 6 kicked off the sequence of events. The former director of the Congressional Budget Office and then Brookings Institution senior fellow, Robert D. Reischauer, PhD, talked about "Reducing the Deficit: Past Efforts and Future Challenges." Although Frank Engle had not personally attended a lecture since 1992, he enjoyed watching them on video tape. He died the day after the 19th Engle Lecture at his home in Tulsa, Oklahoma, at the age of 98.[69]

Frank M. Engle is a story of his own. This highly successful life insurance agent, entrepreneur, and stock market investor was born in 1898, which was before his native Oklahoma became a state. Through the encouragement of his considerably younger friend and partner, Jack Gatewood, CLU, Engle became interested in The American College's mission relatively late in his life and began contributing to the College in 1976 with the institution of the acclaimed Engle Lecture series. The Chair in Economic Security was created in 1983 with his initial gift of $500,000. In 1985 he raised the endowment to $1 million and at his death, his contributions to the College exceeded $1.8 million. Although he was not a Chartered Life Underwriter, Frank M. Engle was committed to professional education and believed that too many knew too little about economics. He was still going to the office every day until he contracted a brief illness that led to his death. His oil portrait hangs in the hallway of MDRT Foundation Hall as a lasting tribute to this great friend of the College.

Other May events included the 1996 Art in Exhibition program (which this year featured paintings from the Art League of Delaware County) and the second annual Lang Dixon Professional Education Day presented by the African-

American Advisory Committee and coordinated by the College Multicultrual Activities Director David A. Lester.[70] The College also introduced its Home Page on the World Wide Web, thereby joining some 3,000 other colleges and universities in this contemporary communication technique. The College could now explain its programs and answer the most frequently asked questions via an "Information for Students" section.[71]

Two important campus events occurred in June 1996. On June 2d, the College and the National Press Foundation began a 3 1/2-day conference to give reporters who cover the insurance industry a balanced educational foundation for their writing. This was part of a larger nationwide program of the Life and Health Insurance Foundation for Education, more popularly known as LIFE, which sponsored and financed the event and provided the financial support for the attendees.

The other important event that month—the campus groundbreaking ceremony for Mitchell Hall and MONY Plaza—took place on June 20 and was significant for two reasons. First, it showcased the College's fresh initiative and continued growth. Second, it signified still another episode in the long, happy relationship between the College and Mutual of New York. MONY and The American College had been helping each other, working together, and enjoying reciprocal benefits since the days of Julian S. Myrick, one of MONY's top managers and a longtime (1938–1960) College trustee chairman.

Other MONY officials had also served on the board, and MONY efforts later produced the Roger Hull-James S. Bingay Chair of Leadership. Now, company officials and College leaders posed together at the construction site with their shovels. A smiling board chairman, Glenn A. Britt, stood between the two chief executives—Samuel H. Weese for the College and Samuel J. Foti for MONY—to mark the historic occasion. The College, said Dr. Weese, "was most fortunate to have such support from the Mutual of New York family." Samuel Foti generously replied, "Without The American College, Mutual of New York could not have grown as it has."[72]

The new facility will house the registrar and the Student Services, Agency Services, and Student Development Departments. "In addition," Dr. Weese explained, "we see MONY Plaza as the new hub of campus activity, providing an ideal location to entertain alumni and guests."[73] The new structure will be dedicated in May 1997 as part of the College's 70th anniversary celebration.

Sixty-eight men and women received their MSFS or MSM degrees from the College's Graduate School of Financial Sciences and the Richard D. Irwin Graduate School of Management on June 21, 1996. The class is particularly interesting in that it included one of the College's newest trustees, Anita J. Hsiao of Prudential Life; Multicultural Activities Director David A. Lester; two women from British Columbia, Canada; and 14 people from New York Life Insurance Company.[74] Harry J. Hohn, chairman of the board and CEO of New York Life, was the commencement speaker. Because he had served 6 years on the College board, it was, in some ways, a brief homecoming for him. He was an enthusiastic supporter of the New York Life Masters of Science program; it was therefore fitting that he was the speaker when the first of these Masters of Science graduates received their degrees.

*   *   *

As the year 1997 emerges, The American College is poised to celebrate its 70th anniversary during the week of May 19–24 in downtown Philadelphia and on its Bryn Mawr campus.

There is much to celebrate. The College's place of business has grown from a file drawer in the office of Solomon S. Huebner to a campus of its own, which includes seven modern buildings on 35 beautiful suburban acres—complete with a winding stream, hundreds of magnificent trees, and countless shrubs and flowers. The College has expanded from a single office with a few dedicated individuals to an academically accredited educational institution with a full-time professional faculty including five endowed chairs, a full-sized library that is one of the best of its kind in the country, a stable and experienced support staff, and a talented management team that provides the operational efficiency necessary for success in today's highly competitive world of education.

The number of alumni has grown from 21 CLU designees the first year to more than 80,000 CLUs, 30,000 ChFCs, and 1,800 masters degree graduates. The Golden Key Society, which had just a few hundred members when it was created in 1960, has increased to over 7,000 members today. Examination procedures have progressed from twice-a-year, paper-and-pencil exams at select locations to year-round computerized examinations at more than 500 sites both domestically and internationally.

Even more important than the increases in size and statistics is that the College has consistently enhanced its credibility and prestige as a quality educational institution, maintaining exceptionally high standards through depressions, wars, and industry turmoil. Earning a designation from The American College has never been an easy task—for every 10 students who matriculate with the College, only three earn their designation. For the past 2 decades the average length of time it has taken to earn the CLU designation has been 5 years. It is little wonder that those who earn a designation or degree from The American College are extremely proud of their accomplishments and their alma mater.

A recent survey of graduates across the nation from many different classes shows widespread enthusiasm for the Bryn Mawr institution. Bradford D. Hazeltine, CLU, ChFC, of Boston, Massachusetts, is "thrilled to see how the College has grown." Jane A. Christison, CLU, of Overland Park, Kansas, and Frank C. Clapp, from Lafayette, California, agree that it is difficult to think of any weaknesses the College might have. Arlene R. Foreman, CLU, ChFC, Fort Myers, Florida, praises the College's "high educational integrity and well-communicated information."

The College deserves the accolades. Its steadfast adherence to independence and academic freedom for its faculty has set the College apart from all other support organizations in the life insurance industry. Over the long run, this unbiased, objective approach to the subjects and issues of the day has deepened the respect the esteemed institution has earned.

The 70th anniversary in May will provide another reason to celebrate when the College pays off its remaining long-term debt. The American College will then be debt free for the first time in more than 25 years and on schedule to invest over $7 million in capital improvements on its physical properties over the next few years—without incurring additional debt.

The most significant aspect of the 70th anniversary celebration, however, is that it sets the stage for the future. The American College is well positioned for a new millennium that will offer unlimited opportunities. As the boundaries between banks, securities, and insurance break down and an integrated financial services industry emerges, the College's potential constituency will be far larger than simply the traditional life insurance industry.

Throughout most of the 70-year history of The American College, distance education has been viewed as nontraditional education. Today, however, the gulf between traditional education and distance education is rapidly disappearing. Traditional colleges and universities are now recognizing the legitimacy of distance education and its ability to meet the needs of enormous numbers of students without diminishing the quality or effectiveness of the learning process. The vast possibilities to use computers for education via the Internet and World Wide Web are just beginning to unfold.

The American College has been a pioneering leader in distance education in this country for 7 decades. Moreover, it expects to be the pioneering leader for the next 7 decades and beyond. It is well equipped for the role it intends to play in the professional development of those in the financial services industry. The College has the governance, the management, the organizational structure, and the financial stability to enable it to be even more successful in the future than it has been in the past.

It all began with the Power of One, but it will be carried forward by the commitment of thousands.

NOTES

1. *World Almanac and Book of Facts* (Mahwah, NJ: World Almanac Books) 1996, p. 510.
2. Announcement of *McGill's Life Insurance*, 1994.
3. *Book of Honors,* The American College Archives, Kentucky Room.
4. *Society Page,* American Society of CLU & ChFC, June 1994, p. 1.
5. Ibid.
6. Samuel H. Weese memo to College employees, May 4, 1994.
7. *The American College Outlook,* fall 1994, p. 10.
8. "President's Update," August 16, 1994, p. 3.
9. Ibid., p. 2.
10. *Annual Report,* The American College, 1994, pp. 2, 3.
11. "President's Update," November 17, 1994, p. 1.

12. *Outlook,* fall 1994, p. 3.
13. *Society Page,* August 1994, p. 1.
14. Ibid., December 1994, p. 2.
15. Ibid., p. 5.
16. *Outlook,* fall 1994, p. 8.
17. The American College news release, August 29, 1994.
18. D. David Eisenhower, commencement address, October 29, 1994.
19. Barry Kaye Media Center dedication program.
20. *Outlook,* fall 1994, p. 8.
21. *World Almanac,* 1996, pp. 338, 332.
22. LOMA Opinion Survey, November 1994, p. 1.
23. "President's Update," January 30, 1995.
24. *Annual Report,* 1994, pp. 2, 3.
25. Ibid., pp. 4, 6.
26. "President's Update," January 30, 1995.
27. The American College news release, January 5, 1995.
28. *World Almanac,* 1996, pp. 47, 52, 54.
29. Calendar of 1995 Events, p. 2.
30. "Facilities Audit Report," Burt Hill Kosar Rittlemann Associates, 1995, p. 1.
31. *Annual Report,* 1995, p. 2.
32. Samuel H. Weese, interview with the author, July 26, 1995.
33. Samuel H. Weese memo to College employees, April 10, 1995.
34. "The Implications of NAFTA," Frank M. Engle Lecture, The American College, May 1, 1995.
35. Ibid.
36. *Outlook,* spring 1995, p. 10.
37. Commencement program, June 1995, pp. 1, 3.
38. *Outlook,* fall 1995, p. 10.
39. The American College news release, November 19, 1995.
40. *World Almanac,* 1996, p. 66.
41. Gary K. Stone, interview with the author, March 16, 1995.
42. Ibid.
43. The American College news release, August 31, 1995.
44. Ibid.
45. Ibid., October 27, 1995.
46. Ibid., October 18, 1995.
47. *Wall Street Journal,* August 15, 1995, p. A4.
48. *Philadelphia Inquirer,* September 18, 1995, p. F1.
49. Gordon K. Rose, interview with the author, March 9, 1995.
50. *Philadelphia Inquirer,* October 7, 1995.
51. The American College news release, November 1995.
52. Ibid., November 22, 1995.
53. Samuel H. Weese, interview with the author.
54. *Annual Report,* 1995.
55. "Life Insurers Launch Campaigns," *Wall Street Journal,* January 31, 1996.
56. *Trusts & Estates,* April 1996, p. 59.
57. "Home News," *London Times,* June 25, 1996, p. 9.
58. Burke A. Christensen, "The Evaluation of Life Insurance," *Trusts & Estates,* May 1995, p. 55.
59. Ibid.
60. *Wall Street Journal,* March 1, 1995, p. C1.
61. Ibid., January 19, 1995, p. A3.
62. *Atlantic Monthly,* November 1994, p. 53.
63. The American College news release, January 19, 1996.

64. The Association of Governing Boards of Universities and Colleges and the Pew Higher Education Roundtable "Perspectives," July 1995, p. 3.
65. The American College news release, January 29, 1996.
66. Ibid., February 23, 1996.
67. Michael S. Klim, *Trusts & Estates,* May 1996, p. 4.
68. The American College news release, April 15, 1996.
69. *Outlook,* spring 1996, p. 11.
70. The American College news release, April 8, 1996.
71. Ibid., May 20, 1996.
72. *Main Line Life*, July 11, 1996.
73. The American College news release, July 5, 1996.
74. Ibid., July 15, 1996.

At the dinner following the inauguration of Samuel H. Weese as the seventh president of The American College, Dr. Weese; his wife Ellen; and John R. Driskill, executive vice president and managing director of the American Society of CLU & ChFC, admire the painting given to the Weeses by the College in honor of the occasion.

Chairman of the Board of The American College John B. Carter presents the symbol of office to Samuel H. Weese, PhD, CLU, at his inauguration in 1988.

Dr. Weese delivers his acceptance address upon being inaugurated as the seventh president of The American College.

226

Fred E. Wright, former professor of insurance at West Virginia University, friend and mentor of his former student Sam Weese, at Dr. Weese's inauguration.

Maxine B. Niemeyer, former president of the American Society of CLU & ChFC and life trustee of The American College, speaking at the inauguration of Samuel H. Weese as president of the College.

The American College's fifth president, Davis W. Gregg, congratulates the College's incoming seventh president, Samuel H. Weese, at his inauguration.

The American College hosted the plenary session of the 1996 American Risk and Insurance Association annual meeting, The Future of Life Insurance Distribution, moderated by President Weese. Panelists, pictured left to right, were Dr. Walter H. Zultowski, LIMRA; Samuel J. Foti, CLU, Mutual of New York; and Glenn A. Britt, State Farm Life Insurance Company.

The American College's annual Ben Feldman Forum educational teleconference honors a legend in life insurance. Pictured left to right during the 1995 event are Stephen D. Tarr, Stanley Liss, Marvin Feldman, Ethel Feldman, Stephan R. Leimberg, and Samuel H. Weese. Inset: Professor Stephan R. Leimberg delivers Feldman Lecture.

Gary K. Stone, PhD, CLU, vice president of academics, joined the College in 1988. In 1994, he directed the revision and publication of *McGill's Life Insurance*, the most comprehensive text in the field and a major addition to the College curriculum.

Dr. Glenn Boseman, CLU, chairholder of the Roger Hull-James S. Bingay Chair of Leadership, teaches a seminar in leadership.

Samuel H. Weese and Marvin D. Bower cut the ribbon to dedicate the Archives Room in the Gregg Educational Conference Center honoring Bower, the retired chairman of State Farm Life Insurance Company and The American College (October 1993).

The American College's 35-acre campus. Industry leaders and thousands of alumni have consistently supported the College with their commitment and financial generosity.

At a dinner on October 29, 1996, Dr. Dan M. McGill and President Samuel H. Weese announced the College's newly established Joseph E. Boettner Chair in Financial Gerontology, endowed through a gift to the College from the estates of Joseph E. and Ruth Boettner. Dr. McGill taught both Dr. Weese and Dr. Gary K. Stone, vice president of academics, while they were students at the Wharton School.

Anita Jin-Ming Hsiao, trustee of The American College, has served as a member of the College's Asian-American Advisory Committee since the committee's inception in 1992.

The Department of Multicultural Activities was founded at the College in 1993 to develop CLU and ChFC growth among minority segments of the population. Pictured left to right are William T. Parker and Humberto Torres, committee chairmen; Samuel H. Weese; Richard Chen; and David A. Lester, department director.

Life Trustee Brian S. Brown, CLU, chairman of the Development Committee of the College's Board of Trustees, demonstrates strategic planning.

The American College Mitchell Hall/MONY Plaza groundbreaking ceremony took place on June 20, 1996. Pictured left to right are Stephen D. Tarr, Ellen Seaman, Stephen J. Hall, Allen Skogebo, Samuel J. Foti, Glenn A. Britt, Samuel H. Weese, Eugene J. Seaman, Connie McCole, Cornelius McCole, Brian S. Brown, and Sally McCole Wheat.

Ribbon cutting for the Barry Kaye Media Center, a state-of-the-art audiovisual production facility, took place in 1994. Pictured left to right are the Kayes' daughter, Barry and Carole Kaye, and their grandchildren (in the foreground). President Weese and Board Chairman Denis F. Mullane look on.

Following a year-long restoration process and landscaping, the Bette and Thomas J. Wolff ponds, dedicated in May 1997, are a major feature of The American College campus and arboretum.

The American College Trustees
Past and Present

Alfred J. Johannsen	1935 – 1936
Henry E. North	1936 – 1958
Robert Dechert	1936 – 1957
	1959 – 1975
Kellogg Van Winkle	1937 – 1938
George H. Chace	1938 – 1947
George L. Hunt	1938 – 1954
George A. Patton	1938 – 1944
Joseph H. Reese, Sr.	1938 – 1939
	1943 – 1968
Earle W. Brailey	1939 – 1940
Sewell W. Hodge	1939 – 1966
Cecil J. North	1939 – 1963
Benjamin Alk	1940 – 1941
Henry E. North	1940 – 1958
John D. Moynahan	1941 – 1942
Charles J. Zimmerman	1941 – 1944
	1951 – 1994
Chester O. Fischer	1943 – 1957
James Elton Bragg	1945 – 1958
Paul W. Cook	1944 – 1956
Dudley Dowell	1944 – 1953
Roger Hull	1944 – 1972
Clifford H. Orr	1944 – 1946
Roland D. Hinkle	1945 – 1947
Walter A. Craig	1946 – 1947
William S. Leighton	1947 – 1949
Martin I. Scott	1947 – 1950
Harold M. Stewart	1947 – 1957
Karl K. Krogue	1948 – 1951
Howard H. Cammack	1949 – 1952
Vincent B. Coffin	1949 – 1966
E.M. McConney	1949 – 1951
Clarence B. Metzger	1949 – 1964
Charles W. Campbell	1950 – 1965
M. Albert Linton	1950 – 1955
Carl M. Spero	1950 – 1953
Davis W. Gregg	1951 – 1993
James W. Smither, Jr.	1951 – 1954
Frank Cooper	1953 – 1956
Wm. Eugene Hays	1953 – 1972
Raymond C. Johnson	1953 – 1982
Karl H. Kreder	1953 – 1954
Hugh S. Bell	1954 – 1963
William T. Grant	1954 – 1955

Vane B. Lucas	1969	– 1977
Miles McNally	1969	– 1972
James J. O'Leary	1969	– 1974
Warren M. Pace	1969	– 1972
Donald S. MacNaughton	1970	– 1978
Bernard S. Rosen	1970	– 1979
Richard R. Shinn	1970	– 1979
Thomas C. Simons	1970	– 1979
Leroy G. Steinbeck	1970	– 1976
Raymond F. Triplett	1970	– 1973
Clarence C. Walton	1970	– 1979
Edward B. Bates	1971	– 1980
William A. Clement	1971	– 1980
Sumner Rodman	1971	– 1974
Frank P. Samford, Jr.	1971	– 1980
Robert Woods	1971	– 1980
Robert M. Best	1972	– 1985
James S. Bingay	1972	– 1976
Dean W. Jeffers	1972	– 1975
Joseph C. Ladd	1972	– 1981
Jack L. Nix	1972	– 1975
	1979	– 1988
Louis B. Perry	1972	– 1981
Eli Shapiro	1972	– 1981
Marvin D. Bower	1973	– 1982
	1985	– 1992
Armand G. Stalnaker	1973	– 1982
Robert P. Gatewood	1974	– 1982
Sidney P. Marland Jr.	1974	– 1990
J. Edwin Matz	1974	– 1982
Harris L. Wofford, Jr.	1974	– 1982
William J. Braun	1975	– 1978
Walter L. Downing	1975	– 1980
John H. Filer	1975	– 1978
Dan M. McGill	1975	– 1984
Lester A. Rosen	1975	– 1981
Bernard H. Zais	1976	– 1979
Robert B. Williams	1977	– 1980
Jarrett L. Davis	1978	– 1981
	1985	– 1995
George J. Hauptfuhrer, Jr.	1978	– 1987
	1988	– 1990
Harold S. Hook	1978	– 1984
William B. Wallace	1978	–
Robert A. Beck	1979	– 1988

Harry Hohn	1988 – 1996
Sidney Kess	1988 – 1990
Samuel H. Weese	1988 –
Jon W. Webber	1988 – 1991
Robert W. Barth	1989 – 1991
Robert E. Carlson	1989 – 1995
Warren W. Deakins	1989 – 1995
Edwin T. Johnson	1989 –
Donald H. Mehlig	1989 – 1992
Stewart G. Nagler	1989 – 1995
Jerry S. Rosenbloom	1989 – 1995
Curtis W. Tarr	1989 – 1992
Brian S. Brown	1990 –
Richard R. Collins	1990 – 1993
Kenneth L. Fry, Jr.	1990 – 1993
Wilmer S. Poyner, III	1990 –
Rex B. Shannon	1990 – 1993
Thomas J. Wolff	1990 –
David F. Woods	1990 –
Vincent C. Bowhers	1991 –
Glenn A. Britt	1991 –
Louis G. Lower, II	1991 –
John B. Peyton	1991 –
Paul J. Shevlin	1991 –
Richard E. Stewart	1991 – 1993
John D. Campbell	1991 – 1994
Robert D. Bates	1992 – 1995
Bert Collins	1992 –
Alan Press	1992 –
Robert A. Shafto	1992 – 1994
Raymond A. Silva	1992 – 1995
Donald G. Southwell	1992 –
Lawrence L. Grypp	1993 – 1996
Howard C. Humphrey	1993 – 1995
Ann E. Smith	1993 –
James M. Benson	1995 –
Robert W. Fiondella	1995 – 1996
Curtis B. Ford	1994 –
James A. Mitchell	1995 –
L.J. Rowell, Jr.	1995 –
Jack B. Turner	1995 –
Harold B. Skipper	1995 –
Stuart G. Tugman, Jr.	1995 –
Victor E. Millar	1995 –

Solomon S. Huebner
Gold Medal Winners

1975	C. Lamont Post	1984	Kenneth Black, Jr.
1976	William T. Beadles Charles J. Zimmerman	1985	Frank M. Engle James B. Irvine
1977	William H. Andrews, Jr Paul F. Clark David McCahan Dan M. McGill Julian S. Myrick	1986	Robert A. Beck Clarence C. Walton
		1987	Vane B. Lucas Lester Rosen
1978	Ernest J. Clark John O. Todd Edward A. Woods	1988	Richard D. Irwin Benjamin N. Woodson
		1989	Leo R. Futia Sidney P. Marland
1979	Davis W. Gregg Raymond C. Johnson	1990	Helen L. Schmidt William B. Wallace
1980	Roger Hull Paul S. Mills	1991	Marvin D. Bower
1981	Joseph E. Boettner Mildred F. Stone	1992	John B. Carter
1982	John T. Fey Gen Hirose	1993	Edmund L. Zalinski
		1994	Maxine B. Niemeyer
1983	Robert M. Best J. Carlton Smith	1995	Stanley Liss

1996   Brian S. Brown

Dates to Remember
in the History of The American College

1927   College incorporated as The American College of Life Underwriters
      in District of Columbia
    Edward A. Woods installed as president

1928   Ernest J. Clark installed as president
    First CLU designations conferred
    American Society of CLU & ChFC founded

1931   College moves from Professor Solomon S. Huebner's office at the
      University of Pennsylvania to nearby bank building

1934   Solomon S. Huebner elected president
    Ernest J. Clark elected board chairman

1938   Julian S. Myrick elected board chairman

1948   College moves to first permanent headquarters at 3924 Walnut Street,
      Philadelphia

1952   David McCahan elected president

1954   Davis W. Gregg elected president

1959   College purchases 10-acre estate in Bryn Mawr to create new
      headquarters
    Groundbreaking for Huebner Hall

1960   Golden Key Society created

1961   College moves to Bryn Mawr campus
    Huebner Hall dedicated
    Paul F. Clark elected board chairman

1965   Julian S. Myrick Pavilion dedicated
        Charles J. Zimmerman elected board chairman

1966   Trustees commission Mitchell/Giurgola Associates to design
            architects' campus master plan

1969   Groundbreaking for MDRT Foundation Hall
        Roger Hull named board chairman

1972   Dedication of MDRT Foundation Hall
        Hull Foundation established
        John T. Fey elected board chairman

1973   Faculty established
        Clarence C. Walton's study, *Nontraditional Education in Contemporary
            America,* published

1975   First Solomon S. Huebner Gold Medal awarded to C. Lamont Post
        Authority to grant masters degree given by Commonwealth of
            Pennsylvania

1976   James S. Bingay Chair of Creative Leadership combines with Hull
            Foundation
        Reincorporation of The American College in the Commonwealth of
            Pennsylvania (new charter)

1977   College awards first Master of Science in Financial Services (MSFS)
            degree

1978   Accreditation by Middle States Association of Colleges and Schools
        First Frank M. Engle Lecture delivered

1981   Trustees authorize Chartered Financial Consultant (ChFC) designation
        Dedication of Davis W. Gregg Educational Conference Center (first
            called Graduate Studies Center)

1982   Examinations on Demand (EOD) program initiated

1983   Edward G. Jordan installed as president
        Robert A. Beck named board chairman
        First Master of Science in Management (MSM) degree awarded
        Introduction of Premier School customized education

1984   College adopts Code of Ethics embodying Professional Pledge

1986   Boettner Institute founded
John B. Carter named board chairman

1988   Samuel H. Weese installed as president
George G. Joseph Chair in Management Education established

1989   Professional Achievement in Continuing Education (PACE) established
Marvin D. Bower named board chairman

1991   William B. Wallace named board chairman

1993   Computerized Registration Information System (CRIS) installed

1994   First Registered Health Underwriter (RHU) and Registered Employee Benefits Consultant (REBC) designations offered through the College

1996   Charles J. Zimmerman Chair of Life Insurance Education established
Joseph E. Boettner Chair in Financial Gerontology established
Glenn A. Britt named board chairman

1997   The American College celebrates 70th anniversary
Dedication of Mitchell Hall/MONY Plaza

Index